American Imagination and Symbolist Painting

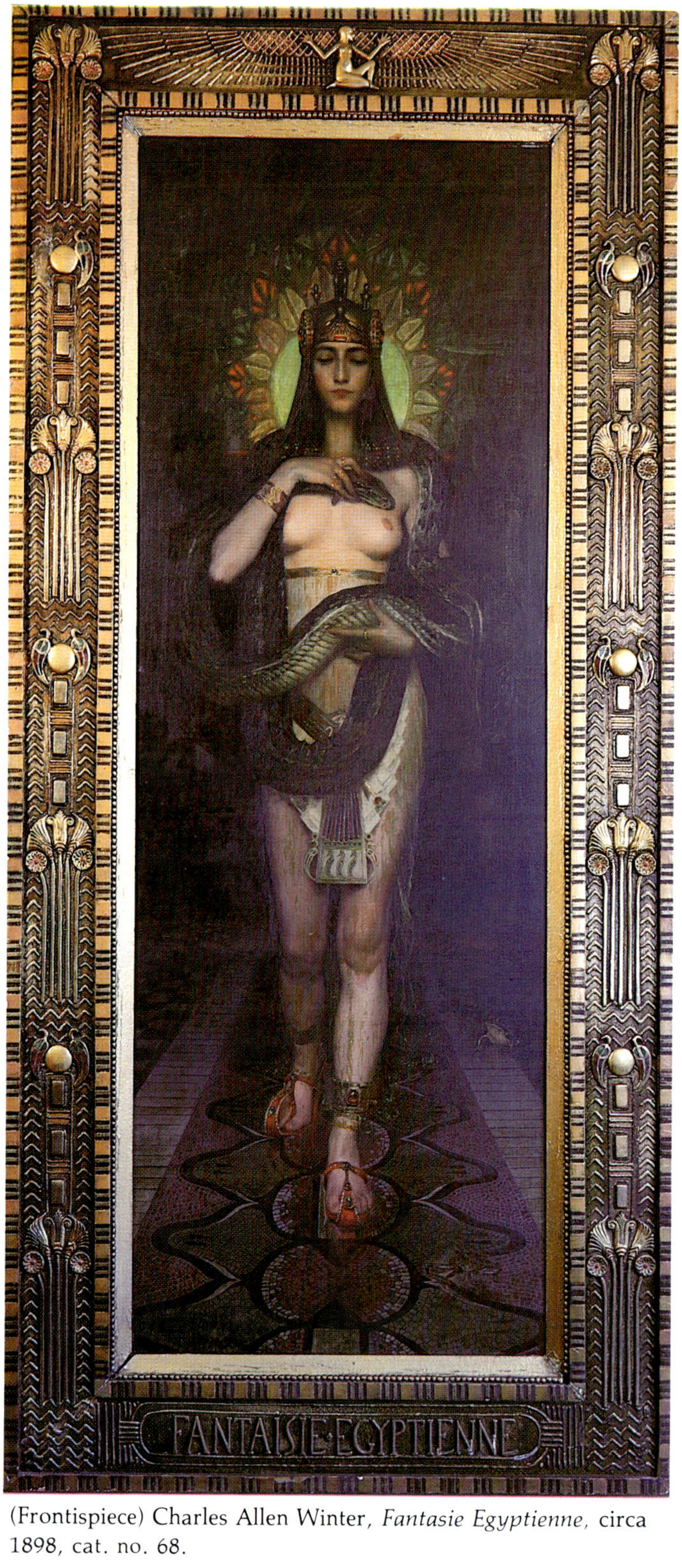

(Frontispiece) Charles Allen Winter, *Fantasie Egyptienne,* circa 1898, cat. no. 68.

American Imagination and Symbolist Painting

Charles C. Eldredge

GREY ART GALLERY AND STUDY CENTER, NEW YORK UNIVERSITY

Cover: Moonlit Pool *by Philip L. Hale (26). Photo by H. P. Vose.*

Library of Congress Catalogue Card Number 79-55429

This exhibition and publication are made possible by a grant from the National Endowment for the Arts, a Federal agency, and from the Kansas University Endowment Association.

All exhibitions at the Grey Art Gallery and Study Center are made possible with public funds from the New York State Council on the Arts.

A portion of the Spencer Museum of Art's general operating funds for this fiscal year are made available through a grant from the Institute of Museum Services, a Federal agency in the Department of Health, Education and Welfare, which offers operating and program support to the nation's museums.

Printed and bound by the University of Kansas Printing Service, Lawrence, Kansas. Color plates by Laser Ltd., Lawrence, Kansas.

Designed by Ruth Lawner

Published in conjunction with the exhibition of
American Imagination and Symbolist Painting

Grey Art Gallery and Study Center, New York University
October 24 - December 8, 1979

Helen Foresman Spencer Museum of Art
The University of Kansas
January 20 - March 2, 1980

To Jane, Gifford and Janann

Contents

Lenders to the Exhibition

The Art Institute of Chicago, Chicago, Illinois
Baker-Pisano Collection
Brandeis University Art Collections, Rose Art Museum, Waltham, Massachusetts
The Brooklyn Museum, New York, New York
Brooks Memorial Art Gallery, Memphis, Tennessee
Mrs. Claude Buck
The Cleveland Museum of Art, Cleveland, Ohio
Robert P. Coggins, M.D.
Columbus Museum of Art, Columbus, Ohio
Rozelle Cooper, New York, New York
Dr. and Mrs. Edwin J. De Costa
Elvehjem Art Museum, University of Wisconsin-Madison
Everson Museum of Art, Syracuse, New York
Fall River Public Library, Fall River, Massachusetts
Fine Arts Museum of San Francisco, San Francisco, California
Franklin P. Folts
Barry Friedman
Jean and Kahlil Gibran
Graham Gallery, New York, New York
Guennol Collection
The Hyde Collection, Glens Falls, New York
Kennedy Galleries, New York, New York
Lyme Historical Society, Inc., Old Lyme, Connecticut
The Metropolitan Museum of Art, New York, New York
The Museum of African Art, Washington, D.C.
Museum of Art, Rhode Island School of Design, Providence
Museum of Fine Arts, Boston, Massachusetts
The Museum of Modern Art, New York, New York
National Collection of Fine Arts, Smithsonian Institution, Washington, D.C.
The National Park Service
The Oakland Museum, Oakland, California
The Phillips Collection, Washington, D.C.
Stuart Pivar
Raydon Gallery, New York, New York
Beverly and Ray Sacks
Sheldon Memorial Art Gallery, University of Nebraska, Lincoln
Victor Spark, New York, New York
Helen Foresman Spencer Museum of Art, The University of Kansas, Lawrence
Stanford University Art Museum, Stanford, California
Alfred Stieglitz Archive, Collection of American Literature, Beinecke Rare Book and Manuscript Library, Yale University, New Haven, Connecticut
Whitney Museum of American Art, New York, New York
Worcester Art Museum, Worcester, Massachusetts
Anonymous lender

Foreword

This is the first detailed examination of the parallels between American imaginative painting of the turn-of-the-century and contemporaneous Symbolist art in Europe. In reviewing this exhibition's progression to reach this, its final form, there are numerous individuals and institutions whose advice, goodwill and generous help we wish to acknowledge.

As with any loan exhibition, the project would have been impossible without the kind willingness of owners to share their artworks. In this instance particularly, their help was essential in ferreting out little-known paintings and in preparing them for the show, which in several instances required extensive conservation. To all the lenders, who are listed elsewhere in this publication, we extend sincere thanks for their great cooperation in this venture.

The research for this publication and implementation of the exhibition was made possible by the munificent support of several organizations. The National Endowment for the Arts, a Federal agency, provided grants to both sponsoring museums for the planning and preparation of the show.

The idea of assembling paintings demonstrating an American manifestation of Symbolist activity was originally proposed to us by Stuart Pivar, collector and inventor. This first attempt had to be postponed and during the interlude, Charles Eldredge's interest and research into this particular topic was made known to us through the good offices of Professor William Gerdts, of the CUNY Graduate Center. Our exhibition plans coincided, and we trust that this resultant whole will be greater than the sum of its parts otherwise might have been. We particularly want to single out the assistance and encouragement of those mentioned below for their very special aid and attentions during all phases of this exhibition: Mary Anne Goley, Robert Preato of Grand Central Galleries and Patrick Roger-Binet for their scholarly aid; Linda Ferber and Deirdre Lawrence of The Brooklyn Museum, Rowland Elzea of The Delaware Art Museum, Doreen Bolger Burke and Natalie Spaskie of The Metropolitan Museum of Art for their special courtesies; Sandra Leff of Graham Gallery, Stuart Feld and Jane Richards of Hirsch & Adler, Vance Jordan and Todd Volpe of Jordan-Volpe Gallery, Deedee Wigmore and Gerold M. Wunderlic of Kennedy Galleries, Inc., Mildred Thaler of Marbella Gallery, Alexander Raydon of Raydon Gallery and Mr. and Mrs. Victor D. Spark for their combined advise and special attention.

Robert Littman, Director
Grey Art Gallery and Study Center
New York University

Acknowledgments

The preparation of this exhibition has been made easier and more pleasurable by the generous interest and assistance of numerous individuals and organizations. Support from the University of Kansas Faculty Research Fund and from the Kansas University Endowment Association was instrumental in the early development of this venture. The University of Kansas generously awarded me a sabbatical leave in 1979, which allowed the precious time to bring this project to conclusion. The Smithsonian Institution's award of a postdoctoral Fellowship as Visiting Museum Scholar insured that that time would be profitably spent in completing the research and preparing the manuscript for publication. The National Endowment for the Arts, a Federal agency, provided grants to both sponsoring museums to allow implementation of the exhibition plans. Additional assistance from the Corporate and Business Membership Program of the Spencer Museum of Art permitted the presentation of the exhibition at The University of Kansas. I am grateful to all those sponsors for their generous support which was essential to the realization of this venture.

Funding alone, however, does not an exhibition make. Without the huge assistance of colleagues around the country, who freely and repeatedly offered their valued expertise on all manner of issues, this project would have been stillborn. Most especially I am indebted to two friends who from the outset have provided the encouragement and considerable knowledge which helped to nurture the venture, Jeanne Stump and Joshua Taylor. Dr. Stump, chairperson of the Kress Foundation Department of Art History at the University of Kansas, is a specialist in French nineteenth-century painting, and her understanding of the European scene at the *fin de siècle,* which she has freely shared, has been of immeasurable benefit to me. Dr. Taylor, director of the National Collection of Fine Arts, also took an early interest in this project and generously offered both the resources and the intellectual stimulation required to complete it.

Many other colleagues in Washington, Lawrence, New York and elsewhere have helped with valuable criticisms and substantive advice along the way; for their particular interest and assistance I am grateful to Michele Bogart, Elizabeth Broun, Leslie Buck, Doreen Bolger Burke, Wanda Corn,

David Curry, David Deitcher, Lois Marie Fink, Susan Hobbs, Douglas Hyland, Ruth Lawner, Richard Murray, Marilyn Stokstad, John and Marsha Vine, James Yarnall, and Jean Fagin Yellin. Over the years numerous graduate students at The University of Kansas have shared my pleasures of discovery in the preparation of this exhibition, and I particularly acknowledge with gratitude the assistance of Hollis Goodall, Pamela Herrick, Stephen Nelson, Susan Pickel, Susan Pollard and Lea Rosson.

As any scholar knows, a good librarian can be one's best friend. I have been particularly blessed with the excellent cooperation and assistance of William Walker, Katherine Ratzenberger and the staff at the library of the National Collection of Fine Arts; Martha Kehde, Marianne Griffin and their colleagues at The University of Kansas Library; Garnett McCoy and his associates at the Archives of American Art; Martha Andrews and her assistants at the Smithsonian Inventory of American Painting; and the many helpful staff members of the Library of Congress.

I am also most appreciative of the help offered by Douglas Tilghman, assistant director of the Spencer Museum, and the rest of my colleagues here who ably carried on the institution's operations during the period of my absence, and who have all contributed importantly to this exhibition's presentation at The University of Kansas.

Last, but certainly far from least, I am enormously grateful to my wife and children who patiently suffered the trials of separations, selfishness and quirkish behavior which mark the scholarly birth process. This publication is for them.

These many midwives have all contributed valued and greatly appreciated service to the safe delivery of this exhibition and publication. Where the "child" shows signs of good health, it is due to their careful attendance; its ailments, however, are congenital and the fault of the parent, not to be blamed on the assistants.

Charles C. Eldredge, Director
Spencer Museum of Art
The University of Kansas

Author's Preface

What? An exhibition of turn-of-the-century American painting without Eakins, without Homer, without Henri? How can it be? The genesis for this study came a decade or so ago as I was trying to understand the early works of Georgia O'Keeffe. Clearly, her remarkable watercolors and drawings of 1915-1916 owed little to the so-called realist tradition in American art, as represented by Eakins, Homer and company. Yet the explanation of her early abstractions as something which erupted spontaneously on the isolated plains of North Texas also seemed difficult to buy. At that time I struggled with the issue but never achieved a satisfactory resolution.

More recently the problem of O'Keeffe's early work and the similarly difficult origins of her modernist colleagues Marsden Hartley and Arthur Dove was recalled as I worked with the troublesome oeuvre of Albert Ryder. Although differing greatly on the surface, the similarity in spirit among certain of their works intrigued me, as did the evident admiration which Hartley and others of his generation held for the older master. I was especially struck by the inadequacy of standard histories of American painting to explain the singular contributions and challenges posed by the paintings of both the mature Ryder and the early O'Keeffe.

In a general way their works bracket the extended turn of the century here examined. Ryder's mature phase began roughly simultaneously with the emergence of the French Symbolists, about 1885. His death in 1917 coincided with O'Keeffe's first one-woman show at Alfred Stieglitz's "291" Gallery. In the same year a little-known group of imaginative New York artists calling themselves the Introspectives made their debut. Also in 1917, and probably most significant of all, America entered the First World War, an involvement that irrevocably altered not only American art, but its larger history as well.

From this period—circa 1885-1917—emerged a fascinating group of artists, many of whom are now forgotten and whose oeuvre constitutes a neglected chapter in accounts of American art history. Painters, sculptors, illustrators and muralists—artists in many media contributed to the flourishing of imagination which characterized the era. Over the years my files expanded and with them grew the accumulation of random images and miscellaneous documents. Gradually a pattern began to emerge which would ultimately provide the outline for an alternative view of the turn of the century—not the realists', but one defined by a more introspective and imaginative spirit.

About five years ago, while he was visiting at The University of Kansas, Irving Sandler informally remarked on the proximate interests of my colleague, Professor Jeanne Stump, and myself, and off-handedly wondered about the possibility of there having been an American variant of French Symbolism. While he had little idea of what it would yield, and can in no way be held accountable for the results, Professor Sandler's chance comment provided the requisite catalyst which began to pull the miscellany into focus.

Stimulated by his remark, my research gained a new direction and was no longer merely an accumulation. However, in making the transition from general investigation to specific exhibition, many other decisions had to be made. The chronological span of the show had already been generally determined, but the exhibition itself depended upon the availability of the works. The number and diversity of those works in themselves presented a problem, and ultimately it was decided to limit the study to American painting. For logistical reasons, most murals of the period which might have been appropriate were unavailable; the work of American illustrators of the period which might have suited the exhibition had been or could be examined in other ways; American sculptors, with a few significant exceptions, seemed to have lagged behind their fellow painters in developing the introspective strain in their art.

The resulting view of American painting in the decades embracing the year 1900 consciously excludes the so-called realists. This omission is in no way intended as a denigration of their significant role. Instead it is hoped that this exhibition will be viewed and this catalogue read as a companion to the abundant scholarship which has already secured an important place for the objectively oriented painters from America's past.

Because the painters themselves were often involved with contemporaneous events and attitudes outside the narrow realm of painting, I believe that considerations of such phenomena are of great importance in understanding their long-neglected accomplishments. Accordingly, perhaps, more than the usual amount of background information is given in the first part of the essay, which I hope will enhance the understanding of the paintings discussed in the second part.

The full appreciation of the imaginative spirit as manifested in the exhibition is complicated by the need to focus upon the subjects or content rather than upon familiar formalist concerns. This in turn often requires a re-examination of traditional canons of style and taste. Upon re-examination the major contributions of a Ryder, a Davies or an O'Keeffe are happily re-validated in a new light, while the contributions of some of their forgotten contemporaries are resuscitated. This is not to claim equal stature for all the painters here loosely grouped, for certainly variations in achievement can and should continue to be recognized. However, the resulting wider view of artistic activity at the end of the nineteenth and beginning of the twentieth centuries does add to our understanding of a complex era too seldom or too simply examined in the past.

Each generation, of course, revises its view of the past in accordance with its present values and biases. I hope that this study may make some small contribution to the renewed appreciation of America's rich cultural life at the turn of the century, and may suggest other doors to be opened and avenues followed as the re-examination of the period continues.

C. C. E.
July 1979

I: The Background

Introduction

In recent years turn-of-the-century American art has enjoyed renewed attention on the part of historians, students and collectors. One new study of late nineteenth-century American painting states that "our patrons seem to have rejected the purer forms of Symbolism with its avowedly decadent and often Roman Catholic themes and few Americans were attracted to Europe to follow this style."[1] Such a pronouncement is of interest on three counts: first, it is unlikely that until very recently Symbolist connections to American would even have been considered by historians, in view of the general neglect which late nineteenth-century alternatives to the realist mode have suffered in studies of American art; second, the statement illuminates the specific confusion of esoteric subjects and Symbolist "style," and the general misapprehension regarding Symbolist aesthetics, which still persist in many commentaries on the *fin de siècle;* and third, the author implies that Symbolism was a uniquely European phenomenon, for acquaintance with which our artists would necessarily have to travel to the Continent.

Despite the spate of Symbolist studies in recent years, consensus is still lacking on a definition and dating of the movement. The problem is complicated by recent popularizations of some of the more bizarre and extreme manifestations of the Symbolist mood in the specialized contributions to the Paris Salons de la Rose+Croix and the Brussels exhibitions of Les XX and Libre Aesthetique in the 1890s. The application of the Symbolist label to movements in both literature and the visual arts has further confused the issue. Similarly, the plethora of sometimes contradictory manifestos and declarations by Symbolist writers and artists and by their critics and historians has clouded more than clarified our appreciation of their contributions.

Out of the confusing welter of theory and apologia, however, certain things have become clear, namely that there was little stylistic coherence to the Symbolist movement, and that our usual tools of formal analysis are frustrated by the highly subjective iconography and individual technique which characterize Symbolist painting. It is only on the basis of their subjects, or more precisely their attitudes toward their subjects, and their mood—an even more elusive and indefinable quantity—that these artists show any group coherence. The Symbolist poets and painters of the late nineteenth century were united in their common reaction against what they saw as the dominant materialist, naturalist and determinist ethos of the epoch. By focusing on the internal, symbolical world rather than the external, empirical one, by resorting to introspection rather than observation, they sought escapes from the tyranny of Fact and the denunciation of Soul which threatened to extinguish the life of the Imagination.

Theirs was, then, an art based upon the subjective suggestion of ideas, often made through an appeal to the senses, rather than the factual statement of things. The tendency toward subjectivity and introspection often led to personal and enigmatic visions and mystical themes expressed through private symbol rather than public, consensual allegory or metaphor. In the sense urged by Baudelaire and Mallarmé, their art was suggestive rather than nominative, resulting in obliquely defined equivalence of depicted objects and their correspondent ideals. Symbolist aesthetics prized ideographic content over purely formal statements, reflecting the primacy of spirit, soul or imagination over both the realist's dictionary of natural phenomena and the aesthete's manipulation of form without content. The Symbolist would applaud John La Farge's stated resolve to "give something more than a study or a handsome arrangement," and would agree with Elihu Vedder when he wrote that "for my part I must always admire a good arrangement of ideas as much as a good symphony in pale green and yellow."[2]

Although similar to the early nineteenth century's Romantics in their reactive stance, the Symbolists differed from their precursors both in the causes for their reaction and in their relation to their environment. Whereas the Romantic movement, generally speaking, arose in response to the dominant rationalist heritage of the Age of Enlightenment, Symbolism grew in reaction to the materialist values of the *fin de siècle.* The Romantic response was characterized by struggle and engagement with the world, while the Symbolist reacted by withdrawal and a carefully cultivated detachment from his time and place. The *fin-de-siècle* retreat into the life of the imagination and the world of private symbols knew no national boundaries nor restrictions to specific art forms. While the poets who were first labelled "Symbolists" were based in Paris, the reaction they represented was manifested nearly simultaneously from St. Petersburg to San Francisco, and cut across forms of artistic expression to embrace music, literature, theater and opera, as well as the visual arts. By focusing upon American painting from the mid-1880s to the First World War, both the native roots and the European parallels for this country's introspective Symbolist mood may be better understood.

Americans and the Symbolist International

Ever since Benjamin West stepped ashore at Livorno in 1760, American artists have been travelling to Europe for study. In the last twenty-five years of the nineteenth century, this trans-Atlantic traffic increased greatly: transit was facilitated by more and better steamships; the illustrated art press served to familiarize more Americans with the works of their European contemporaries, thereby increasing the desire for travel to the Old World; European art, especially French, enjoyed unprecedented popularity among American collectors and patrons, again sharpening American artists' focus upon the works of their competitors in the marketplace; and, the American economy's rebound from the Civil War made European *Wanderjahre* more feasible for our young artists.[1]

For most American artists in Europe after about 1875, Paris was the primary destination, so much so that in the early 1880s J.-K. Huysmans worried that the French capital was becoming a "sinister Chicago."[2] The case, however, had not always been so. Following his Italian sojourn, Benjamin West settled permanently in London, thereby establishing a vogue for that capital as a mecca for American painters well into the early decades of the nineteenth century. In turn, Rome and the Arcadian landscape of the Italian Campagna, then Düsseldorf, and later Munich and Venice had all enjoyed attention as important art centers for travelling American painters; for sculptors, Florence as well had been a major center of activity from the late 1820s through the end of the century.[3] Periodically American travel abroad was interrupted by economic recessions, or by European revolutions and wars, such as those in 1848 and 1870-71; and in this country the Civil War and occasional waves of xenophobic nationalism from time to time detoured some of our painters from the Campagna to the Catskills. Despite these periodic barriers to cultural intercourse with Europe, the century as a whole was marked by the growing involvement of Americans in general, and our artists in particular, with the international community; indeed, recalling his first European tour at the very end of the century, Van Wyck Brooks wrote that "it was understood in the world I knew that a voyage to Europe was the panacea for every known illness and discontent . . ."[4]

In the years immediately following the turmoil of the Civil War and the Franco-Prussian War, the United States and France both experienced remarkable growth politically and artistically. By the mid-1870s, Munich was the only European art center which could rival Paris in terms of its attractions for American travellers. However, even Frank Duveneck, the

American painter most closely identified with the Bavarian art capital, had to admit by 1877 that "Munich is very much played out in the way of art. There is nothing done whatever and no pictures bought at all and I don't know but what I would do better to get out of Munich as soon as possible."[5] He and his compatriot, William Merritt Chase, were contemplating a move to Paris as an escape from the Bavarian backwater.

France, and Paris in particular, had been increasingly important since mid-century, both as a specific destination for American artists and as a general force in European art. The increasing prominence of French influence on American art led to successive or simultaneous vogues for Millet-like landscapes and peasant pictures, for slick Salon compositions, for color- and light-filled landscapes in the Impressionist mode, and other variations upon French themes. In recent years the Franco-American connections have been the subject of a number of important studies focusing upon American art in the Barbizon mood, on American academic painting, on American Impressionism, and other Gallic imports.[6]

Curiously, however, in the on-going review of late-century parallels between Europe and America little heed has been paid to American artists' relations with the European Symbolists. The general neglect which Symbolism has suffered may account for this oversight. For nearly half a century critics and historians have focused on the formal innovations of the European modernists, often at the expense of the highly subjective, content-laden and frequently esoteric works of the Symbolists. This neglect of Symbolist sources is not surprising in view of the fact that the movement has been seen as embracing phenomena as diverse as the synthetism of the Pont-Aven school centered on Paul Gauguin and Emile Bernard, the decadent and chimerical visions of Fernand Khnopff and Jean Delville, and the abstruse iconographies of Sâr Joséphin Peladan's Rosicrucian Salon exhibitors. In general, however, such artists, and the writers connected with the movement—Stephane Mallarmé, Paul Verlaine, Joris-Karl Huysmans, Maurice Maeterlinck, and others—were linked by a personal, subjective and not infrequently visionary aesthetic which ran counter to the prevailing naturalism and materialism of late nineteenth-century culture.

Neglect of Symbolist parallels between European and American art is all the more remarkable in light of the numerous and meaningful contacts which existed between subjectivist artists on both sides of the Atlantic. In fact, two of the leading writers among the Parisian Symbolists were Americans by birth, Stuart Merrill and Francis Vielé-Griffin. The former especially came to be known to his compatriots through his poetry and commentary; between 1887 and 1890 he was resident in New York where, with mixed success, he proselytized the cause of his Parisian colleagues in the American press and among American authors. In Paris, the *Mercure de France* revived at the end of the century and became an hospitable organ for the dissemination of Symbolist literature and theory; in its pages American writers such as Merrill found occasional outlets for their works, along side those of their better-known French colleagues. For instance, Mrs. Fiske-Warren of Boston published a drama in the December, 1894, issue, which one Chicago reviewer praised as "mystical enough for Maeterlinck himself, and exquisite enough to add to her various successes."[7]

The analogy to the Belgian mystic, Maeterlinck, is not surprising in view of the broad impact which his thought and writings had on turn-of-the-century America. In later years the painter-photographer Edward Steichen described himself as "terribly romantic and passionate in my early painting days . . . Maeterlinck's essay 'Silence' stirred me, [and] I went out to paint pictures of night and silence in that mood."[8] In Paris between 1900 and 1902, Steichen sought out Maeterlinck and prevailed upon him to sit for his portrait, one of a series of masterful photographs which he made of leading writers and artists. Many of Steichen's subjects in those years were notable for their imaginative contributions to the arts, and provide a gauge of the young American's taste: George Frederick Watts, Auguste Rodin, Franz von Stuck, Alphonse Mucha, as well as Maeterlinck.[9]

Perhaps nowhere in America were the ideas of the "Belgian Shakespeare" more sympathetically received than in Boston. There the still-potent legacy of Ralph Waldo Emerson created a responsive audience for Maeterlinck's belief in the "oneness of the individual with the absolute."[10] Through the medium of the Back Bay aesthete, F. Holland Day, a circle of Boston writers and artists was introduced to the Belgian's work. Among Day's protégés was the Lebanese mystic, poet and painter, Kahlil Gibran, for whom Maeterlinck became a special idol with an enduring influence.

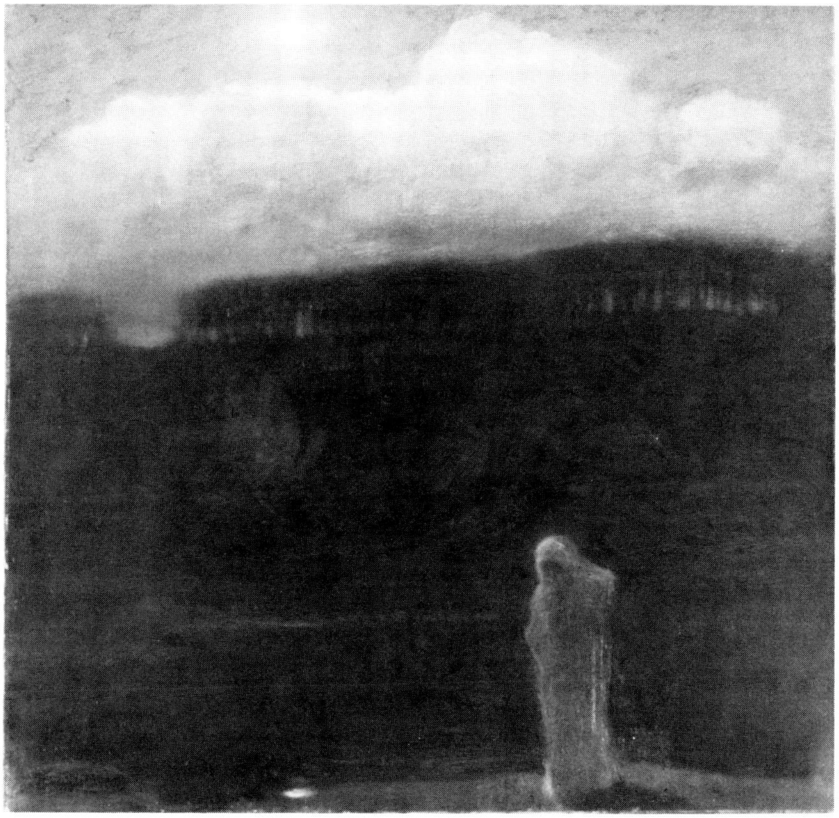

1. Edward Steichen, *Shrouded Figure in Moonlight,* 1907, cat. no. 58.

Eclipsed financially by New York and the brash boom towns of the prairie, especially Chicago, Boston by the end of the century was well into its decline. Yet Boston conceded nothing intellectually to the rest of America, and in its waning the seeds of introspective thought and the decadence readily took root. Aubrey Beardsley, like Maeterlinck, found an enthusiastic audience there. In 1894, Harvard undergraduates lampooned their founding father in a caricature of John Harvard purportedly reproduced from *The Chip-Book* and *The Blue Book* and signed by one Daubley Beardless. The editor of the new *Chap-Book,* whose prominence was early indicated in this cartoon, commented on the parody of the notorious illustrator for the London *Yellow Book:* "It may have been easy to do, but it was well done. Few people know Beardsley's work at all, outside of grotesque abnormal massed blacks and whites. Even in them is always the original and distinctive line; but he has executed many drawings which are full of elaborated beauty and nothing else, and some little wild pastoral designs with figures which stand midway between Cellini and the Greek potters. Meanwhile it pays to be queer."[11]

Even the aging Boston realist, William Dean Howells, succumbed to the charm of the subjectivist Europeans. At the request of his countryman, Stuart Merrill, Howells wrote the introduction to *Pastels in Prose,* an English translation of prose poems by French writers, including Baudelaire, Mallarmé, Huysmans, Maurice de Guérin and others. "The very life of the [prose poem] form is its aerial delicacy," wrote Howells, "its soul is that perfume of thought, of emotion, which these masters here have never suffered to become an argument. Its wonderful refinement, which is almost fragility, is happily suggested in the notion of 'Pastels' . . . I have felt, in going over these little pieces, that the slightest rudeness of touch might shake the bloom, the color, from them. As it is, I am certain they must be approached with sympathy by whoever would get their lovely grace, their charm that comes and goes like the light in beautiful eyes."[12]

Through such translations and commentary, educated American readers of the 1880s and later became familiar with the work of the European Symbolist writers. *The Chap-Book,* which was begun by Herbert Stone and Ingalls Kimball while still undergraduates at Harvard, and later moved to Chicago, became one of the leading American outlets for such literature, and Stone and Kimball proselytized enthusiastically for the Symbolist cause, especially in the early years of the publication. For instance, they were the American representatives for Mallarmé's campaign to raise funds for a monument to the late Paul Verlaine; while they admitted that "the number of persons in this country who knew and appreciated Verlaine's work is not great," they urged their readers to avail themselves of "the opportunity to assist in raising a monument to the greatest poet of modern France and one of the most perfect poets of all time . . . "[13] Earlier, *The Chap-Book* had published "A Feminine Appreciation" of Verlaine, the "incarnate of the mad poet . . . the first poet of France . . . "[14] Many Americans might have lamented, as did Theodore Child, the *fin-de-siècle* attitudes of the French Symbolists; Child damned the "disposition to dreaminess and perverse meditation over the past, the bitter sadness that comes from the loss of illusions of all kinds . . . , the negative and non- creative mental attitudes . . . [and] the subtle and amusing poison of Renanism" which he saw as indications that "the French soul is undergoing a transformation . . . that implies withal the disappearance of those qualities which gave to France her intellectual supremacy of old."[15] Contrary to such conservative reactions, *The Chap-Book* editor prided himself on his belief that "the decadent movement as a whole is significant and sincere . . ."[16] In its pages *The Chap-Book* extolled the "Uses of Perversity," argued arcane points of precedence in the use of accentuated repetition by Mallarmé and Maeterlinck, and, with tongue in cheek, cited *The Jabberwocky* as the first Symbolist poem and its author, Lewis Carroll, as the "new chief of the Symbolists!"[17] An early American commentator noted that "such part of the wide public as the Symbolists can reach . . . is a very restricted part, at best . . . "[18] So too was the audience for *The Chap-Book's* articles, poems, illustrations and editorials a somewhat limited one.[19] Nevertheless, the fact that it flourished from 1894 to 1898 and exercised a huge impact on other little magazines suggests the presence of an educated, cosmopolitan and sympathetic audience for the advanced literary and artistic theories published therein.

A year after *The Chap-Book's* appearance, H. T. Peck introduced *The Bookman, An Illustrated Literary Journal* in New York. Although its focus was more narrowly upon contemporary writers, Peck's journal, and particularly his own columns in it, displayed a cultivated mind and courageous taste similar to Kimball's and Stone's. Peck departed from the usual reliance upon British criticism of the Parisian writers, and his 1898 commentary on Mallarmé remains one of the most perceptive early appreciations of the poet's work.[20]

Even those who were not initiates of *The Chap-Book's* or *The Bookman's* theories could not escape the wide publicity given to the Symbolist writers and painters. "And who have not escaped the contagion?" asked Theodore Child in *Harper's*. "Very few, indeed, of the brilliant and active minds," he complained.[21] Consequently, considerable attention was paid to the Parisian vogue by the popular American press, although much of it echoed the negative appraisal offered by Child. There were, however, partisans of the Symbolist movement who tried carefully to explain its tenets to American readers. In 1893, Aline Gorren offered her readers in *Scribner's* a lengthy and perceptive examination of the French Symbolist writers.[22] Given the speed with which Maeterlinck's and other Symbolist writings were translated into English, some *Scribner's* subscribers may already have read the texts which Miss Gorren so insightfully reviewed.

Perhaps the most important proselyte in the popular press was the critic, James Gibbons Huneker. His commentary on contemporary art, literature and music filled the pages of specialized publications and popular journals from the early 1890s until the First World War, and many of his impressions were reprinted in volumes of collected essays during his lifetime. While music was his main love,[23] Huneker was also a regular reporter on events in the literary and artistic circles of New York and Europe. With Vance

Thompson he co-edited *Mlle. New York* which made its debut in August 1895. This most Francophile of American journals sought to broaden its readers' comprehension of the Symbolist literary revolution beyond the limits of the small circle to which their acquaintance was largely limited. *Mlle. New York* published writings and criticism of Jules Laforgue, Remy de Gourmont, Paul Fort, Marcel Schwob and other less well-known authors in

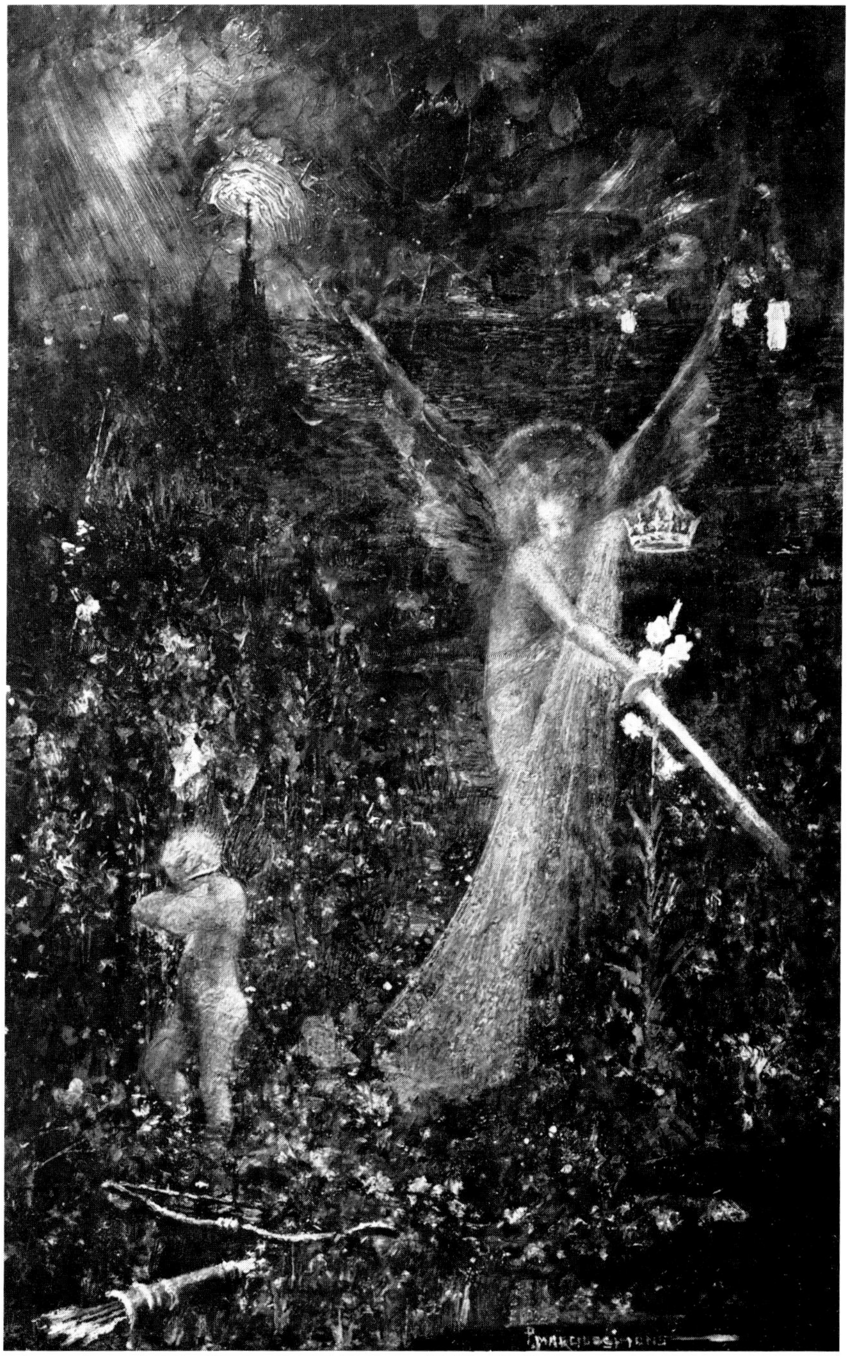

2. Pinckney Marcius-Simons, *Cupid and the Flowers,* circa 1895, cat. no. 37.

an effort to rebut the notion of Symbolist literature as difficult and troublesome, and to correct the common misapprehension of the movement as being limited to Baudelaire, Verlaine, Mallarmé and Maeterlinck.[24] Huneker also contributed frequent articles to *Harper's Bazar, Harper's Weekly, Scribner's* and other periodicals directed toward a large audience, discussing Huysmans, Baudelaire, Maeterlinck, Wagner, Rodin and other heroes of the Symbolist camp.[25] In many of these cases his reactions to the art were informed by his frequent meetings and personal friendships with the artists in Europe. While Huneker's writings on art were less numerous than his musical and literary commentaries, and are consequently and regrettably less well known today, they are infected with the same romantic enthusiasm, visionary spirit and musical vocabulary as his critiques of other media.

Personal contacts, translations and commentary familiarized educated Americans with the Symbolist writers. So too did friendships, exhibitions and journalistic accounts acquaint them with painters working in Paris, Brussels and elsewhere in Europe. In many reports of artists' early years in Paris and London, the expatriate painter, James McNeill Whistler, figures prominently. Having created sensation after sensation with his striking canvases of the 1860s and '70s, he became a logical focus for American artists abroad. Through Whistler, painters such as Alice Barney were introduced to the rarified ambience of Mallarmé's circle.

Puvis de Chavannes was another object of Americans' interests. Although Puvis was never comfortable with the Symbolist label, his work was greatly admired by many artists of the period, and among them none were more vociferous in their acclaim than the subjectively oriented Symbolists. More important perhaps than Puvis' own self-definition may have been the way others saw him; in that regard his was clearly a major influence on the Symbolists, who particularly admired the dreamy vagueness of his paintings. Americans echoed this praise of the independent French master and were influenced by his work, sometimes to the point of adulation. Puvis gave a "courteous and intimate" reception to his occasional American pupils, a trait which must have been appreciated by young men who might otherwise have encountered a scornful reproach like that offered by Gérôme who told one American that "[I] would better have stayed in my own savage country and planted cabbages than have come all the way to Paris to study drawing."[26] Arthur Wesley Dow praised Puvis as the "greatest painter of modern times," a sentiment echoed by other American artists as well as by the critic, Theodore Child; he found Puvis' to be the "grandest and most considerable work of the present century."[27] That Child, who had previously deplored the Symbolists' "dreaminess and perverse meditations," could honor the accomplishments of one of their heroes, suggests something of the ambivalent position which Puvis de Chavannes occupied in late-century French painting.

Even the more extreme manifestations of the Symbolist spirit claimed their American admirers. The Salons de la Rose+Croix were organized in Paris between 1892 and 1897 by the French mystic and self-styled "Sâr,"

Joséphin Peladan. Both the man and his exhibitions were among the most extraordinary phenomena of *fin-de-siècle* France. The quirkish guidelines which Peladan established for exhibitors at the Rosicrucian Salon eliminated many of the more independent and innovative talents at work in Paris during the decade of the 1890s. Even in his Salons, however, which were possibly the most esoteric manifestation of the Symbolist mood anywhere in Europe, an American was included—the now-forgotten Pinckney Marcius-Simons, who displayed work in the Rosicrucian Salons of 1893-1895 and again in the final exhibit in 1897. More surprising than Marcius-Simons' inclusion was the rumored support which was pledged to Peladan by a wealthy American sympathizer, who planned to provide the Sâr's Ordre de la Rose+Croix with its own abbey. Unfortunately for the order, Peladan was detained overnight on smuggling charges by Belgian customs officials upon trying to re-enter France, thereby missing his scheduled appointment with his would-be sponsor. With that incident in November 1893 vanished hopes for American benefaction of the Rosicrucians.[28]

As with the writers', so too could the ideas of Symbolist painters become familiar to segments of the public in this country through reports appearing in the daily press and periodicals. Accounts of the Salon d'Automne and other European exhibitions were regular features in the art press, which was enjoying a boom in the period from the 1890s onward. For obvious reasons the actual paintings by Gauguin and Moreau, Redon and Khnoppf, and others of similar persuasions, did not travel to these shores with the same ease or regularity as translations of Symbolist literature; but through written commentary and continually improving quality of reproduction in the art press, their works were not entirely unknown. One French visitor to Boston in 1893 was surprised to hear Gustave Moreau's work knowledgably discussed with a "suppleness of intellect."[29]

Despite the occasional appearance of their paintings in American exhibitions or collections from the 1890s onward, despite major commissions for Puvis de Chavannes at the Boston Public Library in 1890, and despite the availability of their canvases to American students and buyers in Paris, it was not until the fabled Armory Show of 1913 that many Americans had a belated opportunity to encounter the Symbolist artists in their finest form and in full force. The organizers of the Armory Show delighted in the anticipation of the surprising introduction of Odilon Redon to American audiences, who were not previously familiar with his visionary work; in fact, Redon had the largest single representation in the exhibition, with 75 prints and paintings included. While Marcel Duchamp and the Cubists may have stolen the show, as far as the general public and the New York press were concerned, there were those for whom the encounter with the Symbolist exhibitors was even more meaningful. After seeing the show in Boston, Kahlil Gibran noted that Redon "has a mind and has greatness—he grasps widely, inclusively . . . " Gauguin he found "the most interesting of the others . . . (other than Redon)."[30] That the Boston visionary should have responded to Redon and Gauguin is not, perhaps, surprising; but he was not alone in his response. For others also the encounter with "the individualists of Pont-Aven and their compelling radicalism" effected a conversion which was to alter American tastes in the years immediately following the Armory Show.[31]

The synthetist experiments which Paul Gauguin and Emile Bernard conducted in Pont-Aven in 1888 provided stimulus for Maurice Denis and his "brothers" in *les Nabis.* In 1890 Denis made the first effort to codify his difficult version of a modern aesthetic emerging from the Symbolist milieu. Denis' famed "Définition du néo-traditionnisme" stressed the hermetic and formal world of the picture itself, divorced from naturalistic concerns for the external world.[32] The Symbolist concerns of Gauguin and his followers were brilliantly argued by the tragically short-lived critic and apologist, Albert Aurier, most especially in his well-known critique of "Le symbolisme en peinture—Paul Gauguin." There Aurier made the often repeated argument that ". . . the work of art . . . should be:

1) Idea-ist, because its unique idea would be the expression of the Idea;
2) Symbolist, because it would express this idea through forms;
3) Synthetic, because it would write these forms, these signs, following a method of general comprehension;
4) Subjective, because the object would never be considered as an object, but only as a sign of the idea perceived by the subject;

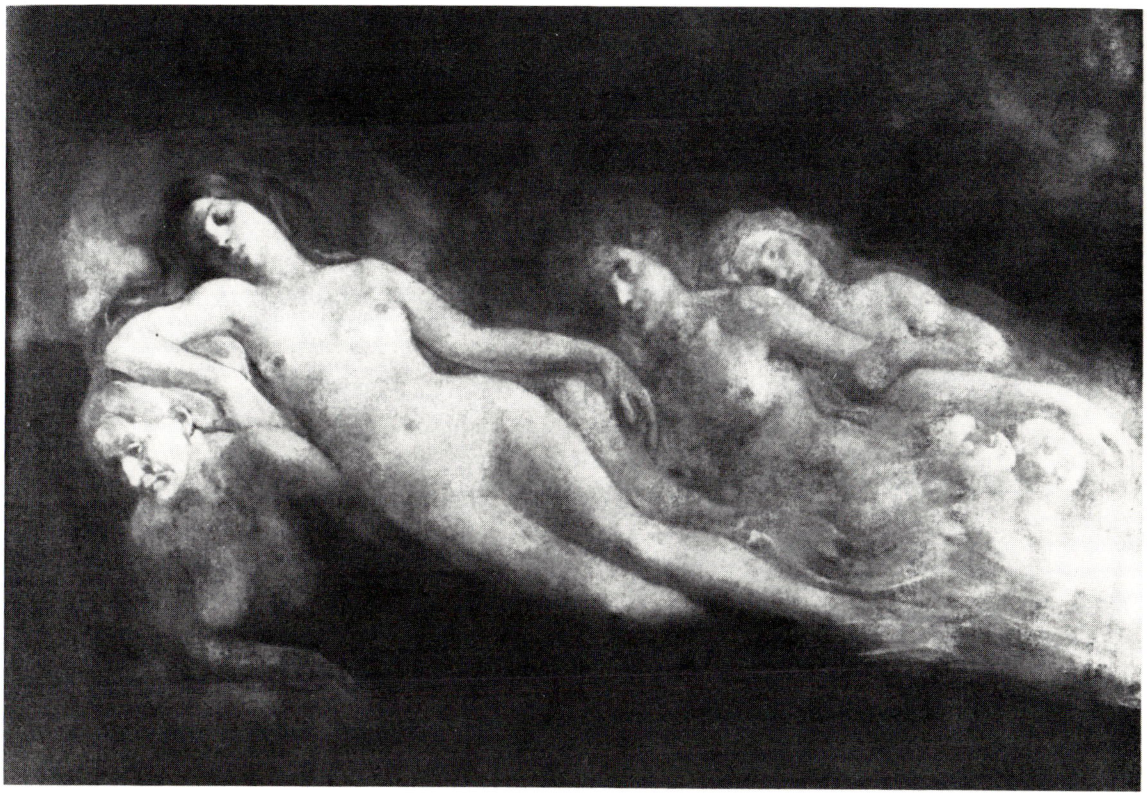

3. Kahlil Gibran, *The Ages of Women,* 1910, cat. no. 24.

5) (This is a consequence) *decorative*—for decorative painting, accurately described, as it was understood by the Egyptians, most likely the Greeks and the Primitives, is nothing else than a manifestation of art that is all at once subjective, synthetic, symbolist and idea-ist."[33]

Simultaneous with Denis' and Aurier's efforts to develop a modern or Symbolist aesthetic, Joséphin Peladan was preparing his creed for the Salon de la Rose+Croix. In lieu of the Nabis' formally subjective concerns, Peladan emphasized the propriety of selected pictorial subjects; similar to Aurier's and Denis' arguments, however, was Peladan's proscription of mere observation and recording of empirical reality. Instead the Sâr sought "to ruin realism, reform Latin taste and create a school of idealist art." Therefore, from his Rosicrucian Salons, the following were "rejected subjects, no matter how well executed, even if perfectly:

1) History painting, prosaic and from a textbook, like Delaroche;
2) Patriotic and military painting, such as by Meissonier, Neuville, Detaille;
3) All representations of contemporary, private or public life;
4) The portrait—except if it is not dateable by costume and achieves style;
5) All rustic scenes;
6) All landscape, except those composed in the manner of Poussin;
7) Seascape; sailors;
8) All humorous things;
9) Merely picturesque orientalism;
10) All domestic animals and those relating to sport;
11) Flowers, still life, accessories and other exercises that painters ordinarily have the effrontery to exhibit."[34]

Following the breakup of Impressionism, other European innovators sought inspiration in Whistler's vague and suggestive aestheticism, in the obliqueness of Symbolist verse, in an escape from the present into idylls remote in time or place, and in similar retreats from the dominant objectivism of the day. Initially this Symbolist episode was viewed as largely a French phenomenon, with important contributions from Belgium. Increasingly, however, more recent historians have noted Symbolism's manifestations across the whole of Europe. As the aggressive self-confidence of mid-century became infected with the nascent malaise of the *fin de siècle*, the result knew no national boundaries. In its various regional manifestations, the Symbolist spirit became an international symptom of the struggle of introspection with observation, of imagination with fact.

American artists, especially those present in such numbers in Paris at the end of the century, were not immune to the mood of the period. Until recently, however, few have been the references to Symbolist sources for American art and thought at the turn of the century. To identify their creations with a philosophy or aesthetic which was frequently pessimistic or

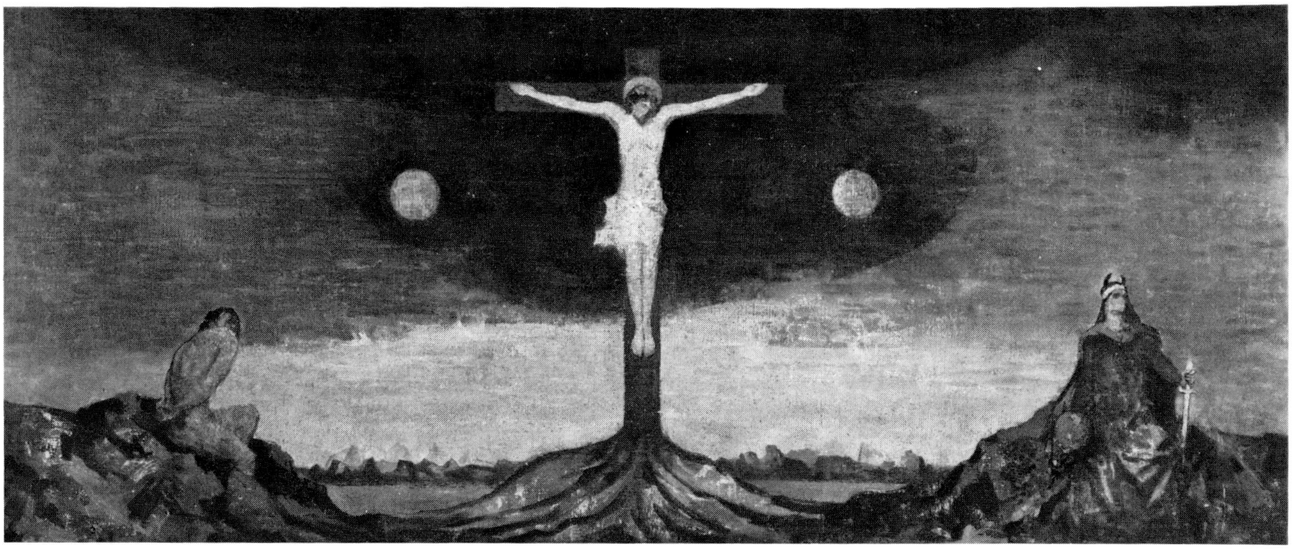

4. Augustus Vincent Tack, *Mystical Crucifixion,* before 1924, cat. no. 61.

negative, if not perverse, would be to contradict the isolated and optimistic faith in which Americans prided themselves. Henry Adams' pessimistic *Education* is clearly at odds with the buoyant optimism of his distinguished Federalist forebears, and the legacy of the earlier Adams generations remained deeply ingrained in the national consciousness well into the present century. The factual and empirical bias of America's hagiographers allowed little room for the canonization of mystics, visionaries, dreamers and escapists of a Symbolist stripe. Consequently, the references to artists' relations with the subjective and introspective alien aesthetic remained few, and in general have been made only with specific focus upon individual alliances or affinities so as not to despoil the main drift of American historiography.

The exceptional visionaries among American painters had been recognized as anomalies by their contemporaries, and often continue to be so regarded today. Men such as Albert Ryder and Arthur B. Davies were esteemed despite, or because of, their separation from the mainstream of perceptual art. Whistler provides another case in point: "These nocturnes," wrote one critic in 1892, " . . . have disconcerted people more than anything Mr. Whistler has painted . . . for sometimes they reach the very limits of the painter's art, and even penetrate beyond into the artificial paradises of Poe and Baudelaire."[35] Other such Franco-American analogies, with suggestions of Symbolist overtones, abound in the literature of the period. Of Gibran one Boston contemporary wrote: "Maeterlinck has lived on, and at present he is drawing and writing Arabic poems and essays."[36] In 1917, the long-neglected work of Robert Newman was praised as having "an elusive charm . . . easily missed unless one is peculiarly sensitive to the sensations of color and to the suggestion of forms used mainly as symbols in a manner of expression somewhat similar to that of . . . Rodin."[37] Duncan Phillips believed that Augustus Tack's "philosophy is that of the universal mystic . . . [showing] affinity with the improvisations of Odilon Redon . . . who discovered the brooding mind of man as a rich vein of raw material for the artist."[38]

More recently parallels have been drawn, for instance, between Maurice Prendergast's titling of his pictures and the nomenclature used by Symbolist artists, and Thomas Dewing's use of studio props to evoke a state of mind has been compared to the analogous use of correspondences by the French Symbolists.[39] The specificity of all these references, however, is suggestive of the isolation in which historians and critics have tended to view such affinities.[40] Perhaps only now, as we near another *fin de siècle,* and as Symbolist studies continue to burgeon, is it possible to appreciate fully the impact which the Symbolist mood made upon American art at the turn of the century, to recognize the parallels which existed between the American tradition which preceded and the Symbolist aesthetic which was imported, and to understand the legacy which the mingling of native tradition and Symbolist aesthetics created for twentieth-century art in America.

The Imaginative Tradition in American Literature

That Symbolist sources for American painting might have been overlooked in the past is not, perhaps, surprising in view of the general tone of writings on American art. From their beginning with William Dunlap's *History of the Rise and Progress of the Arts of Design in the United States,* published in 1834, and continuing through much of the nineteenth century, accounts of the arts in America were marked by a heavy reliance upon biographical details and anecdotes. Today the writings of such mid- and late-century historians and critics as Henry Tuckerman, James Jackson Jarves and Maria G. van Rensselaer stand out and are important for their insights into individual artists and their general grasp of aesthetic issues of the day; however, such commentators as these were the exception rather than the rule for most of the century. Even the rapid growth in illustrated art journals at the end of the century did not perceptibly raise the general level of art commentary in this country. In welcoming the appearance of *The American Art Review's* initial issue of 1879, a writer for another journal astutely noted that "art criticism in this country has been too much mixed up with journalism, and journalism has come to mean hasty and unformed writing. We have a few cultured and two or three able and brilliant writers who have devoted themselves particularly to this branch of periodical literature, but there is no body of men competent both to criticize and to write, and thoroughly versed not only in the technique of art, but in that of art criticism as well." The reviewer concluded on a curious note: "There is time enough, however. Criticism, it has often been pointed out, is a later growth, succeeding a period of production, and criticism of our art would only be premature at this time."[1]

Premature or no, critical writing flourished in quantity if not in quality at the end of the nineteenth century, and the journalistic debates regarding tradition versus innovation in the art of painting preoccupied writers and readers on both sides of the Atlantic. Paralleling trends in much of the painting, critical language became increasingly subjective as the battles of Realism and Idealism, Impressionism and Academicism were waged in periodicals, catalogues and manifestos. Following the lead of Whistler's musical notations for his "Symphonies" and "Harmonies," many American critics adopted similar jargon to describe their subjective responses to painted compositions. The writings of the versatile Huneker, of Charles Caffin, of Sadakichi Hartmann and other turn-of-the-century commentators on

American aesthetics abound in such references. Where coupled with true understanding and appreciation of the works, they occasionally achieve meaningful insight; but in less capable mouths, such language ultimately served to muddle distinctions and to debase criticism.

In this country such an evocative critical vocabulary continued well into the present century with writers such as Paul Rosenfeld and Marsden Hartley, who especially applied it to the achievements of the Stieglitz circle, with which they were both allied. But the 1920s—the era of Rosenfeld, Hartley, *et al.*—also saw the emergence of a maturing historical perspective on American art. Simultaneous with the vogue for Americana in the 1920s and '30s came serious efforts to organize and interpret the artistic past, by writers like Suzanne LaFollette, Alan Burroughs and Frank J. Mather; these early histories of American art built upon and amplified the sequence initially laid out by Samuel Isham in his landmark study of 1905, *The History of American Painting.* The populist tone of American art between the Wars, the Americana revival, and the generational proximity to the painters of the turn of the century all contributed to what today might be considered curious selections indicating some myopia with regard to art of the turn of the century.

Significantly, however, the trinity of Homer, Eakins and Ryder was already established in the writing of the 1920s as representative of the highest accomplishments of the nineteenth-century American artist, and in such capacity they were canonized by the Museum of Modern Art in 1930.[2] While it would be foolhardy to demean the contributions which Homer and Eakins made to the realist tradition in this country, it is nevertheless worthwhile recalling the spirit of the times in which historians first acclaimed their titanic role; and it should also be noted that two-thirds of this American Trinity were acclaimed for their realism, their naturalism, their powers of observation. Ryder's place alongside Homer and Eakins was problematic to many observers in his own day, and subsequently. The dreamy vagueness, the mystical overtones, the literary subjects did not neatly harmonize with the emerging creed of the American vision as an empirically realistic one.

The objective canon was developed early; even in the 1890s observers noted "the truly American gift of direct vision; they see things and not the ideas of things. Furthermore, their ever-active life develops in them the virtue of an immediate relation with reality."[3] By the time the turn of the century was achieving historical status, the objectivist view had become the consensus of many writers. In 1927 Mather lamented the fact that "the American mind is concrete and little disposed to let itself wander, and as little to mystical concentration. Hence the mood of vision is as rare in our painting as in our literature."[4] Royal Cortissoz agreed, noting that "the prevailing tendency in American art has been toward an objective treatment of the facts of nature. This renders all the more conspicuous—and valuable—the work of a man rich in imagination."[5] Later, Perry Miller among others reiterated this evaluation; America, he wrote, is "the land of enterprise and industry, where the 'Romantic movement' could never penetrate more deeply into the life of the Republic than into the fragile brains of a pathetically few intellectuals."[6] Against this persistent litany of American objectivism, the neglect of the visionary, sensual fantasts of the late nineteenth century becomes more understandable.

Another problem has complicated and delayed the appreciation of late-century subjectivism in this country. In a classic case of generations' differences in tastes, Russell Lynes speculated on the problems of distance in time as a prerequisite for the appreciation of one's parents' tastes. "It was a long leap back for my generation to rediscover the delights of the mid-nineteenth century and to try to sort out the quality from the chaff," he wrote. But the end of the century presented even greater difficulties: " . . . we continued to consider the genteel attitudes and platitudes that characterized so much of Victorian and Edwardian art as the frosting on a cake which we suspected had a file concealed in it. At least we hoped it did, for it seemed to us like an age imprisoned in its conventions and content not to escape." Only with the passage of decades was Lynes able to arrive at the hope "that I can be talked out of my prejudices and my scepticism toward the taste of my parents from which I did my best forty-odd years ago to escape."[7] With the passage of years the children and more especially the grandchildren of the late Victorians have come to recognize the rich diversity of turn-of-the-century culture in America, and to till what Lynes belatedly recognized as "a lovely fertile and largely uncultivated field waiting for the scholarly plough to dig it up and the scholarly harvesters to pluck its blossoms . . . "[8]

Although Homer and Eakins still loom large in the artistic landscape—and rightfully so—no longer is their achievement seen in quite such isolation; no longer can they be understood as isolated, realist peaks against the vast and undistinguished salt flats of sentiment. Other peaks, and other valleys, have been discovered which fill out the landscape; now Mount Homer and Mount Eakins can be better understood in relation to their foothills, and their true elevations can be better measured. Recent studies have also changed and increased our understanding of Albert Ryder; instead of an isolated pinnacle against an eroded art-scape, Mount Ryder now forms the centerpiece of the Imaginative Range, within which is the mother lode American painters—visionaries, fantasts, and Symbolists—mined at the turn of the century.

The imaginative range of our literature was fully appreciated earlier. Ever since Charles Brockden Brown's publication of *Wieland* in 1798, American authors have shown interest in *Gothick* fantasy, although the tendency has been periodically balanced by more naturalistic or moralistic concerns. Edgar Allen Poe represents the century's most complete statement of this mode. His favored themes—death's awesome and mysterious face, the terror of insanity or remorse—show a preoccupation with the grotesque, the chimerical and the phantasmagoric. His thematic obsessions resulted in an art of narrow range, but great intensity. According to Edmund Stedman, the leading Poe scholar of the late nineteenth century, "Poe was not a single-poem poet, but the poet of a single mood. His materials were rather a small stock in trade, chiefly of angels and demons, with an attendance of Dreams, Echoes, Ghouls, Gnomes and Mimes ready, at hand.

He selected or coined, for use and re-use, a number of . . . 'beautiful words'—'albatross,' 'halcyon,' 'scintillant,' 'Ligeia,' 'Weir,' 'Yaanek,' D'Elormie,' and the like. Everything was subordinate to sound. But his poetry, as it places us under the spell of the senses, enables us to enter, through their reaction upon the spirit, his indefinable mood . . ."[9]

It is this last quality which formed the basis of Poe's appeal to Charles Baudelaire, who discovered the American's work in 1847. That discovery, and Baudelaire's subsequent translations of Poe into French, were events of signal importance in the evolution of the Symbolist movement in French literature. The euphony of Poe's verse, the uniqueness of his vision, and the evocative language he utilized were all of appeal to the Symbolists in later years. Of special interest here is the American source for the genesis of European Symbolism, implying a certain parallelism between American and French literature at mid-century. In *Axel's Castle,* his landmark study of Symbolist literature, Edmund Wilson noted this simultaneity. "It was in general true," he wrote, "that, by the middle of the century, the Romantic writers in the United States—Poe, Hawthorne, Melville, Whitman, and even Emerson—were . . . developing in the direction of Symbolism; and one of the events of prime importance in the early history of the Symbolist movement was the discovery of Poe by Baudelaire."[10]

Wilson's coupling of Poe and Hawthorne is particularly apposite. A year before the publication of *Axel's Castle,* Mathew Josephson had similarly paired the two American authors. From the vantage point of the early 1930s, when the rediscovery of our native literary tradition was gaining full momentum, Josephson observed that "in a large measure the strain of morbidity in Hawthorne and Poe seems to have been handed on. The obsession with evil, early sorrow and death appears astonishingly native to the American muse, which often continues, during the later period, to live by preference in the enchanted and supernatural air of Arthur Gordon Pym—as if in an effort to escape from hateful realities. 'Whatever the American men of genius are,' an English critic observed, 'they are not young gods making a young world'."[11]

The "young-ness" of America posed a special challenge to America's romantic authors. The darker visions which inhabited the minds of a Poe or a Hawthorne were at odds with the freshness and sunlight of the American present. Charles Baudelaire once noted that "what one sees in full sunlight is always less interesting . . . "[12] This was the predicament Hawthorne summarized in his famed preface to the *Marble Faun,* published in 1860. The author set his romance in Italy, "where actualities would not be so terribly insisted upon as they are, and must needs be, in America. No author, without a trial," wrote Hawthorne, "can conceive of the difficulty of writing a romance about a country where there is no shadow, no antiquity, no mystery, no picturesque and gloomy wrong, nor anything but a commonplace prosperity, in broad and simple daylight, as is happily the case with my dear native land. It will be very long, I trust, before romance writers may find congenial and easily handled themes, either in the annals of our stalwart republic, or in any characteristic and probable events of our individual lives. Romance and poetry, ivy, lichens and wall-flowers, need ruins to make them grow."[13]

The romance writer's retreat from the insistent actualities revealed by "broad and simple daylight" was echoed in the selection of many subsequent writers' and painters' motifs. A generation after Hawthorne, Paul Bourget, a turn-of-the-century de Tocqueville, still could perceive "the sense of need of a more distant background in this country, where all is present and actual."[14] As the century moved toward its conclusion, artists in increasing numbers turned from the simple narrative tale or genre picture to motifs and locales remote in time and place from the present. The antiquarian's refuge in lost civilizations of the ancient world, Hawthorne's romantic resort to shadowed ruins, Poe's wanderings in the morbid corridors of his mind, and the Symbolists' retreat into private visions all share in this aspect of escapism from the here and now. It was Sâr Peladan, perhaps, who codified the principle most tersely in his rules for Rosicrucian exhibitors: "All representations of contemporary, private or public life" were excluded.[15] His prohibition was, however, simply the reflection of a widespread antipathy to the material facts of contemporary life, shared by artists otherwise remote from the occult concerns of the Rosicrucians.

Hawthorne's romantic avoidance of the actualities manifested itself not only in the locale of his *Marble Faun* but also, on another plane, in the ontological concerns which characterized his most profound writings. More given to metaphysics than to phantasms, Hawthorne at his best might be seen as a precursor of the correspondent vision of the later Symbolists. Even Poe's sympathetic biographer, Edmund Stedman, admitted that it was the New Englander, not the Southerner, who conveyed the greater "spiritual meaning." "[Poe] relied upon his externals, making the utmost of their gorgeousness of color, their splendor and gloom of light and shade. Hawthorne found the secret meaning of common things and knew how to capture, from the plainest aspects of life, an essence of evasive beauty which the senses of Poe were unable to perceive. It was Hawthorne who heard the melodies too fine for mortal ear."[16]

Similar to the favorable response given to Hawthorne's tales in the Boston area was the reception accorded the Transcendentalist faith of his Concord neighbor, Ralph Waldo Emerson. Both evolved from the Puritan background which provided the strength and inspiration for their art and thought, either as a source for their mature work or as a philosophical tradition against which they could react. The vitality of the Transcendentalist faith stands in striking contrast to the vagaries of fortune which Poe's reputation suffered posthumously.[17] Forty years after his death Poe's work was still disdained by the Brahmins; in 1888 one critic observed that the Baltimore poet was "still unforgiven in New England. 'Those singularly valueless verses of Poe,' was the now celebrated *dictum* of one Boston prophet. . . . There were many sides on which Poe was likely to be long distasteful to Boston, Cambridge, and Concord. The intellectual weight of the man, although unduly minimized in New England, was inconsiderable by the side of that of Emerson."[18]

In his writing, Poe placed prime importance upon sensual or emotional response to the visions related in verse or prose. He argued against the importance of the idea in poetry, and especially against a didactic aesthetic; the immediacy of response, evoked by sound and image, was the basis for his art, and constituted his appeal to Baudelaire and the Symbolists. Emersonian Transcendentalism, by contrast, stressed the moral character of natural facts, which was effected by establishing correspondences between the material facts of this world and the spiritual facts of another. Sensual response could aid in making this metaphysical translation, but unlike Poe, such emphases were not the writer's primary aim. To the Concord philosopher the notion of correspondences validated the material, objective, natural fact both with regard to the human mind and to the moral universe. As had the Puritan theologian, Jonathan Edwards, Emerson used the observation of the natural fact to arrive at a moral conclusion, a form of correlative argument at which Henry David Thoreau was to become a master.

The quest for metaphysical ideals, so persistently conducted by Emerson and his colleagues, differed greatly then from Poe's artistic intentions. The allure of the Southern poet for French writers and intellectuals has been suggested already. Less well recognized is the extent to which Transcendentalist philosophy helped to prepare Boston and America for the reception of Symbolist beliefs imported at the end of the century. Significantly, Emersonian thought enjoyed something of a revival in *fin-de-siècle* Paris, as well as continuing to exert its influence on many American intellectuals, especially in New England. American Transcendentalism and its emphasis upon the individual's perception of and communion with the world offered an alternative to Darwinian determinism rampant in Western culture. By placing stress upon the unique volition of individual imagination and intellect, neo-Emersonians sought to stay the implacable determinism derived from Darwin and his interpreters. Remy de Gourmont, who, after Albert Aurier's death and Jean Moréas' defection, became the main spokesman for the literary Symbolists in Paris, defined the writer's art as "not merely a reflection but a magnified reflection of his own personality. The only excuse a man can have for writing is to write himself, to reveal to others the sort of world that is mirrored in his own individuality. His only excuse is to be original . . . . He must create his own aesthetic. . . . Let us therefore admit that symbolism, though it may be excessive, though it may be inconvenient, though it may be pretentious, is the expression of individualism in art."[19] In America as well, the Transcendentalist tradition continued to exercise its influence. In 1888 it was noted that "Bryant, Holmes and Emerson exist, and were never more prominent than today. . . ."[20] That prominence continued into the next decade at least; one of F. Holland Day's circle of Boston aesthetes described his poetic colleagues as "not, strictly speaking, a school at all. . . . They cannot be catalogued under one formula. . . ." As with the writers championed by Remy de Gourmont, the Boston poets' "greatest unity lies in the stress of individuality. . . ." Among these writers, "materialism seems almost without a representative, the tendency being to the other extreme of mysticism as in the native symbolism of [Bliss] Carman

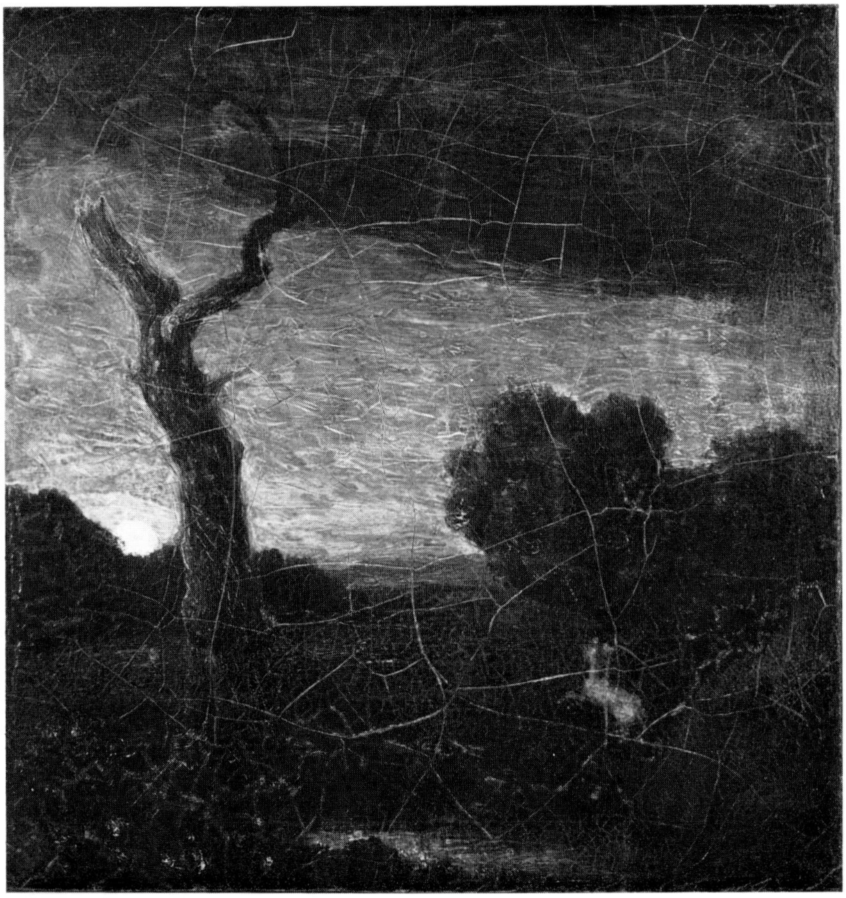

5. Albert P. Ryder,
Stag in the Forest of Arden
(or *Landscape with Centaur*),
circa 1897, cat. no. 53.
(Photo by Joseph Levy)

or Maeterlinck's strange new development of Neo-Platonic thought."[21] Also in the 1890s, one of the Parisian reviews serialized Emerson's writings, and Maeterlinck published in translation a volume by the Concord thinker.[22] This reciprocal admiration of Parisians for Emerson and Bostonians for Maeterlinck suggests that the romantic or, as Edmund Wilson called it, "proto-Symbolist" spirit evinced by our mid-nineteenth-century writers had, by the end of the century, become fused with a mature Symbolist aesthetic as part of an international mood of introspection.

Scholarship on the imaginative romantic tradition in American literature abounds. Research into a comparable spirit in our painting, however, has been relatively less extensive. Albert Ryder survived to enjoy a measure of critical acclaim at the end of his life. It is significant, however, that in seeking to explicate his apparently unique work, interpreters more often drew analogies to America's romantic writers—Poe, Hawthorne, Melville—or to European imaginative artists—Blake, Moreau, Boecklin, Matthijs Maris—than to his fellow American painters of the late nineteenth century. Such comparisons are symptomatic of a tendency to view American imaginative or visionary painters as "exceptional." Ryder's predecessors, such as Allston, Quidor and Page, and his contemporaries, such as George Fuller, Vedder and La Farge, were often examined *in vacuo,* lacking apparent parallels within American experience. Because such introspective artists perforce rely upon their individual imaginations it was easy to overlook the relationships among them and to treat them as isolates. Twentieth-century studies, however, have helped us to recognize that a century of "unique" contributions *does* serve to constitute a tradition in our native art.

Beginning with the landmark exhibition which James Thrall Soby organized for the Museum of Modern Art in 1943, the romantic tradition in American art has come in recent decades to enjoy more intense scrutiny, comparable to that which had previously been granted to its literary counterpart.[23] In addition to Ryder, numerous Americans of similar artistic temper—although not necessarily of comparable achievement—have been the subjects of monographic studies since the mid-twentieth century.[24] A new appreciation of the complexities of American art in the last century has resulted from these collective studies, which no longer makes it convenient, or even possible, to dismiss the visionary, romantic spirit as the mere underside of the realist coin. A century of imaginative and evocative productions on the part of our writers and our painters helped to prepare America for the *fin-de-siècle* manifestations of the Symbolist spirit.

The tradition of romanticism was vital for the Symbolist growth, and the situation in America offers numerous, provocative parallels to that in Europe, especially France. Revolutions in the late eighteenth century established the basis for new nationalistic fervor in both countries, and concomitant expressions of that national pride in artistic images and forms appropriate to the local situation. Catastrophic upheavals in the 1860s and '70s scarred the optimistic faith of each nation. In their recoveries from the Civil War and the Franco-Prussian War and Commune, both America and France experienced rapid industrial and economic growth, the phenomenal success of which made the periodic financial recessions all the more striking and stressful by contrast. In their postwar booms, America and France, and indeed much of Europe, saw traditional values being threatened by the rampant materialism which accompanied economic growth, and the determinist philosophies which sprang from Darwin's precepts as amplified by Herbert Spencer and others.

While such sweeping generalizations are admittedly fraught with peril, the striking similarities in American and European social, cultural and economic conditions at the end of the nineteenth century did seem to yield related reactionary movements. Late-century pessimism regarding cultural "progress" was felt on both sides of the Atlantic, and with it came an inevitable reaction against the reigning materialist culture. "I believe only in art," wrote Ralph Adams Cram, " . . . the ultimate expression of all that is spiritual, religious and divine in the soul of man. I hate material prosperity, I refuse to justify machinery, I cannot pardon public opinion. I desire absolute individuality and the triumph of idealism."[25]

In Europe such anti-materialist reactions have been related to the Symbolist mood; in America, they have been called Idealism, the Genteel Tradition, and other even less flattering terms. By whatever name, the flourishing of idealism and introspective imagination at the end of the nineteenth century was decidedly international in scope, and paralleled the romantic response of nearly a century earlier. The Symbolist movement might be considered as a revived romanticism, but with important differences from its earlier manifestation. Edmund Wilson's distinctions between Symbolism and Romanticism in literature might equally well be applied to the visual arts: " . . . we see plainly the fundamental difference between Symbolism and Romanticism," he wrote. "The later movement . . . was an antidote to nineteenth-century Naturalism, as the earlier had been an antidote to the neo-classicism of the seventeenth and eighteenth centuries: Symbolism corresponds to Romanticism, and it is in fact an outgrowth from it. But whereas it was characteristic of the Romantics to seek experience for its own sake—love, travel, politics—to try the possibilities of life; the Symbolists though they also hate formulas, though they also discard conventions, carry on their experimentation in the field of literature [or painting, as the case may be,] alone; and though they too, are essentially explorers, explore only the possibilities of imagination and thought. And whereas the Romantic, in his individualism, had usually revolted against or defied that society with which he felt himself at odds, the Symbolist had detached himself from society and schools himself in indifference to it: he will cultivate his unique personal sensibility even beyond the point to which the Romantics did, but he will not assert his individual will—he will end by shifting the field of literature [or art] altogether . . . from an objective to a subjective world, from an experience shared with society to an experience savored in solitude."[26]

The imaginative tradition in American art, the romantic writings of American authors in the mid-nineteenth century, and the aversion to a dominant materialism and naturalism at the end of the century all contributed to the development of an introspective American aesthetic which appeared simultaneously with, and inspired by many of the same causes as, European Symbolism.

Mystics and Humanists

The decades which embraced the turn of the century were then, and continue to be, regarded as a "watershed period" dividing two distinct and at times antipathetic cultures in America. As the century wound down, Tradition suffered a series of rude assaults in the miasmic flux of cultural revolution. Van Wyck Brooks offered an early review of America at odds with itself; in his *America's Coming of Age* (1915) he reflected upon the cultural polarities of the transitional period, on which our 1917 entry into World War was about to close a chapter.

Brooks, like George Santayana and other insightful commentators of the day, defined the central problem of the age as the competition of two cultures, the one based upon tradition, the other upon innovation. Since the revolutions of mid-century, traditional thought had sought accommodation with an unparalleled series of novel concepts, ranging from Charles Darwin's landmark thesis on the origin of species (1859), to Herbert Spencer's application of Darwinian precepts to the social organism, to William James' uniquely American Pragmatic solution to the dilemma of the times. The triumph of industrialism, with its social ramifications, which were justified in part by Spencerian arguments, colored the age which came to be known as "gilded." Scientific thought, and its pseudo-scientific handmaidens, undermined the shibboleths of traditional faith. Confronted by this conjunction of scientism, empiricism and the resulting naturalist ethos, beleaguered traditionalists resorted to self-definition by negation and retreated into inviolate cathedrals of imagination.

The reactions against modern culture were manifested internationally in the anti-materialist, anti-determinist, and anti-rational spirit of the late nineteenth century. Reactionary expressions ranged from political anarchism to religious evangelism, phenomena which arose across western Europe and America in the closing decades of the century. The quest for unity in the face of the modern age's fragmentation found artistic expression in both Bayreuth and Boston, in Wagner's *Gesamkunstwerk* and Richardson's collaborative which created Trinity Church. The force of history, which led Henry Adams to his pessimistic crisis of 1900, precipitated by the Paris Exposition, drove other artists deeper into the self and to a greater reliance upon individual imagination in lieu of a social orientation and an empirical observation. It was this interiorization of thought, this refusal to deal with the world as fact but rather as symbol, this imaginative flight from the empirical to the intuitive and sensual, which came to characterize the introspective Symbolist mood internationally at the turn of the century.

European and American fascination with the great expositions of the second half of the nineteenth century is well documented. Beginning with London's Crystal Palace Exposition of 1851, these extravaganzas occurred with increasing frequency through the balance of the century. Such fairs gave opportunity to air nationalistic pride, to expose technological and artistic advances and to revel in self-congratulation on cultural and technical progress. Although each fair had its own circumstances, history and results, there were factors common to most, if not all; among the most significant of these was the special enthusiasm shown for displays of technological innovations, by which society could in concrete fashion measure its advancements. As the century waned, the earlier positive reactions to such inventions were compromised by alternative responses. Reacting to the Galerie des Machines at the Paris Exposition of 1889, the French philosopher Eugene Melchior de Vogüé explained that "the Exhibition is an interminable object-lesson, whose first effect is to overwhelm all the perceptive faculties, whether physical or moral . . . The discovery we have undertaken [at the Galerie des Machines] is nothing less than the discovery of ourselves. This miscalled 'Centenary' of successive material facts would be a mere childish diversion if it were not, as it is in truth, a profound examination of conscience." For De Vogüé, the exhibition represented not so much a retrospective view of past accomplishment, but a preview; "it contains the embryo of the world's future. . . . In this lies the riddle of its irresistible charm." It was not the singular exhibition which impressed him, but rather "the Idea lying latent under the form which has so possessed us that no room is left to examine or care for the objects presented to our view. The Exhibition is only what it is, and so enthralling as it is, because it represents such an immense, such an infinite and marvelous storage of Ideas!"[1]

De Vogüé's response to the 1889 exhibition is marked by the predominance of Idea over Fact; in this he curiously portends Henry Adams' famous reaction to the Paris Exposition of eleven years later, in which the American's historical neck was broken by the modern Dynamo, confirming his nostalgia for the thirteenth-century Virgin, symbol of the unity of the medieval world of Mont Saint-Michel and Chartres. Unlike the pessimistic Adams, however, De Vogüé voiced the optimistic "hope that science will one day reveal the Central Motor, the motor whence are derived the sometimes conflicting applications of power." With that revelation would come the condemnation of the scientific principle as lacking "Sovereign Energy" and moral values. "The laws of the outward universe are but the reflex of the moral world within, and the Universal Force, once adequately distributed into its proper channels, will inspire the human heart for all the purposes of human life. In this new order of things Force must regain its noble, ancient name; with us, as with the Roman, it must be called Virtue."[2]

De Vogüé was a leader of the movement cumbersomely known as the Spiritualization of Thought in France, which was marked by a strong antimaterialist idealism. Although evidently short-lived in France, its basic concepts had at the time a wide appeal, extending well beyond Paris. The British *Contemporary Review* reported sympathetically and at length on the new tendency, and in America De Vogüé's tenets reached receptive ears as well. The Boston *Journal* editorialized on the significance of "Transcendentalism in France," and located its impetus in "a revulsion from the emptiness of current French belief, or more accurately, want of belief. It is an attempt to seek for the roots of the real in the invisible." While parallels to the American situation were left unstated by the *Journal's* editor, the implied

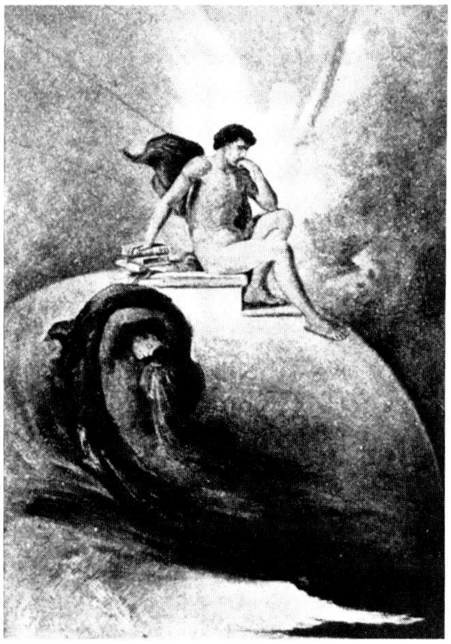

6. Ella F. Pell,
The Evolution of Soul,
circa 1896, location unknown.

critique of the French circumstances might relate as well to this country's: "Science became their religion. Just in conjunction with this came the application of the theory of realism to literature. Under these two influences France has struggled for more than a quarter century."[3] The editor of *Harper's Monthly* was readier to draw the analogy between the two nations. "Spiritualization of thought in France . . . is not a religious propaganda. . . . I adjure you, says the lecturer, to cultivate poetry and the ideal life. Of course, this is not a call to the verse-makers. It is not the art of rhyming that is to save us either in France or America," he wrote. Rather, "it is the poetic side of life that is to be cultivated; the newly enlisted army is to fight materialism, for it is seen how Realism, more and more sordid, has been playing into the hands of the materialistic age, killing poetry, killing aspiration, with its gospel of the equal value of all facts."[4]

In a similar vein, *Scribner's Magazine* offered a Christmas contemplation to its readers in 1902. The editor prescribed distraction from details and concentration on generalities, which "fetches incidentals into perspective and gives them their proper proportions. . . . The mechanisms of living abound so enormously nowadays," he lamented, "that we are in constant danger of losing sight, and even thought, of life from too rapt and incessant contemplation of its complicated apparatus. We don't invite our souls enough."[5]

The invocation of the "soul" had, with the concern for the ideal, characterized spiritualistic thought in France. Emile Faguet had dethroned Voltaire and the rationalist tradition with a single sentence: "*Voltaire n'a pas d'âme.* (Voltaire has no soul.)" This clarion call crystallized the sentiment of many in Fauget's *fin-de-siècle* generation. It "electrified France," according to *Harper's.* "It sent through it a thrill of conviction. At this phrase the whole soulless fabric of the eighteenth century tumbled into ruins. Over these ruins rose, like a star, the dictum of Tolstoi, till then unheeded, 'It is necessary to have a soul'."[6] Armed then with imagination, ideal and soul, reactionaries against the modern condition waged battle internationally with the hegemonic naturalism, empiricism and rationalism of the late nineteenth century. "The reaction against the rationalism of the eighteenth century has mingled with a reaction against the materialism of the nineteenth century," observed William Butler Yeats in 1897, and in the wedding of these two strains he found "certainly the only movement that is saying new things."[7]

The gospels of naturalism, social Darwinism and materialism had combined to drive many of our artists overseas during the 1870s and '80s. These refugees from the "Gilded Age" sought more hospitable ground for the cultivation of their artistic concept. "We are the disinherited of Art!" railed Theobald, Henry James' fictional expatriate. "We are condemned to be superficial! We are excluded from the magic circle. The soil of American perception is a poor little barren, artificial deposit. Yes! we are wedded to imperfection. An American, to excel, has just ten times as much to learn as a European. We lack the deeper sense. We have neither taste, not tact, nor power. How should we have them? Our crude and garish climate, our silent past, our deafening present, the constant pressure about us of unlovely circumstance, are as void of all that nourishes and prompts and inspires the artists, as my sad heart is devoid of bitterness in saying so! We poor aspirants must live in perpetual exile."[8] James' plaint of 1880 came at the high water mark of the expatriate movement, and it represented his most acerbic view of America's cultural barrenness. While expatriates continued to leave these shores well into the twentieth century, and in fact still do so today, their numbers greatly declined after 1900, ending what has been termed the "general expulsion of the civilized type."[9] By the 1890s, American painters' interests had shifted subtly but significantly; in place of Breton peasants, Alpine scenery and Roman ruins, more imaginative—that is, less geographically and temporally specific—subjects came to be of greater interest to contemporary artists. Although many still found it more congenial, the pursuit of purely imaginative motifs and subjective handlings did not mandate permanent exile.[10]

The flourishing of imagination affected all the arts in varying degrees. In what may have been a premature celebration, coming as it did just after Frank Norris' publication of *The Octopus* , one critic rejoiced that "the realism—the literalism—of both Zola and Mr. Howells perhaps belongs to a literary mood that has passed."[11] The naturalist's view, and the materialist concern for things, had ruled American taste for the preceding generation or more. In 1892 Henry Adams expressed remorse that the "banker's Olympus . . . had become, for five-and-twenty years, more and more despotic over Esop's frog empire."[12] Yet Esop's empire was not vanquished, and in certain circles began to prosper anew, even as Adams penned his rueful remarks.

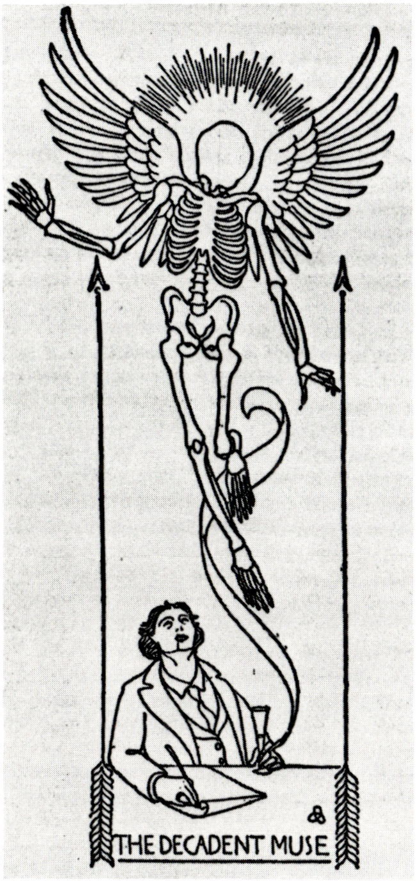

7. Claude Bragdon, *The Decadent Muse*, published in The Chap-Book, IV:6 (1895).

In Boston, for instance, Back Bay decadents were investigating theosophy and other alternatives to the dominant culture of the day. "The Theosophical Society, though backed by the wisdom of the ages, has, thus far, been unable to satisfy the hot yearnings skyward of some of its members," reported one unsympathetic observer in 1889; " . . . they have turned to churches, 'rosecrucian,' 'gnostic,' and 'esoteric' societies, with 'mahatmas' warm enough for the chilliest woman, and with short cuts to bliss!"[13] In addition to pseudo-Buddhism, Bostonians sought bliss through drugs, absinthe, and other decadent devices. William James described his experiences with mescal, which was distributed to his friends by Dr. S. Weir Mitchell, who "had himself been 'in fairyland.' It gives the most glamorous visions of color—every object thought of appears in a jewelled splendor unknown to the natural world. It disturbs the stomach somewhat, but that, according to W.M., was a cheap price, etc. I took one bud three days ago," reported the pragmatic Professor James, "and was violently sick for twenty four hours, and had no other symptom whatever except that and the *Katzenjammer* the following day. I will take the visions on trust!"[14]

One Boston aesthete catalogued the means for escaping the oppressive mood of the period: "We have tried . . . to reform the world, to induce mankind to turn now and then from the mad chase after Almighty Dollar, and smoke cigarettes and read Oscar Wilde. We have taken sides against electric cars, bicycles, and Mr. Howells. We have played at theosophy because we found it amusing. . . . We have sung the praises of cigarettes and coffee, not for themselves alone, but because they stand for a mood opposed to the prevailing tone of our times which turns life into an express train and makes old men at forty."[15] In Boston and elsewhere, sensitive artists and thinkers sought to escape the quotidian dullness they felt surrounding them. Whether by mescal or Wilde, cigarettes or theosophy, the goal was the same: to achieve release in the imagination, in dreams, in "fairyland." The release from the here and now, achieved through such means, made life worthwhile, indeed bearable. Otherwise, "living is a drab transaction, a concatenation of unimportant events," wrote the novelist, James Branch Cabell; "man is impotent and aimless; beauty, and indeed all the fine things which you desiderate in literature [or art]—and in your personal existence . . .—are nowhere attainable save in imagination. To the problem of living romance propounds the only possible answer, which is, not understanding, but escape. And the method of that escape is . . . the creation of a pleasing dream, which will somehow engender a reality as lovely."[16]

While Dr. Mitchell toyed with drug-induced hallucinations, other dream worlds were pursued with equal or even greater frequency. Brahmin mysticism, described by *The Buddhist Ray,* was symptomatic of an international fascination with the occult and with psychic phenomena which thrived at the turn of the century. James Huneker, who had a predilection for such matters, called man a metaphysical animal. Speaking of William James' prominence in Boston, Huneker was delighted to find that "the artistic spider that spins the dark cells of every thinker's brain is already at work with the pragmatic idea. . . . You may expel metaphysics by way of the door, yet it will enter through the window or come down the chimney. . . . Faith being the Fourth Dimension of the human intellect, the Cambridge professor [James] dismisses it under the rubric of 'Over-belief.' Yet mysticism rages mightily down Boston way."[17]

To the mystically minded many prophets were available. Among the most flamboyant was Madame Helena Petrovna de Blavatsky, the leader of Russian occultism and the founder in 1875 of the Theosophical Society. After abandoning her husband in 1848, Madame Blavatsky fled Russia and for a quarter century wandered the world, spreading her mystical gospel, before settling in New York City in 1873. In Europe as in this country there were receptive audiences for her message, which in part stressed man's origin in various lost civilizations of mythology, thereby offering an alternative to Darwin's brutalizing explanation of the origin of the species. Artists were not immune to her sensational appeal; as recalled by his daughter, the American painter William Dodge, for instance, "was steeped in these theories during his student days in Paris and the seed was planted there for his enduring interest in archaeology."[18] Madame Blavatsky's impact on America—where she lived from 1873 to 1882, becoming a naturalized citizen —was not limited to the selection of painters' motifs; indeed, in this country she found a culture peculiarly susceptible to her theosophical philosophy which accorded well with the general spiritualization of

American thought in the late nineteenth century. A subsequent Russian visitor to these shores, the mystic composer Alexander Scriabin, was heartened by the mood he found in New York. At the end of his notorious stay during the winter of 1906-1907, he bade farewell with the proclamation that "America has a great future. There is a very strong mystic movement there."[19]

Concurrent with Blavatsky's mystical appeal was the continuing fascination with spiritualism. While spiritualism as a faith enjoyed fluctuating allegiance by Americans from the mid-century onwards, its greater attention came as a field for scientific investigations. The first such experiments were conducted at the University of Pennsylvania in 1853; the investigations gained momentum with the founding of the Society for Psychical Research in England in 1882, and the organization of an American branch of the society—in Boston, of course!—two years later.[20] Hamlin Garland was an influential member of the executive board of the American Psychical Society, and utilized his novel, *The Shadow World,* written in the author's first person, as an apologia for his interests in psychic phenomena, telekinesis, spiritualists and mediums. The book attempts to illuminate the "shadow world" which, according to Garland, "lies very close to the sunny, so-called normal day."[21]

Relationships between the shadow world and normal day were sought by artists and intellectuals in Europe and America. The Neo-Platonic quest for correspondences between the unknowable ideal and the observable fact occasioned a revived interest in the philosophy of the eighteenth-century Swedish theologian, Emmanuel Swedenborg. Emerson had been introduced to Swedenborgianism in 1847, the same year as Baudelaire's discovery of Poe, establishing another key link in the inter-relationship of nineteenth century intellectual history in Europe and America. Emerson was attracted by the combination of scientific inquiry, which had been Swedenborg's early interest, and the visionary preaching of his later years, and acclaimed the Swede's effort "to put science and the soul, long estranged from each other, at one again."[22] Swedenborg's appeal grew in America, especially during the troubled decade of Civil War, and his visionary doctrine of equation between a perfect divine or celestial world and the imperfect terrestrial one had an understandable allure for Americans fatigued or distressed by their modern environment. To its adherents Swedenborgianism offered a consoling sense of immanence in its stress upon the unity of perceived and ideal realms. In addition to Emersonian philosophers, Swedenborg's thought also came to have a tremendous importance for numbers of American artists, particularly Hiram Powers, William Page and George Inness.

Most Americans were neither so learned nor so involved as to be able to detect the parallels between Swedenborgian philosophy and other faiths, such as the link to Buddhism described by Philangi Dasa. Dasa, an American convert to the Indian faith, published in California for seven years *The Buddhist Ray,* in which he proselytized for the Oriental philosophy. In its inaugural issue and continuing over a period of several months, the journal analyzed the Swedenborg-Buddhist relationship. Dasa noted that "Sweden-

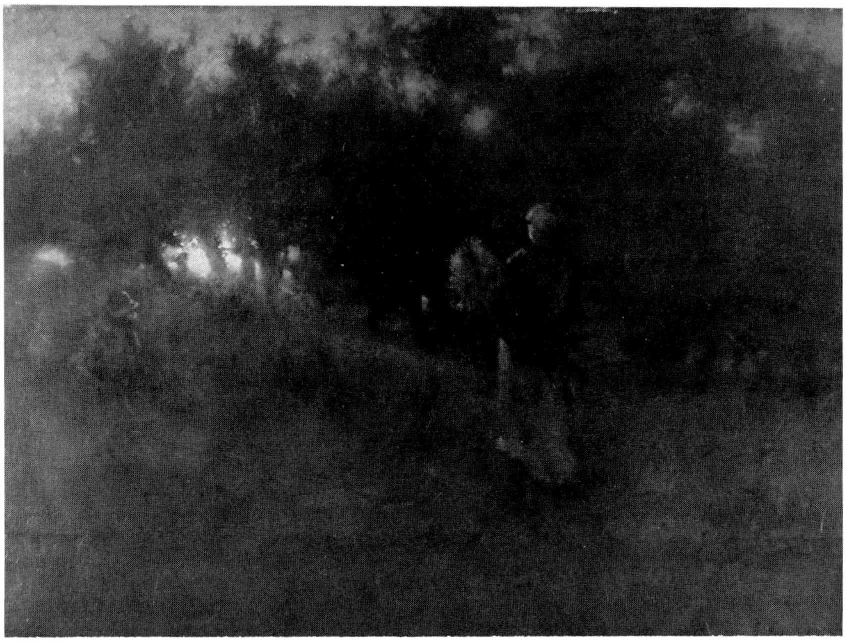

8. George Inness, *The Gleaners*, 1893, cat. no. 31.

borg began . . . under the cover of the Jewish-Christian scriptures, whose 'spiritual sense' he purported to give, to write and publish his spiritual experiences, and to proclaim the establishment of a 'New Jerusalem Church.' . . . He founded, however, no church, sect, or society. Now what did Swedenborg in reality publish? The 'spiritual sense' of the Jewish- Christian scriptures? The 'doctrine' of the Lord's New Church? Fudge! Swedenborg, inspired by *living* Buddhist saints ('Celestial Angels,' as he sometimes called them), published covertly the old, old, old teachings of Buddhism!"[23]

Buddhism and other Oriental philosophies with a meditative, introspective emphasis, received a sympathetic hearing from a significant number of Americans in the late nineteenth century; the Hare Krishna faithful of today have their ancestors in the spiritual crisis of America's Gilded Age. Emerson had carefully studied the *Vedas* and other non-Western religious texts, and patterned some of his best poetry on them. Other Bostonians were similarly attracted to the East; in 1883, Phillips Brooks left his Trinity Church congregation for a tour of India. While the distinguished Episcopalian cleric did not convert, he did concede to the Dehli Brahmans' faith "a wonderful power of appeal to some modes of almost all our natures . . . sufficient to make us understand how it could have been, and still is, held by multitudes of souls."[24] Even in the "Bible Belt," Oriental religion had its sympathizers. About 1888, the Kansas City *Journal* warned that "if our [Christian] spiritual teachers and shepherds expect to stop intelligent people from looking into the ethical, religious, or spiritual system of a people who represent a history . . . older than our own form of religion, they are very much mistaken. . . . The fact must be acknowledged that the Buddhists live nearer the precepts of Jesus than any other people on the globe. And if this is the fact, why not accept it, try to learn its lesson."[25]

While the gulfs separating Madame Blavatsky, Emmanuel Swedenborg and Philangi Dasa are enormous, their respective deviations from the dominant and traditional Christian practice offered alternatives to Americans caught in the cultural flux and philosophical doubts of the *fin de siècle.* In the search for alternative truths, distinctions between divergent philosophies were not always recognized nor carefully maintained. "Mysticism" and "pantheism" were generally used to describe those extreme exceptions to the dominant Christian faith in America. " 'Pantheism' . . . has been familiarly applied to so many utterly diverse systems of thought," complained the theologian, John Fiske, "that it is very hard to tell just what it means." Fiske noted that the term had been applied antithetically to the beliefs of both Stoics and Hindu philosophers. "In recent times it has been used as a vituperative epithet, and hurled indiscriminately at such unpopular opinions as do not seem to call for so heavy a missile as the more cruel term 'atheism.' The writer who sets forth in plain scientific language a physical theory of the universe is liable to be scowled at and called an atheist; but, when the very same ideas are presented in the form of oracular apophthegm or poetic rhapsody, the author is more gently described as 'tinctured with pantheism'."[26]

The revival of mysticism and the survival of pantheism in late nineteenth-century America paralleled the flourishing of artistic imagination and the birth of Symbolist thought. Within the dominant Protestant and Trinitarian American church, such strayings from orthodoxy were regarded with some suspicion, Bishop Brooks notwithstanding. The unsettled times, however, made compelling the search by many Americans for order and for absolutes. Van Wyck Brooks, in analyzing *The Malady of the Ideal,* astutely noted that the "protestant episode of four centuries . . . attempt[s] to regulate the relations between the symbolic [i.e., Roman Catholicism] and the actual [i.e., modern science]. . . . Just there has been the weakness of Protestantism. . . . Symbolic or actual—we may have our preference, but it is the extreme in any form which wins our suffrage."[27]

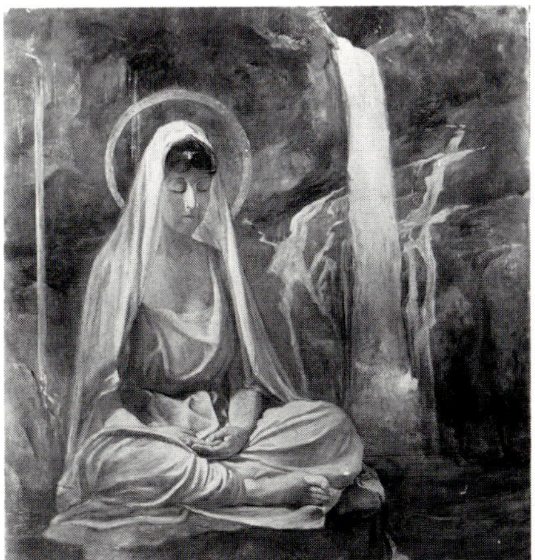

9. John La Farge,
Kwannon, 1887/1908,
The Butler Institute of American Art.
(Photo courtesy of Juley Archive,
National Collection of Fine Arts,
Smithsonian Institution)

Insofar as idealist thought of late nineteenth-century America affected American artists—and the impact was considerable—the effect was to be found particularly in American figure painters' work. The concerns of the age's reactionaries against materialism, scientism and determinism were humanists in their values, and found the best vehicle for expression of such sentiments in the human form itself. Several tendencies combined to accelerate this rise of figure painting at the turn of the century.

As early as 1878, J. Alden Weir had come away from an exhibition of American paintings in Paris with a distaste for the traditional imagery of American artists. "Our exposition is decidedly weak in landscapes . . .," he wrote; in criticizing two of the deans among American painters, Weir issued what might be considered a condemnation of a long tradition of portraiture and landscape art: "Huntington's work looks worse than ever, and so does Church's."[28] Although Weir could still find things to praise at the Paris showing—John La Farge's innovative landscapes, for example—his ennui with the Huntington-Church aesthetic suggests that younger artists were beginning to seek new subjects and approaches for their work.

Landscape painting continued to hold the interest of some American artists at the end of the century. Their treatment of the time-honored motif, however, was marked by a new approach, variously called "Paysage Intime," "Tonalism," "Quietism," "Landscape of Atmosphere," and "Poetic Landscapes of Mood." [29] By whatever term, the painters of the new landscape placed a priority upon personal expression and interpretation rather than factual transcription of nature's forms, as had been the pre-occupation of an earlier generation. One reviewer of the 1890 Society of American Artists' exhibition noted with pleasure that there were only "one or two surviving examples of the 'brown-tree' period" of American landscape painting to be found there.[30]

Moving even further afield from the tradition of Cole and Durand than did the tonalists were the figure painters of the 1880s and later. "Every visitor to the [National] Academy of Design [exhibition of 1882] must remark the increased number of figure pieces," commented one reviewer. "Toward this end everything had been tending for the last ten years."[31] The continuation of this trend was noted again two years later: "In figure painting there is more life and better work on the whole than the early Academy could show . . . " reported another critic.[32] The resurrection of figurative art at the National Academy and elsewhere can be directly related to the rise of academic practice and life studies at the Academy and the Art Students League (established in 1875), as well as to the increased traffic to the Parisian ateliers where concern for such basics as figure drawing had long dominated. The popular appreciation of the figurative subject only further strengthened the artists' tendencies in that direction. By way of introduction to her compendium of American figure painters published in 1886, Maria van Rensselaer noted that "such a book could not well have been given us even a few years ago . . . "[33]

In its initial appearance, the figure was presented in the form of anecdotal genre pictures, popular with the audiences of the day, or in rather straight-forward poses adapted from the *academie*. However, it quickly transcended these narrow limitations and aspired to convey other meanings beyond mere technical finesse and reportage. "Figure painting in America," wrote one critic in 1882, " . . . has gone far beyond the limits reached by popular appreciation. Where it has failed, it has failed in higher aims than can be reached by mere technic or in the selection of felicitous motive."[34] An hierarchical view of artistic subjects was revived by painters of the human figure, placing their favored motif in the upper reaches of painters' concerns. Will Low, for instance, argued that "the representation of the human figure nude or draped in a manner revealing its form has been from the inception of painting as an art the highest achievement of the artist, considered either as a craftsman desirous to test his skill or as a man of imagination wishing to embody his highest thought."[35]

It was the traditional training from the nude, both in European studios and later in New York, which accounted for the craftsmanlike mastery of the figure. It was the imagination which elevated that technical facility to a higher plane, to the extent that by 1889 S. G. W. Benjamin could pride himself on the fact that "we see more evidence of imagination among our artists engaged in this department [figurative art] than in any other branch of our present art . . . "[36]

Re-established in a position of primacy, the human figure, and especially the female nude, came to carry an increasing burden of allegory, personification and symbolic meaning in the decades surrounding the century's turn. The pre-occupation was shared by easel painters with the numerous muralists, illustrators and sculptors of the same period. "The nude human figure is undoubtedly the most beautiful object in the world, but what is it that gives it the highest title to beauty?" asked the Boston critic, William Howe Downs. "What is it that gives it its infinite variety, grace, strength, subtlety, majesty, tenderness, harmony? Is it not the intelligence, the soul, the emotions dwell in it—the God within the machine? Is it not the capacity for work, the capacity for love, the capacity for order and law, for charity and civilization? . . . the more completely the artist is able to express the working of these psychic forces the more completely does he bring out the supreme beauty of the human form."[37]

The placement of abstract virtues in the form of the human figure provided American artists with a sensual release from the repressed imagery of the Victorian era, and a clear alternative to the landscape and genre subjects which had prevailed in an earlier generation. Unfortunately, however, as has often been noted, the new enthusiasm for the figurative brought in its wake a number of lesser talents, whose fascination with the motif never rose much above the naturalistic rendering of the fleshy subject; the late nineteenth century's vogue for Bouguereau and his fellow Parisian academics found pale reflection in the horde of naked ladies which paraded forth from American studios. To the more imaginative, however, the figure, and especially the nude, offered a chance to express the more spiritualized, symbolic aspirations of the age. Speaking of the sculptor George Grey Barnard, one observer wrote: "He has originated what I must call the New Symbolism, a symbolism which goes to the very heart of the life of men and women of to-day, which has to do with the everlasting varieties of life. . . . it is the sheer humanity of his creations which takes hold of us, and gives us a fresh realization of the divinity of human nature, its boundless possibilities, and its glorious destiny. This is what Mr. Barnard's art seem to us, first and last, to stand for."[38]

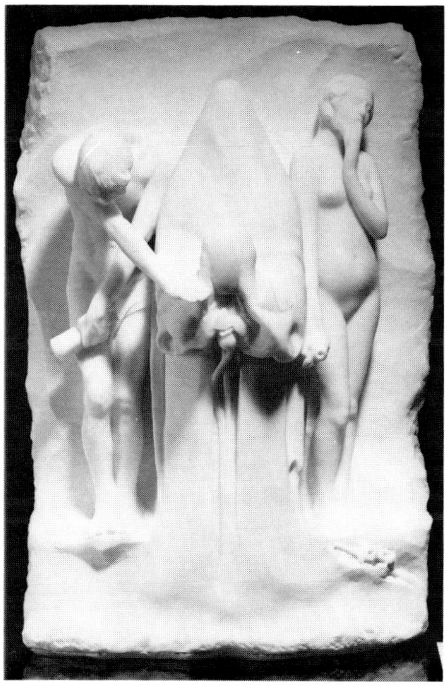

10. George Grey Barnard, *The Mystery of Life,* National Collection of Fine Arts, Smithsonian Institution.

Barnard's sculpture, like the work of American painters in the late years of the nineteenth century, reflects the revived interest in the human figure as a vehicle for expression of sentiments in reaction against the materialistic mood of the day. Much American art of the period also mirrors the various humanistic and mystical strains of thought which characterized the reaction against the tyranny of the modern age. With this conjunction of subjects and attitudes, the stage was set for a native equivalent to the Symbolist aesthetic then evolving in Europe.

Notes

Introduction

1. Michael Quick, *American Expatriate Painters of the Late Nineteenth Century* (Dayton, Ohio: Dayton Art Institute, 1976), 43.
2. La Farge quoted in Helene Barbara Weinberg, "John La Farge: The Relation of His Illustrations to His Ideal Art," *American Art Journal,* V: 1 (May 1973), 62; Vedder to "Dear Madam," declining invitation to speak at Brooklyn Women's Art School, Boston [March 1887], Vedder Papers, Archives of American Art, Smithsonian Institution, Washington, D.C.

Americans and the Symbolist International

1. For a discussion of the increased traffic to Europe, see Michael Quick, *American Expatriate Painters of the Late Nineteenth Century* 15-17.
2. Joris-Karl Huysmans quoted in James Huneker, *Egoists: A Book of Supermen* (New York: Scribner's, 1909), 197.
3. For American travel to European art centers see: London: *Return to Albion: Americans in England, 1740-1940* (Washington: National Portrait Gallery, 1979); Italy: E. P. Richardson and Otto Wittmann, Jr., *Travelers in Arcadia: American Artists in Italy, 1830-1875* (Detroit Institute of Arts and Toledo Museum of Art, 1951), Van Wyck Brooks, *The Dream of Arcadia: American Writers and Artists in Italy, 1760-1915* (New York: Dutton, 1958), and *The Arcadian Landscape: Nineteenth-Century American Painters in Italy* (University of Kansas Museum of Art, Lawrence, 1972); Düsseldorf: The Düsseldorf Academy and the Americans, an Exhibition of Drawings and Watercolors (Atlanta 1973); Munich: *Munich and American Realism in the Nineteenth Century* (E. B. Crocker Art Gallery, Sacramento, 1978); Florence: *The White Marmorean Flock* (Vassar College Art Gallery, Poughkeepsie, N.Y., Merchants Press, 1972).
4. Van Wyck Brooks, *Scenes and Portraits: Memories of Childhood and Youth* (New York: Dutton, 1954), 81.
5. Frank Duveneck to "Dear Dony," Munich, February 17, 1877; John M. Donaldson Papers, Archives of American Art.
6. The most complete account of mid-century Franco-American connections is: Lois M. Fink, "The Role of France in American Art, 1850-1870," unpublished Ph.D. dissertation,University of Chicago, 1970. See also: Peter Bermingham, *American Art in the Barbizon Mood* (Washington: National Collection of Fine Arts, 1975); Joshua C. Taylor and Lois M. Fink, *Academy* (Washington: National Collection of Fine Arts, 1975); Richard Boyle, *American Impressionism* (Boston: New York Graphic Society, 1974).
7. Mrs. Fiske-Warren, "Un Jardin," *Mercure de France,* December 1894; "Notes," *The Chap-Book,* II:12 (1895), 483.

8. Steichen quoted in Joseph Shiffman, "The Alienation of the Artist: Alfred Stieglitz," *American Quarterly,* III (1951), 249-250.
9. Steichen also wanted to photograph James McNeill Whistler and Fernand Khnopff, but was unable to arrange sittings. William Innes Homer, "Edward Steichen as Painter and Photographer, 1897-1908," *The American Art Journal,* VI:2 (November 1974), 49.
10. Maeterlinck quoted in Jean Gibran and Kahlil Gibran, *Kahlil Gibran: His Life and World* (Boston: New York Graphic Society, 1974), 57.
11. "Notes," *The Chap-Book,* II:4 (January 1, 1895), 191.
12. "Introduction" by William Dean Howells, to *Pastels in Prose,* translated by Stuart Merrill (New York: Harper and Brothers, 1890), viii.
13. "Notes," *The Chap-Book,* V:6 (1896), 336.
14. Mrs. Reginald De Koven, "Verlaine:—A Feminine Appreciation," *The Chap-Book,* IV:6 (1895), 286, 289.
15. Theodore Child, "Literary Paris," *Harper's Monthly,* 85:508 (September 1892), 490.
16. "Notes," *The Chap-Book,* V:6 (1896), 287.
17. Lawrence Jerrold, "The Uses of Perversity," *The Chap-Book,* V:5 (1896), 194-198; "Notes," *The Chap-Book,* II:12 (1895), 482-483; "Notes," *The Chap-Book,* II:5 (1895), 231-232.
18. Aline Gorren, "The French Symbolists," *Scribner's Magazine,* XIII:3 (March 1893), 342.
19. *The Chap-Book's* circulation peaked at 16,500 copies in the spring of 1896. Sidney Kramer, *A History of Stone & Kimball and Herbert S. Stone & Co.* (Chicago: Norman W. Forgue, 1940), 53.
20. H. T. Peck, "Stephane Mallarmé," *The Bookman* (November 1898). See also Rene Taupin, *L'Influence du symbolisme français sur la poésie américaine* (Paris: Champion, 1929), 30-31.
21. Child, "Literary Paris," 490.
22. Gorren, "The French Symbolists," 337-352.
23. As music critic for the New York *Sun,* Huneker contributed 425 signed and unsigned articles during the period 1906-1907 alone! Peter Plagens, "The Critics: Hartmann, Huneker, DeCasseres," *Art in America,* 61:4 (July-August 1973), 69.
24. Taupin, 39.
25. For instance, see: "Maeterlinck and the Eternal Womanly," *Harper's Bazar,* 38 (July 1904), 656-669; "Baudelaire Legend," *Scribner's,* 45 (February 1909), 240-249; "Pessimist's Progress: J.-K. Huysmans," *North American Review,* 186 (September 1907), 41-54; "Real Rodin," *Harper's Weekly,* 56 (June 1, 1912), 13-16; "Remy de Gourmont," *North American Review,* 205 (June 1917), 935-942.
26. Henry McCarter quoted in Richard Wattenmaker, *Puvis de Chavannes and the Modern Tradition* (Toronto: Art Gallery of Ontario, 1975), 17; William Lefwitch Dodge quoted in Sarah Dodge Kimbrough, *Drawn From Life* (Jackson: University of Mississippi Press, 1976), 13.
27. Arthur Wesley Dow, letter to the editor of Boston *Evening Transcript,* November 13, 1892, quoted in Frederick C. Moffett, *Arthur Wesley Dow* (Washington: National Collection of Fine Arts, 1977), 61-62; Theodore Child, *Art and Criticism* (New York: Harper & Bros., 1910), 30.

28. Robert Pincus-Witten, *Occult Symbolism in France: Joséphin Peladan and the Salons de la Rose+Croix* (New York: Garland, 1976), 167.

29. Paul Bourget, *Outre-Mer: Impressions of America* (New York: Scribner's, 1895), 361.

30. Gibran and Gibran, 252.

31. Christian Brinton, "Contemporary Art and the Carnegie Institute," *The International Studio,* XLIX:196 (June 1913), 1xxi.

32. Pierre Louis (pseuodonym for Maurice Denis), *Art et Critique* (August 23, 30, 1890), 1f. The concepts initially expressed in 1890 were incorporated into Denis' *Théories, 1890-1910, Du Symbolisme et du Gauguin vers un nouvel ordre classique* (Paris: Bibliotheque de l'Occident, 1912).

33. *Mercure de France* (March 1891), 162-163. The Gauguin commentary was collected with other pieces on Renoir, Van Gogh, and Symbolism and published the year after Aurier's death in *Oeuvres Posthumes* (Paris, 1893).

34. Joséphin Peladan, *Salon de la Rose+Croix, Règle et Monitore* (Paris: Dentu, 1891). Translated and reprinted in Pincus-Witten, *Occult Symbolism . . . ,* 211-216.

35. Child, *Art and Criticism,* 90.

36. Josephine Peabody quoted in Gibran and Gibran, 99.

37. Frederick Fairchild Sherman, *Landscape and Figure Painters of America* (New York: privately printed, 1917), 18.

38. Duncan Phillips, *The Artist Sees Differently* (Washington: Phillips Collection, 1931), 96.

39. Cecily Langdale, "Introduction," in *Charles Conder, Robert Henri, James Morrice, Maurice Prendergast: The Formative Years, Paris, 1890s* (New York: Davis and Long, 1975), n.p.; Susan Hobbs, "The Self-Image of the Artist During the American Renaissance: John La Farge, Abbott Thayer and Thomas Dewing," lecture at National Collection of Fine Arts, Washington, 1978, unpublished typescript, 23.

40. Rather more broad in interpretation was the analogy which Robert Pincus-Witten proposed between "the best of reductivist abstraction—Andre, Judd, LeWitt, Rockburne, Bochner, *et al.*— . . . and the iconography of intelligence rooted in Symbolism and running across the work of Jasper Johns . . . to our own day." Pincus-Witten, "On Target: Symbolist Roots of American Abstraction," *Arts Magazine,* 50:8 (April 1976), 84.

The Imaginative Tradition in American Literature

1. "Literature of the Day," *Lippincott's Magazine,* XXV:145 (January 1880), 133.

2. *Sixth Loan Exhibition: Winslow Homer, Albert P. Ryder, Thomas Eakins* (New York: Museum of Modern Art, 1930).

3. Bourget, *Outre-Mer,* 61-62.

4. Frank Jewett Mather, Charles Rufus Morey and William James Henderson, *The American Spirit in Art* (New Haven: Yale University Press, 1929), 59.

5. Royal Cortissoz, *American Artists* (New York: Scribner's, 1923), 93.

6. Perry Miller, editor, *Margaret Fuller, American Romantic* (Garden City, N.Y.: Doubleday & Co., 1963), xiv.

7. Russell Lynes, "Viewpoints: 'The Genteel Tradition'," *The American Art Journal,* VI:2 (November 1974), 76, 77.

8. Lynes, 77.
9. Edmund Chase Stedman, "Edgar Allen Poe," *Scribner's Monthly,* XX (May 1880), 117.
10. Edmund Wilson, *Axel's Castle* (New York, Scribner's, 1931), 12.
11. Mathew Josephson, *Portrait of the Artist as American* (New York: Octagon Books, 1964), xviii. First published 1930.
12. Charles Baudelaire, "The Windows," in *Pastels in Prose,* 174.
13. Nathaniel Hawthorne, *The Marble Faun, or The Romance of Monte Beni,* in *The Complete Novels and Selected Tales of Nathaniel Hawthorne,* edited by Norman Holmes Pearson (New York: Modern Library, 19), 590.
14. Bourget, *Outre-Mer,* 36.
15. Pincus-Witten, *Occult Symbolism,* . . . 211.
16. Stedman, "Edgar Allen Poe," 118.
17. Poe was neglected by most American critics during his lifetime, and his posthumous reputation varied greatly through the nineteenth century. Despite the generally high regard for his work in France after mid-century, American critics seemed unable to develop a consensus on his achievement, resulting in wide swings of the critical pendulum. As one writer noted, "the Poe Legend . . . puts forth such curious growths from decade to decade." George E. Woodberry, editor, "The Poe-Chivers Papers," *The Century Magazine,* LXV:3 (January 1903), 435.
18. Edmund Gosse, "Has America Produced a Poet?" *The Forum,* 6:2 (October 1888), 185.
19. Remy de Gourmont, introduction to *Livre des Masques,* 1896, quoted in Robert Delevoy, *Symbolists and Symbolism* (New York: Rizzoli, 1978), 157-158.
20. Gosse, "Has America Produced a Poet?", 179.
21. Richard Hovey, "Decadence—or Renascence," *Time and the Hour* (Boston), 6 (December 4, 1897), 14-15.
22. "Notes," *The Chap-Book,* IV:11 (1895), 534.
23. James Thrall Soby, *The Romantic Tradition in American Art* (New York: Museum of Modern Art, 1943). See also, *The American Muse: Parallel Trends in Literature and Art* (Washington, D.C.: Corcoran Gallery, 1959), and *Romantic Painting in America* (Dallas Museum of Fine Arts, 1972).
24. See the bibliographic citations in the catalogue of individual artists included in the exhibition. Also see, for instance; *re.* Allston: *Washington Allston, A Loan Exhibition of Paintings, Drawings and Memorabilia* (Detroit Institute of Arts, 1947), and Edgar P. Richardson, *Washington Allston: A Study of the Romantic Artist in America* (Chicago: University of Chicago Press, 1948); *re.* Page: Joshua C. Taylor, *William Page: The American Titian* (Chicago: University of Chicago Press, 1957); *re.* Quidor: John I. H. Baur, *John Quidor* (New York: Brooklyn Museum, 1942), and David M. Sokol, *John Quidor: Painter of American Legend* (Wichita Art Museum, 1973); *re.* Rimmer: Lincoln Kirstein, *William Rimmer, 1816-1879* (New York: Whitney Museum of American Art, 1946), and Truman Howe Bartlett, *The Art Life of William Rimmer: Sculptor, Painter, Physician* (New York: DaCapo Press, 1970; reprint of 1882 original edition).
25. Ralph Adams Cram, *The Decadent* (Boston: privately printed, 1893), 27.
26. Wilson, 265-266.

Mystics and Humanists

1. De Vogué quoted in Mme. Blaze du Bury, "The Spiritualization of Thought in France," *The Contemporary Review,* LX:311 (November 1891), 642, 643.
2. De Vogué quoted in Du Bury, 643.
3. "Transcendentalism in France," Boston *Journal,* reprinted in *Public Opinion,* XII:7 (January 20, 1892), 430.
4. "Editor's Study," *Harper's Monthly,* 85:507 (August 1892), 477.
5. "The Point of View," *Scribner's Magazine,* XXXII:6 (December 1902), 763.
6. "Editor's Study," *Harper's Monthly,* 477.
7. Yeats quoted in Edmund Wilson, *Axel's Castle,* 22-23.
8. Henry James, "The Madonna of the Future," in *The Madonna of the Future and Other Tales* (New York: Macmillan, 1880), 6-7.
9. Josephson, *Portrait of the Artist as American,* xx.
10. "Another important cause for the decline of the expatriate movement was a general shift in taste and practice away from the special subject matter that had required foreign residence before. . . . The general trend in the 1890s was clearly away from pictorial illusion, detail and serious subject matter and toward imaginative themes and primarily formal considerations." Michael Quick, *American Expatriate Painters of the Late Nineteenth Century,* 43.
11. "Why Zola Was Never Popular in the United States," *World's Work,* V:1 (November 1902), 2715.
12. Henry Adams, *The Education of Henry Adams* (Boston: Houghton Mifflin, 1961), 321. First published 1918.
13. "Boston 'Buddhists' and Tearful Theosophists," *The Buddhist Ray* (Santa Cruz, Cal.), II:3 (March 1889), 17.
14. William James to Henry James, Chocorua, N.H., June 11, 1896, reprinted in *The Gilded Age,* edited by Ari A. Hoogenboom and Olive Hoogenboom (Englewood Cliffs, N.J.: Prentice Hall, 1967), 142.
15. *The Mahogany Tree* (Boston), May 28, 1892, 411.
16. James B. Cabell, *Beyond Life* (New York: Robert M. McBride & Co., 1919), 327.
17. James G. Huneker, *The Pathos of Distance* (London: T. Werner Laurie, n.d.), 351, 366.
18. Kimbrough, *Drawn From Life,* 20-21.
19. Alexander Scriabin quoted in Harold Schonberg, *The Lives of the Great Composers* (New York: Norton, 1970), 503.
20. Luther Weigle, *American Idealism* (New Haven: Yale University Press, 1928), 173.
21. Hamlin Garland, *The Shadow World* (New York: Harper & Bros., 1908), 9.
22. Ralph Waldo Emerson, "Swedenborg; or, The Mystic," in *Representative Men* (Boston: Houghton Mifflin, 1892), 108.
23. Philangi Dasa, "Emmanuel Swedenborg," *The Buddhist Ray,* I:1 (January 1888), 7-8.
24. Brooks quoted in Paul Carter, *The Spiritual Crisis of the Gilded Age* (DeKalb: Northern Illinois University Press, 1971), 205.
25. "Dry Facts," Kansas City *Journal,* n.d., reprinted in *The Buddhist Ray,* I:7 (July 1888), 55.

26. John Fiske, *The Idea of God as Affected by Modern Knowledge* (Boston: Houghton Mifflin, 1886), viii-ix.

27. Van Wyck Brooks, *The Malady of the Ideal* (Philadelphia: University of Pennsylvania Press, 1947), 60-61. First published 1913.

28. J. Alden Weir to his parents, June 16, 1878, in Dorothy Weir Young, *The Life and Letters of J. Alden Weir* (New York: DaCapo, 1971), 143.

29. See Wanda M. Corn, *The Color of Mood: American Tonalism 1880-1910* (San Francisco: H. M. DeYoung Museum, 1972), and Elizabeth G. Broun, "The Poetic Landscapists," in *American Painting and Sculpture in the World's Columbian Exposition, Chicago, 1893,* unpublished Ph.D. dissertation, University of Kansas, Lawrence, 1976, 96-131.

30. "Fine Arts: Society of American Artists," *The Nation,* 50:1297 (May 8, 1890), 381.

31. "Art Notes: Academy of Design," *The Art Journal,* 44 (1882), 189.

32. "Fine Arts: The Academy Exhibition—II," *The Nation,* 38:982 (April 24, 1884), 371.

33. Maria Griswold van Rensselaer, *Book of American Figure Painters* (New York: Garland, 1977), n.p. First published 1886.

34. "Art Notes: Academy of Design," *The Art Journal,* 44 (1882), 189.

35. Will Low, "The Nude," in *Illustrated Catalogue with Short Lectures on Art Topics: Sixty-ninth Annual Exhibition* (New York: National Academy of Design, 1894), 29.

36. S. G. W. Benjamin, "Tendencies of Art in America," in *American Art and American Art Collections,* edited by Walter Montgomery, vol. II (Boston: E. W. Walker, 1889), 1003.

37. William Howe Downs, "George Grey Barnard," *World's Work,* XVII:4 (February 1909), 11268.

38. Downs, "Barnard," 11268.

II: The Paintings

Temples of the Mind: Imaginative Imagery and Symbolist Thought

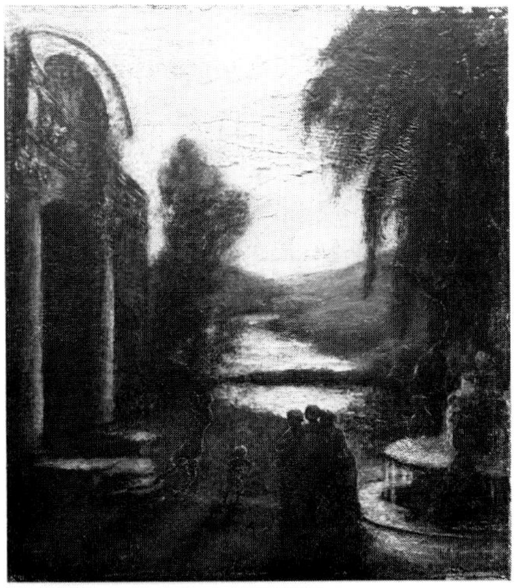

11. Albert P. Ryder,
The Temple of the Mind,
circa 1885,
Albright-Knox Art Gallery.

About 1885, Albert Pinkham Ryder painted one of his best known works, *The Temple of the Mind.*[1] The painting is perhaps the earliest and most complete statement of the artist's mature style, and even in his own lifetime was judged to be one of his masterpieces, as it continues to be today.

The Temple of the Mind provides an ambitious standard against which all imaginative conceptions by American painters might be judged. Even more importantly, it provides a major landmark in the parallelism of Symbolist aesthetics in Europe and America. As with many of the foreign works with which it can be linked in spirit and intent, *The Temple of the Mind* is strongly imbued with a particular mood, here heightened by the artist's rich colorism, nocturnal effects, and generalized forms. The poetic spell cast by the little picture is related to its literary source, a feature common to many European Symbolist paintings as well; and as with some of the major French Symbolist artists and writers, Ryder was inspired by Edgar Allen Poe. Ryder typified the practice of many Symbolists in choosing not simply to illustrate a passage from Poe's text; indeed, the artist took pains to distinguish his invention from the author's grotesque fancy, freely altering details and adding features to his painted creation.

Also parallel to Symbolist practice is Ryder's suggestion of fanciful ritual, evoked by robed maidens in the moonlight before a temple. The temple front is quite unlike anything known in antique architecture, yet the temple itself suggests a setting remote both temporally and geographically from the late nineteenth-century New York in which it was conceived. In typical Symbolist fashion, Ryder flies artistically from the modern, mercantile, materialistic here-and-now to a dreamland, there-and-then, drawn from his imagination.

Poe's poem, *The Haunted Palace,* was first published in 1839, and later incorporated into his *Fall of the House of Usher.* In the verse the author drew an analogy between a deranged mind and a once beautiful classical palace whose inhabitants have been driven out by "a hideous wrong." Poe's literary invention includes neither the three graces nor the faun nor the fountain prominently featured in Ryder's painting; yet the significance conveyed pictorially by the painter closely approximates the mood evoked by the written verse. "The finer attributes of the mind are pictured," explained

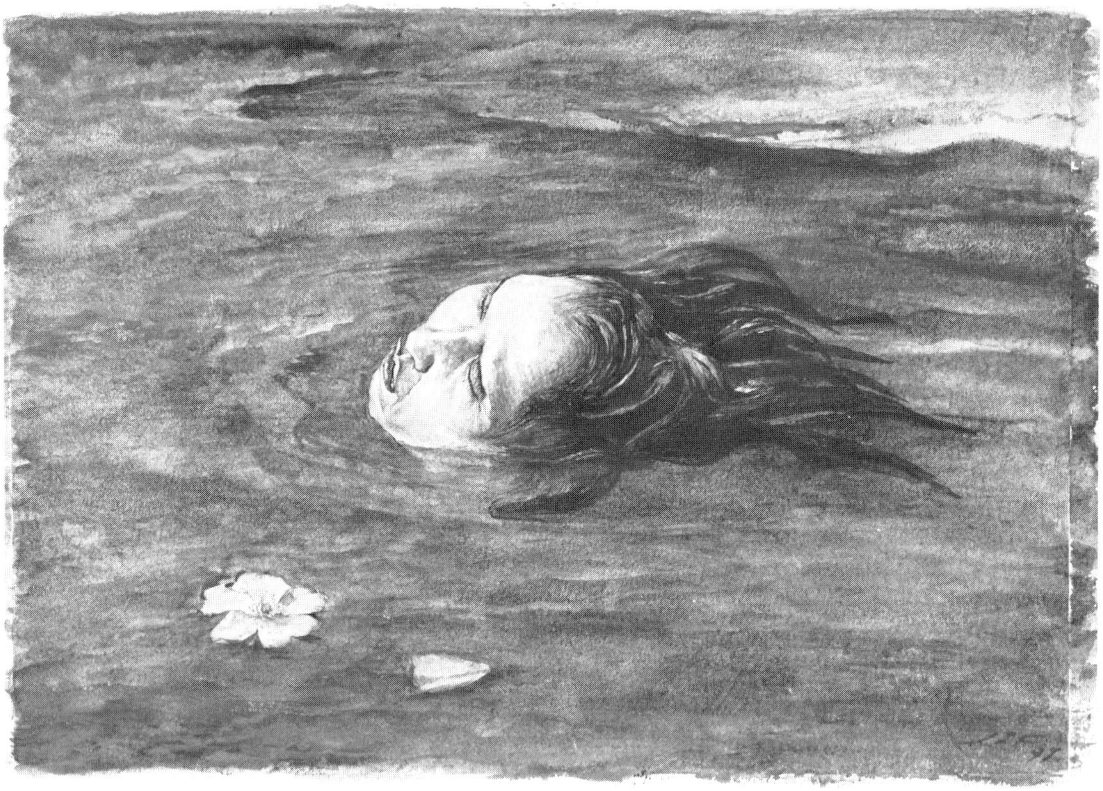

12. John La Farge, *The Strange Little Thing Kiosai Saw in the River,* 1897, cat. no. 34.

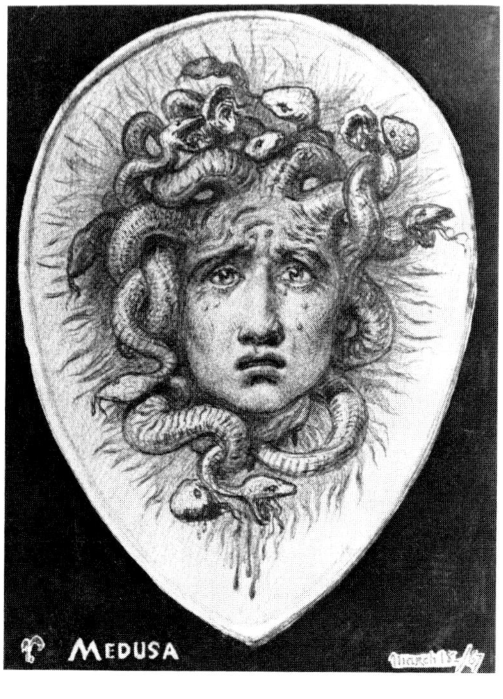

13. Elihu Vedder, *Medusa,* 1867, Collection of Mr. and Mrs. Lawrence Fleischman.

Ryder, "by three graces who stand in the center of the picture. . . . They are waiting for a weeping love to join them. . . . a cloven footed faun dances up the steps snapping his fingers in fiendish glee at having dethroned the erstwhile ruling graces. . . . " The painter recalled having seen the picture at the Cottier Gallery in New York after its sale, and being struck by its "chrystalline purity . . . a new quality."[2] Ryder's response to his conception suggests that the painting nearly had an organic life of its own, which could impress even the creator of the motif. The vitality of its mood, the imaginative conception inspired by, but not illustrative of, Poe's literary source, and the interest in states of mind and sense, and in deratiocination—"dethron[ing] the erstwhile ruling graces"—are interests identical to those prevailing among many imaginative artists in Europe and America during the *fin de siècle.*

In late nineteenth-century painting, the theme of decapitation was frequently essayed by artists from both sides of the Atlantic—the Medusa heads by Vedder, Boecklin, Feuerbach, Khnoppf, and Barney, for instance, or the Orpheus heads by Moreau, Redon and Delville, or the Baptist's head by Tanner and Lévy-Dhurmer. The ubiquity of such gory subjects at the century's end suggests a rooting deep within the general cultural malaise of the epoch. In the hands of such imaginative painters, these essays upon decapitation transcended the romantic appeal to agitated emotions, which had attracted earlier generations of painters to such motifs, and elevated the severed head to a cryptic symbol of modern madness. Confronted with the apparent failure of modern culture—with the dominance of the objective fact over the intuitive spirit, with the divorce of intellect from soul, as lamented by Emile Faguet and others—artists and intellectuals turned away from the world of empirical reality to an inner realm of dreams and visions. The rational heritage of Voltairean thought became suspect, and was challenged by more introspective concerns. The severed head became the symbolic statement for the principle of deratiocination, and it is in this context that Ryder's interpretation of Poe's theme of derangement must be understood. While less gruesome than the bloodied heads, the vacant temple without its reigning graces is equally suggestive of the sterility, indeed fatality, of intellect without imagination, without intuition, without soul.

The obsession with mind, common to many artists at the turn of the century, serves to link Ryder and Vedder to Moreau and Redon, Davies to Denis, and others of a younger generation. The cult of intellect and imagination and its iconography are central to an appreciation of the Symbolist mood at the end of the nineteenth century and the early years of the twentieth. Ryder's *Temple of the Mind* announces and summarizes many of these concerns for American artists. Coming as it did from a painter more independent than most of foreign stylistic influences, Ryder's little picture suggests a native strain similar in both interest and intent to the European Symbolist aesthetic. In the paintings of many of his contemporaries and successors can be found concerns and solutions equivalent to Ryder's, which with his works constitute American temples of the mind, of imagination, and help to define an American Symbolist mood and aesthetic.

Seduction in America: The Dark Lady in American Painting

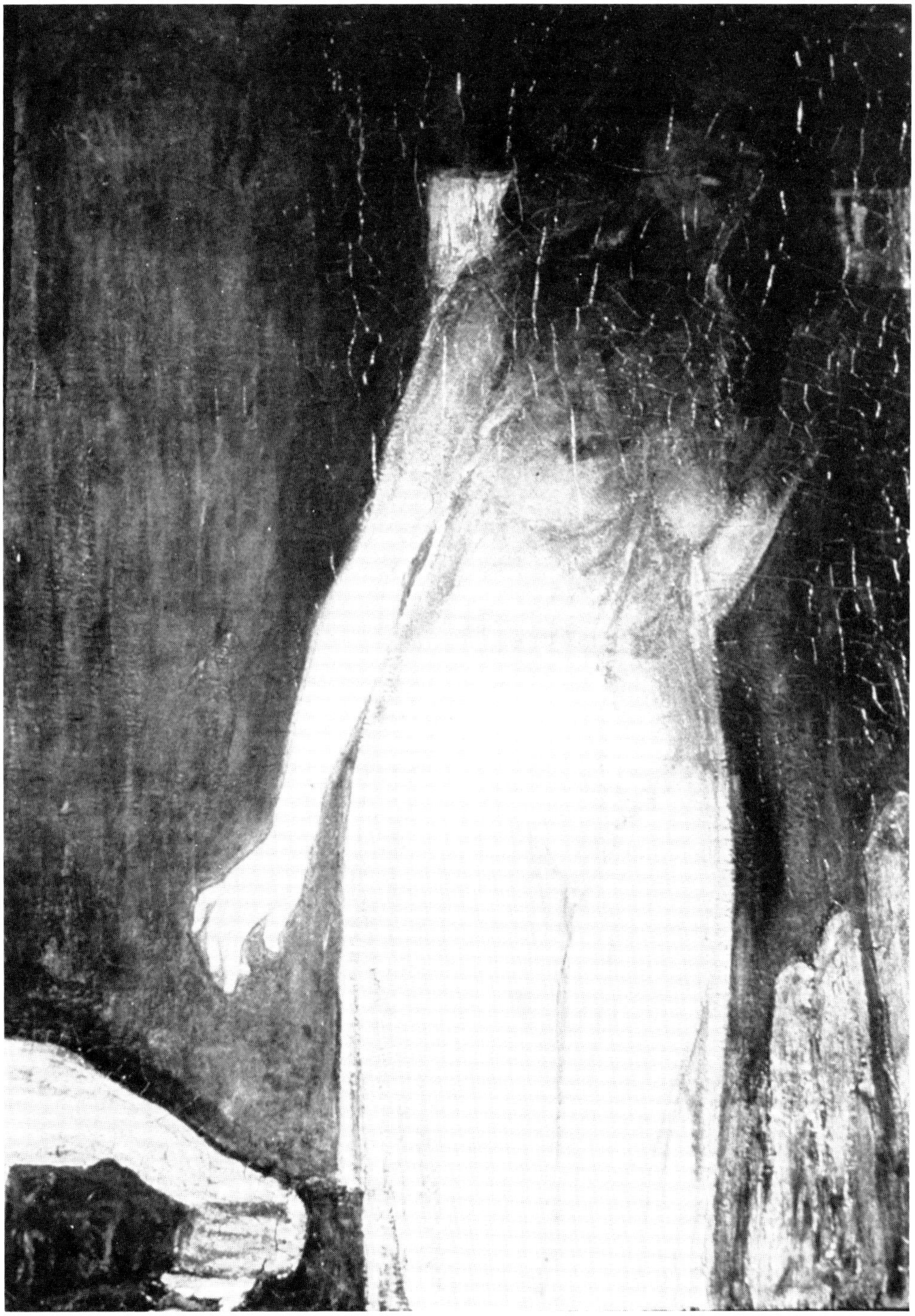

14. Henry O. Tanner, *Salome with the Head of John the Baptist,* cat. no. 62.

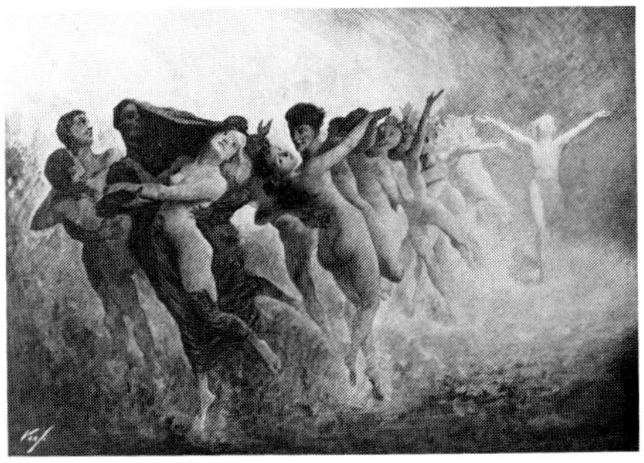

15. S. W. Van Schaick, *Dance of Death*, circa 1886, location unknown.

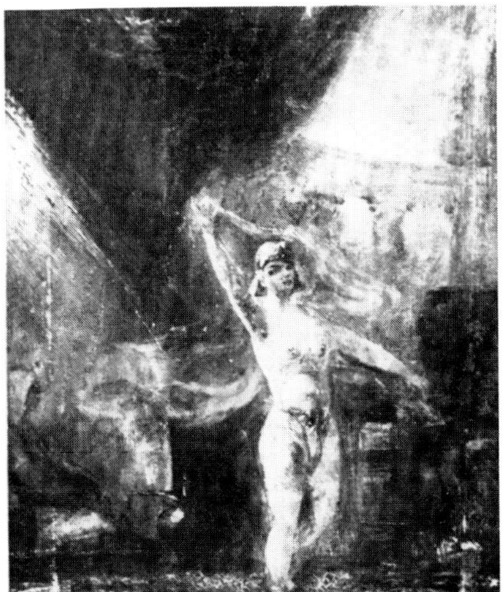

16. Robert L. Newman, *Salome*, location unknown.

Not only the severed head, but the executioner as well fascinated the late nineteenth-century artist. The feminine agents of man's destruction exercised a compulsive sway over the *fin-de-siècle* imagination. In an American society often characterized by its genteel White Ladies, who sometimes paled into angelhood, the Dark Lady of fact and fiction was never far from the artist's mind. Her sources were many and her manifestations were varied, yet her sorority appeared with increasing frequency in our literature and sculpture as well as our painting from mid-century. Leslie Fiedler has brilliantly argued her role in the American novel, identifying the Dark and White Ladies as the essential poles in the complex duality of human nature evolved during the nineteenth century.[1] The role of the *femme fatale* in European art and literature has also been long recognized; however, such embodiments of evil and destruction are less well recognized in America's visual vocabulary.[2]

Gustave Moreau's fascination with the theme of decapitation, especially in his paintings on the Salome theme, betrays an obsession with such decadent motifs in French culture at the end of the century. Salome demonstrated man's impotency in confrontation with the deadly wiles of the female. As the agent of the Baptist's destruction, Salome became the symbol of death and perversity for many of Moreau's generation; in her jewelled and seductive form, painters found expression for their pessimistic statements at the century's conclusion. The obsession with the image was well detailed in Huysman's *A Rebours,* where in describing des Esseintes' collection of artworks, the author gave the best description of Moreau's haunting images available in literature. For American artists, also, the theme had a repulsive fascination. Robert Loftin Newman, inspired by the Moreau examples, painted a small dancing Salome at the end of the century. Henry O. Tanner, working in Paris, was also drawn to the motif, and shortly after the turn of the century painted a frightful Salome; the garish hues of the Tanner oil, combined with the dramatic, almost lurid lighting, serve to heighten the impact of the scene, as Salome at once slinks toward and recoils from the Baptist's severed head. The power of Tanner's conception was rarely repeated in American painting, although his compatriots also treated the subject. Whether drawn from the Scriptural narrative, or from Oscar Wilde's and other imaginative recountings of the incident, painters and illustrators on both sides of the Atlantic found this subject of evil and death a compelling one.

The Bible offered other examples of woman's destructive power and culpability, the most famous of which is the tale of Adam and Eve. Eve, who before Darwin might have been seen as the Mother of the race, was revived by Symbolist artists seeking new re-workings of traditional images dealing with feminine deceit and perversity. In European art, the Original Sinner was elevated nearly to the status of cult object. This view was reflected in American works as well, such as those by Arthur Mathews and Augustus Tack. In America, though, her type never achieved quite the demonic quality of Franz von Stuck's well-known embodiment of *Sin.*

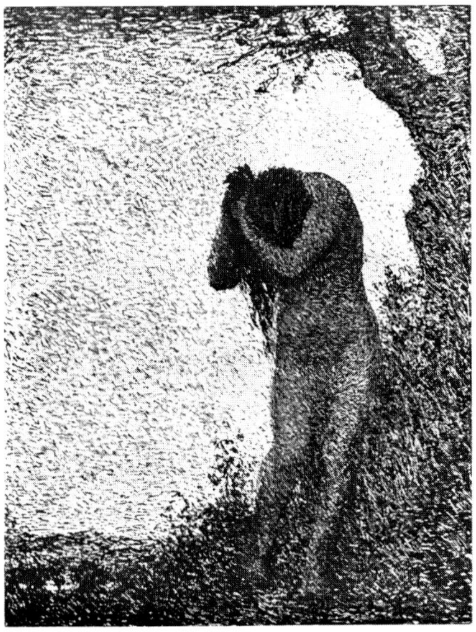

17. Augustus Vincent Tack, *The Remorse of Eve*, circa 1914, National Shrine of the Immaculate Conception, Washington, D.C.

When Stuck's painting was featured in the Saint Louis Exposition's showing of Secessionist painting in 1896, the cataloguers took pains to legitimize the decadent subject for American audiences by reference to the artist's "German interpretation of classic art" and his descent from the lineage of the then-popular Arnold Boecklin and other Teutonic imaginatives.[3] American Eves were more remorseful and less blatant than Stuck's brazen nude. Tack's heavy, earthy figure in *The Remorse of Eve*, painted in a pose borrowed from Rodin's sculpture of the same theme, is in striking contrast to Arthur Mathews' more ethereal vision; yet each, in focusing on the first woman, demonstrates the turn-of-the-century concern for primal femininity. Mathews' figure is depicted in moonlight, nude before a herm figure; the nocturnal setting, the strange silhouette of the herm against the moonlight, the darkened tonalities of the figure in a mysterious landscape, and Eve's arrested pose and comely form all contribute to the highly evocative quality of Mathews' pictorial concept and the suggestion of intimate ritual clandestinely observed.

The Dark Lady abounded in legend and literature as well, and artists drew upon mythology and contemporary writings in developing their archetypal women. Charles Allen Winter's *Fantasie Egyptienne*, exhibited at the Paris Salon of 1898, was derived from Flaubert's *Salammbô*, which attracted a number of American and French painters during the 1890s; *Salammbô's* contorted coupling with the python typified the period's fascination with erotic themes and perverse interpretations of feminine sexuality. Winter's hieratic nude, girdled by the heavy serpent, offered a striking and titillating contrast to the virginal types which recur in the paintings of Alexander, Weir and Dewing, with which American viewers were more familiar and comfortable. When the *Fantasie Egyptienne* was displayed at a New York theater in 1909, the Secretary of the Society for the Suppression of Vice ordered that the astonishing image be turned to the wall! The jewelled colors and richly detailed accoutrements of Winter's figure display a close affinity with the similarly possessed women who populate the canvases of Moreau or Stuck or the early Gustav Klimt.

The seductive classical siren had her Teutonic counterpart in the Lorelei who watched over the Rhine. Her legend was developed in romantic German poetry of the early nineteenth century and formed the theme of Ryder's painting of *The Lorelei*. His depiction of Lorelei's allure does not focus exclusively upon the feminine protagonist; as in other of his dramatic compositions, Ryder employed the entire landscape, with its craggy cliffs, moonlit tempest and mysterious shadowed recesses to support the theme of temptation and psychological storm. Ryder's inventive recasting of legendary incident in works such as *The Lorelei* surpasses the merely illustrative; the painter intuitively recognized both the dramatic potential and the humanistic import of the Germanic legend and his pictorial conception was informed by both concerns. In this he resembles the slightly older Richard Wagner who made comparable use of Northern mythology in his operatic creations. Later Wagnerian apologists noted "the absurdity of asserting that the genius who invented a new form of art . . . set himself no loftier literary and dramatic ideal than to recast old fairy tales as librettos—appeals merely to the ear and eye, regardless of the soul, the intelligence."[4] As with the composer, so too was the painter mindful of both intelligence and soul in creating his moody evocation of Rhine River temptation focusing on the feminine temptress.

The Wagnerian similarities are not surprising in view of the enormous popularity which the German composer's work inspired internationally at the end of the century. In New York in the 1880s, no less than in Paris or Bayreuth, Wagner's genius was proclaimed. While the Bayreuth performances and the Parisian *Revue Wagnérienne* perpetuated the composer's artistic principles in Europe after his death in 1883, American audiences were also being drawn to his operas. Wagner himself believed that his work would be accorded its best reception in the New World where "audiences had not yet become sated with the old operas, but were still open to the reception of the new and beautiful in art and music."[5] The Metropolitan Opera Company offered performances of individual dramas from the *Ring of the Nibelungen* from 1884 onward, and the entire *Ring* cycle was heard for the first time in America in 1889. One American reviewer noted that "not even in Bayreuth have I seen more genuine enthusiasm for Wagner's gigantic work" than at the Metropolitan performance of *Das Rheingold.*[6] Commenting upon the popular pilgrimages which resulted to Wagner's theater, Ludwig Kirschner observed in 1886 that the "American bees swarm with every year in greater numbers about the Bayreuth hive . . . "[7]

While he did not make the Bayreuth trek, Ryder was among those Americans sharing the general enthusiasm for Wagner's art. *The Lorelei* was drawn from sources similar to but independent of those utilized in Wagner's operas; its spirit and mood, however, are repeated in Ryder's paintings inspired by the musical compositions, such as his well-known *Siegfried and the Rhine Maidens.* Like Marcius-Simons, Eilshemius, Davies and others, Ryder found in Wagner's operatic works the critical conjunction of themes and moods appropriate to his introspective art.

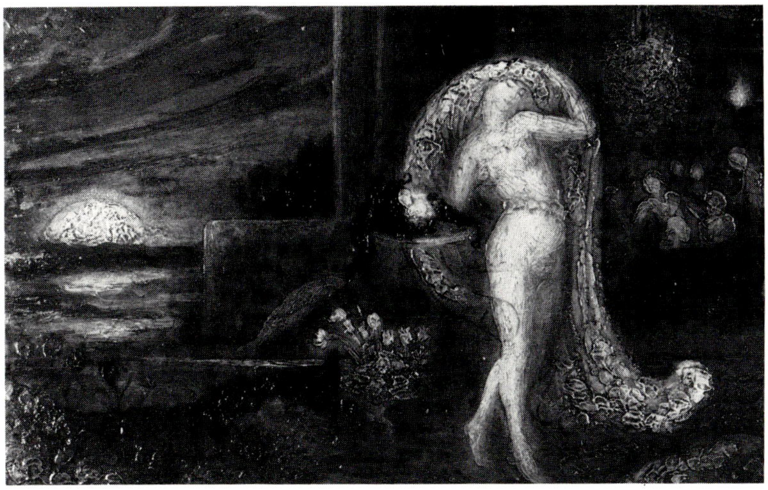

18. Claude Buck, *Salome*, 917, cat. no. 7.

From Sea to Shining Sea: Submarine Fantasies in American Art

The American debut of *Das Rheingold* was extravagantly praised in the New York press; critics especially remarked upon the composer's inventive and ingenious stagecraft, and the "fascinatingly beautiful" pictures which he evoked in his productions. The opening scene of the opera was particularly acclaimed for the depiction of "the gambols of the nixies below the surface of the Rhine," as the Maidens protected the magical gold hoard on the river bottom.[1] The submarine fantasy which Wagner utilized in this striking scene is typical of the period's interest in aquatic imagery, which appeared in prose and poetry, and painting, as well as in opera.

Investigations of the aquatic environment were frequent in the second half of the nineteenth century, both in fact and in fancy. Technological innovations and advances in naval design made explorations of the undersea realm by divers and submarine vessels more feasible. The exploits of the U.S. Navy, however, paled beside the fantastic journeys of Jules Verne's Nautilus and its Captain Nemo, which opened the submarine world to the imaginations of both children and adults. Juvenilia like Charles Kingsley's *Water Babies,* first published in 1863, and Hans Christian Andersen's *Little Mermaid* enjoyed great success with youthful readers and went through multiple editions prior to 1900; in fact, both Kingsley's and Andersen's tales survived well into the present century as staples of childhood literature. For a different audience Tennyson composed verses to *The Mermaid* and *Sea Fairies,* and Wagner incorporated Rhine Maidens into his *Ring* cycle. The American sisters of Rhine Maidens cavorted in *Neptune's Daughter,* a favorite offering of the New York hippodrome in the early years of the present century. In short, the world beneath the sea was explored and exploited by many imaginative artists toward the end of the nineteenth century and provided writers, composers, scene designers and the like with an attractive alternative to terra firma and its phenomena as then being studied by perceptually oriented artists of various persuasions.

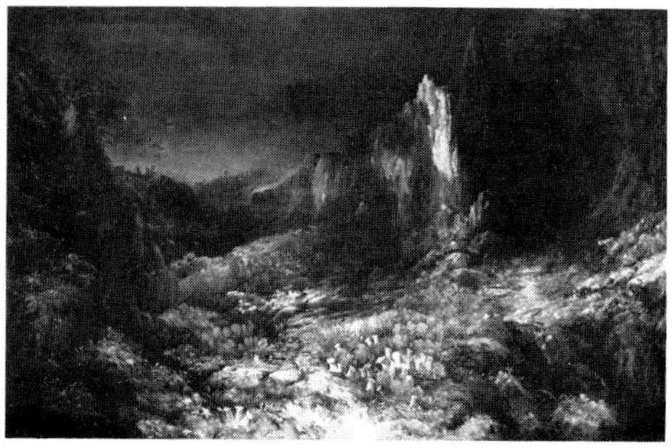

19. Edward Moran, *The Valley in the Sea,* 1892, Indianapolis Museum of Art. (Photo by Maguire Studio, Inc.)

It is no surprise, then, that painters also were drawn to the watery realm. In 1862 Edward Moran painted *The Valley in the Sea,* a striking underwater landscape which stood apart from the equally panoramic views of American scenery which were then the more common exhibition fare. Moran's imaginative journey beneath the sea was, however, a portent of even more fanciful conceptions which were shortly to follow. Classically

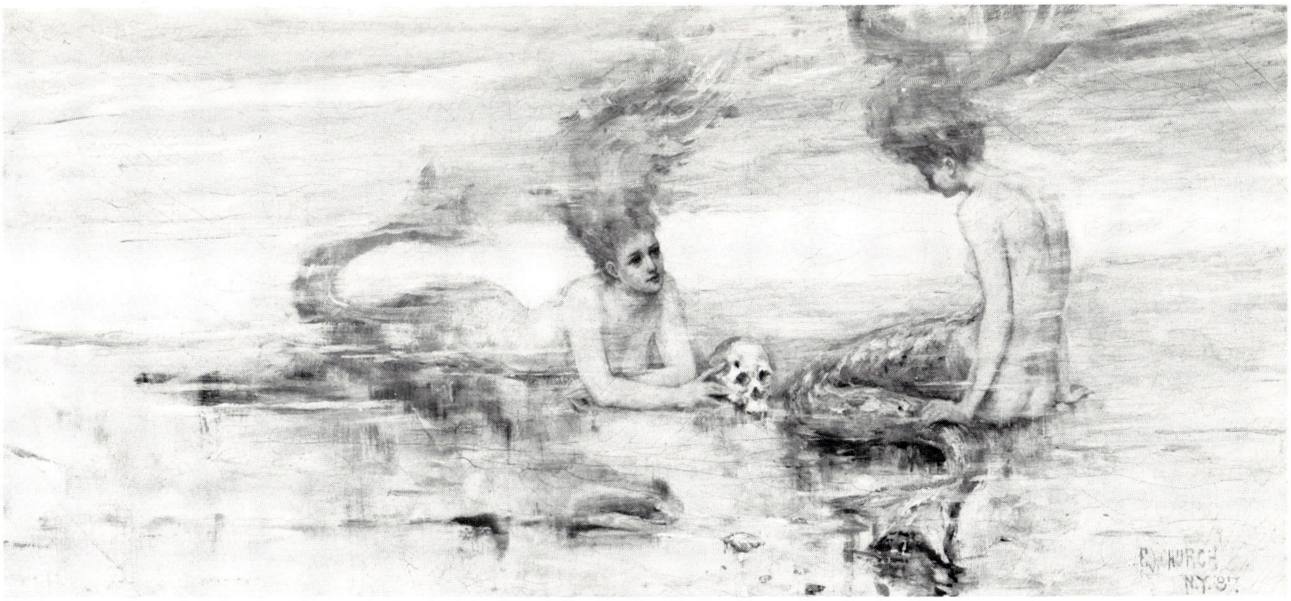

20. Frederick S. Church, *Mermaids*, 1887, cat. no. 9.

derived aquatic subjects, such as Undine or the drowned Sappho, resurfaced with a new appeal for painters of the *fin de siècle.* In both Europe and America the mermaid and, to a lesser extent, the merman provided fanciful subjects for late-century artists. In many cases the mermaid performed a role similar to the seductress acted out by her terrestrial sisters; the submarine enchantress became another symbol for the debilitating and emasculating power of women, made even more alluring by her imaginary life beneath the waves.

The fatal charm of the aquatic temptress was clearly stated by Frederick S. Church in his *Mermaids* of 1887. The attention of the submarine *femmes fatales* is fixed on the skull resting on the ocean floor, presumably representing the remains of one of their hapless sailor-victims. As with their terrestrial sisters, the seductive triumph of the mermaids over man constitutes the theme of the painting.

In this vein Elihu Vedder began his series of illustrations of the *Mermaid and the Fisherman Story* in the 1870s, a motif which he was to pursue in various media over the next three decades. The suggestion made by Vedder's motifs were echoed by other Americans of the period, reflecting an international fascination with aquatic erotica. The longevity of this interest is suggested by the last painting which illustrator Howard Pyle produced, his "Mermaid" of 1910, who rises from the water to embrace and pull down her victim. A curious submarine fantasy from the end of the nineteenth century, by Elihu Vedder, extends the mermaid motif beyond the narrative incident described in Pyle's and other compositions; the figure of a nude, arcing gracefully through her marine world, parallels both formally and symbolically the underwater compositions of Gustav Klimt of a few years later. In the *Submarine Fantasy,* as in Klimt's *Red Fishes* of 1901-1902, the human figure is combined with fish, whose smooth, wet, glistening form was acknowledged by Freud as a strong sexual symbol. In such a symbolic role they were incorporated into Vedder's and Klimt's compositions, elevating an apparently simple marine image into a strong sexual metaphor. Other Klimt equivalents exist in American painting, most especially in the work of the Wisconsin expatriate, Carl Marr. Although better known for his Bavarian genre scenes, Marr's *Mermaids* betray an affinity with the languid ease and sensual forms of Klimt's mermaids in his *Moving Waters* of 1898. The paintings by Vedder, Klimt and Marr evince the priority placed upon instinctive sensual, indeed sexual response evoked by such fleshy subjects, and certainly diverge from the merely anecdotal use of comparable motifs as commonly found in the exhibition halls of Munich, Paris and New York at the end of the century.

Other affinities exist between American mermaids and their European counterparts of the same period. One of George Willoughby Maynard's best known compositions is his *In Strange Seas,* completed in Paris in 1889. His robust mermaids frolic among the waves, their attention momentarily diverted by a passing ship in the distance. The subject's derivation from the classical legend of sirens and sailors is obvious; equally evident is the parallel which Maynard's composition bears with the similar paintings of Arnold Boecklin, especially notable in the sturdy proportions of the females and the tumultuous handling of the seas. Boecklin's work found a receptive audience especially among English-speaking artists, who admired his combination of nightmarish visions and dreamy idylls. Although less favored by the French, Boecklin's work even there excited the imagination, if not the admiration, of critics and painters.[2] The German may not have been the specific source for Maynard's curious conception, but the affinities between the two artists' works suggest similar intentions and imaginations which transgress national boundaries and demonstrate the pervasiveness of the fanciful strain at the end of the century.

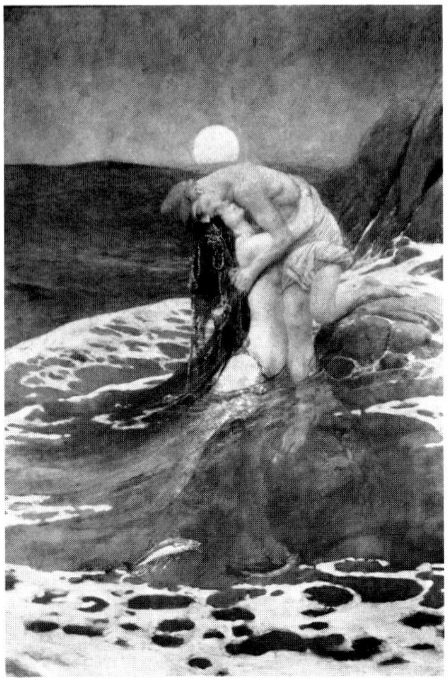

21. Howard Pyle, *The Mermaid,* 1910, Delaware Art Museum.

In French and German painting particularly, aquatic women were also frequently associated with wave forms. As a sexual metaphor, the repeated crashing of white, foamy waves—as suggested by Marr's maritime imagery—had its interest for a generation immersed in evolving sexual symbols. Water, and especially rushing water, were of interest to Freud in just such a symbolic role. The woman-in-wave motif also provided an extension of the submarine-mermaid fantasy schemes of earlier artists. The wave paintings by Pamela Coleman Smith and Arthur Mathews both involve women and water, and yet derive from different inspirations. Formally, the Mathews painting expostulated a patterning similar to Art Nouveau design as then maturing in France; in that regard his woman might be seen as the watery companion to the gracefully composed figure pieces by John W. Alexander—a decoratively arranged treatment of observed incident or posed study. Smith's watercolor, on the other hand, is more inventive in the manner in which the six female forms swirl upward out of the water; here the women are not in the wave, but *become* the wave, more closely bonding image and symbolic statement.

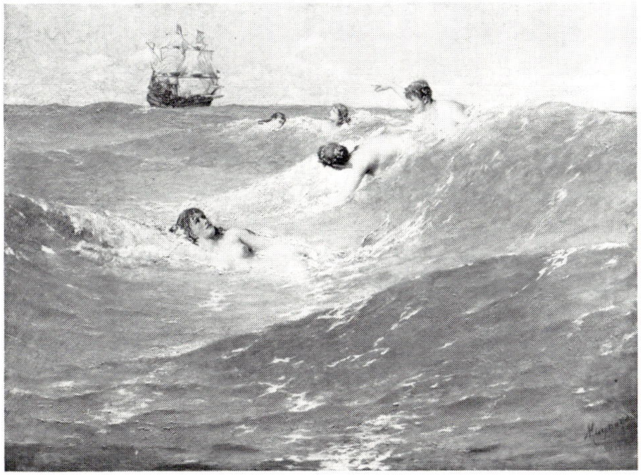

22. George W. Maynard, *In Strange Seas,* 1889, The Metropolitan Museum of Art.

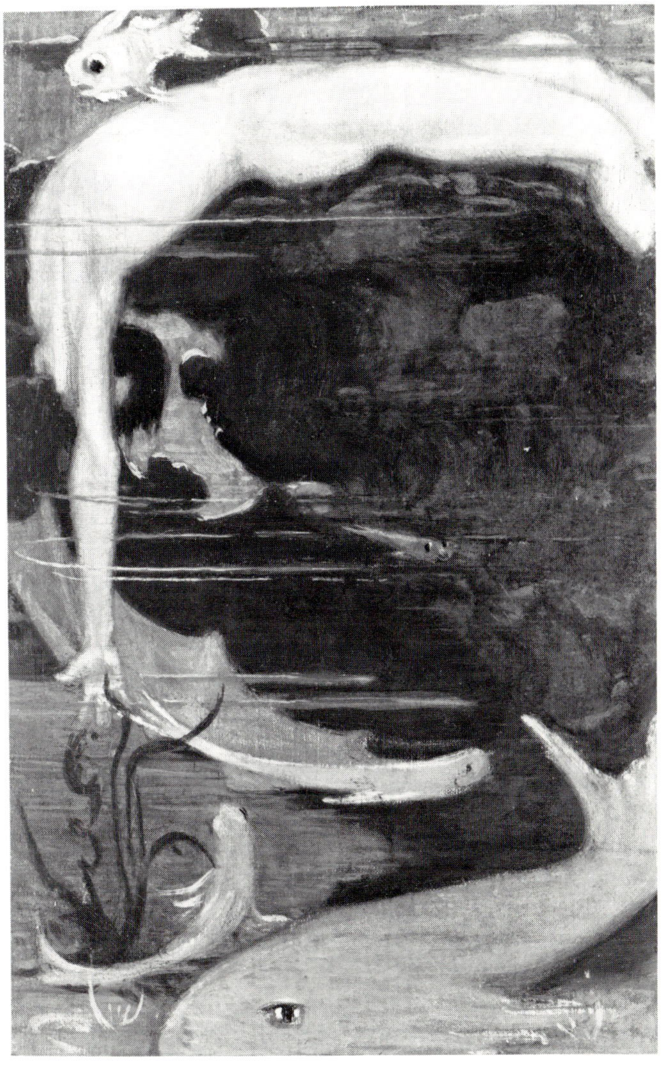

23. Elihu Vedder, *Underwater Fantasy,* circa 1885, cat. no. 64.

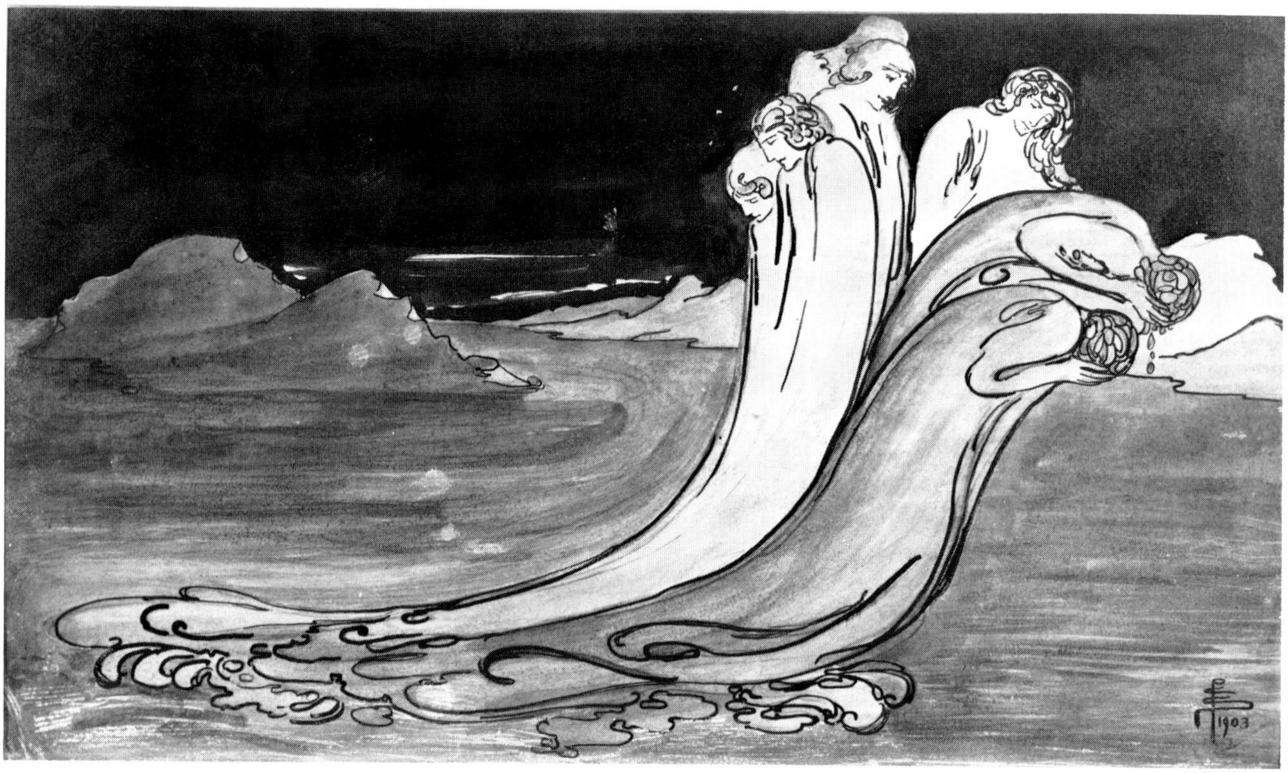

24. Pamela Colman Smith, *The Wave,* 1903, cat. no. 55. (Photo by Geoffrey Clements)

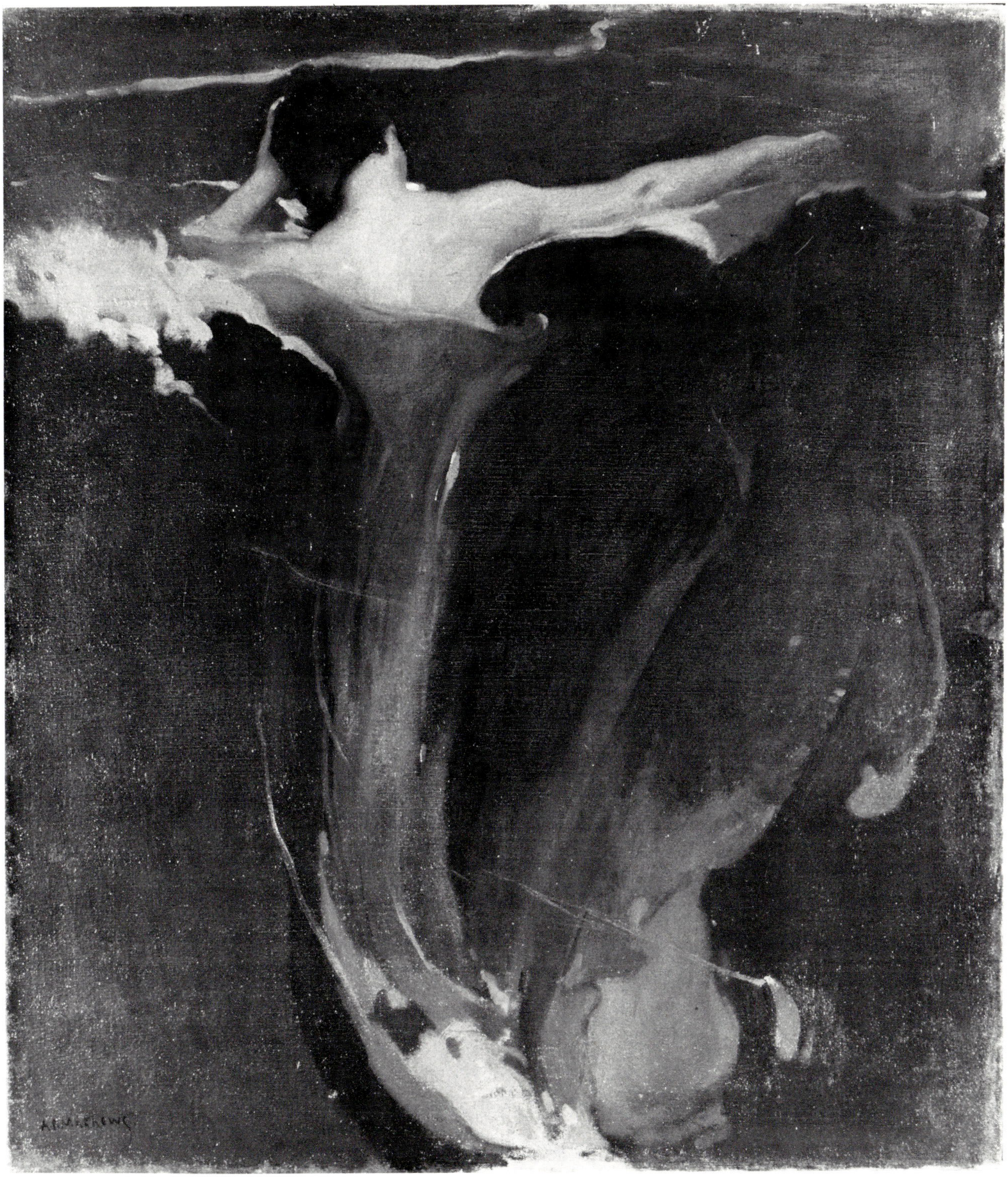

25. Arthur Mathews, *The Wave,* cat. no. 40.

The Virgin and the virgins: The White Lady in American Painting

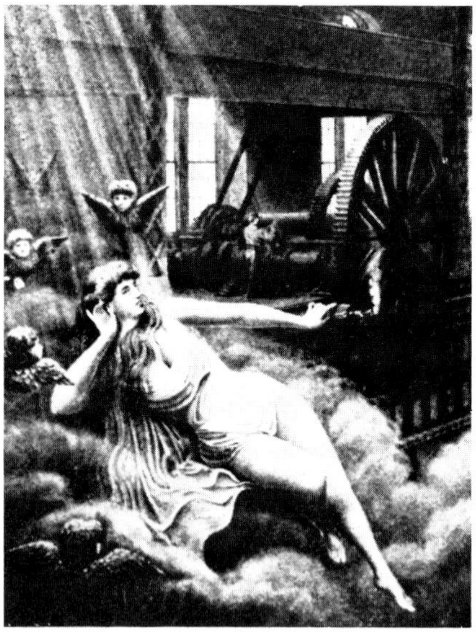

26. P. F. Goist, *Prose and Poetry,* circa 1896, location unknown.

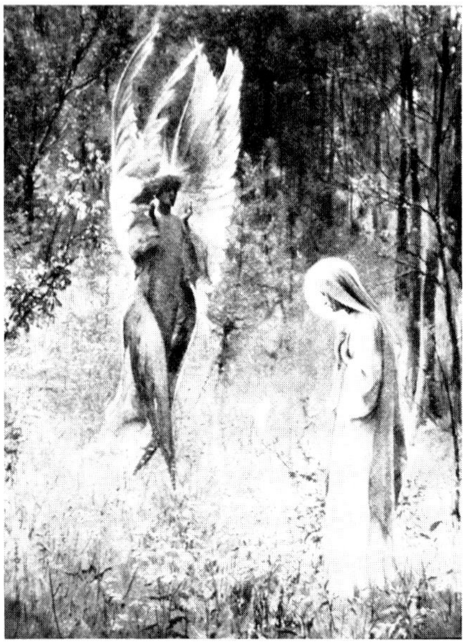

27. Sarah P. B. Dodson, *The Annunciation,* 1906, location unknown.

The counterpart to the demonic woman whether on land or sea was the sweet, virginal, angelic female whose appeal was also powerful for late nineteenth-century artists. These positive virtues of the angelic type constituted the essential other pole in the complex human duality being defined by the period. Her poetic sensitivity balanced man's prosaic pursuits, and in such guise she appeared frequently in paintings and illustrations of the day. Henry Adams' often-quoted response to the Paris Exposition of 1900 was the appeal to the Virgin. To Adams, she represented the unity and grace of the medieval world whose passing he lamented; in contrast to her values stood the complexities of the modern age, as symbolized by the Dynamo. In America at the end of the century, in an era increasingly dominated by the Dynamo, both the Virgin and virginal types enjoyed a renewed popularity as motifs for the writer's pen and the painter's brush.

The strongly Protestant tradition in America had checked the rise of Mariolatry in our churches and in our art. While veneration of the Virgin never achieved here the level of some Catholic cultures, there was at the end of the nineteenth century an increased fascination with her as a symbolic figure. For Adams it was as an emblem of unity that she came to be of interest; for others, the Virgin's Immaculate Conception and the rebirth of mankind through her Son offered an appealing alternative to Darwinian determinism. The Annunciation motif was of particular appeal, partly as a general reaffirmation of virginal values in an era of more tawdry and mechanistic concerns, and partly as a reaffirmation of faith and the promise of a new beginning. The British pre-Raphaelites, particularly Rossetti, had focused upon the theme at mid-century, and some of the devout if not especially inventive Salon exhibitors of later decades had persisted in their essays on the subject. Some Americans continued the basic type pioneered by Rossetti, such as Sarah Dodson whose last painting, an Annunciation left incomplete at her death in 1906, essentially repeated the style developed by Rossetti a half-century earlier. Others among her compatriots sought more innovative handlings of the theme. Henry Tanner's *Annunciation,* for instance, dispensed with the angelic messenger and replaced it with a symbolic blaze of light, from which the Virgin recoils at the startling news. George Hitchcock's Paris Salon entry for 1888 represented the Virgin in a Dutch field of tulips, and, as with Tanner, she is unaccompanied by any divine messenger; at first glance, Hitchcock's Virgin is indistinguishable from the young Dutch girls which generally appeared in his canvases and those of his studio-mate, Gari Melchers, in the 1880s. Related in subject to his Salon painting is another version of the Annunciation in which the Virgin, swathed in white robes of a vaguely North African type, is simply

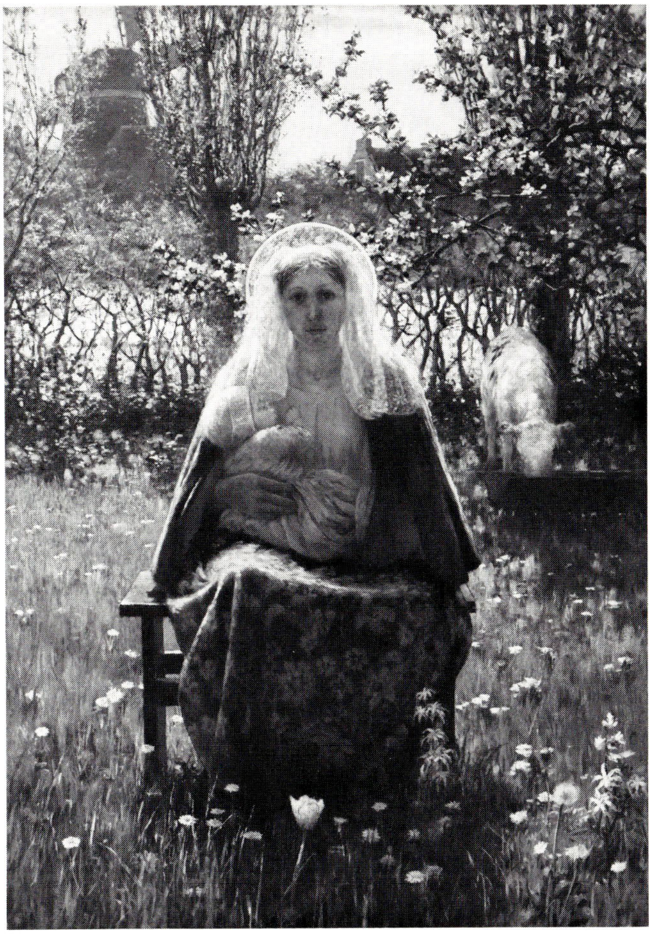

28. George Hitchcock, *Blessed Mother,* 1892, cat. no. 29.

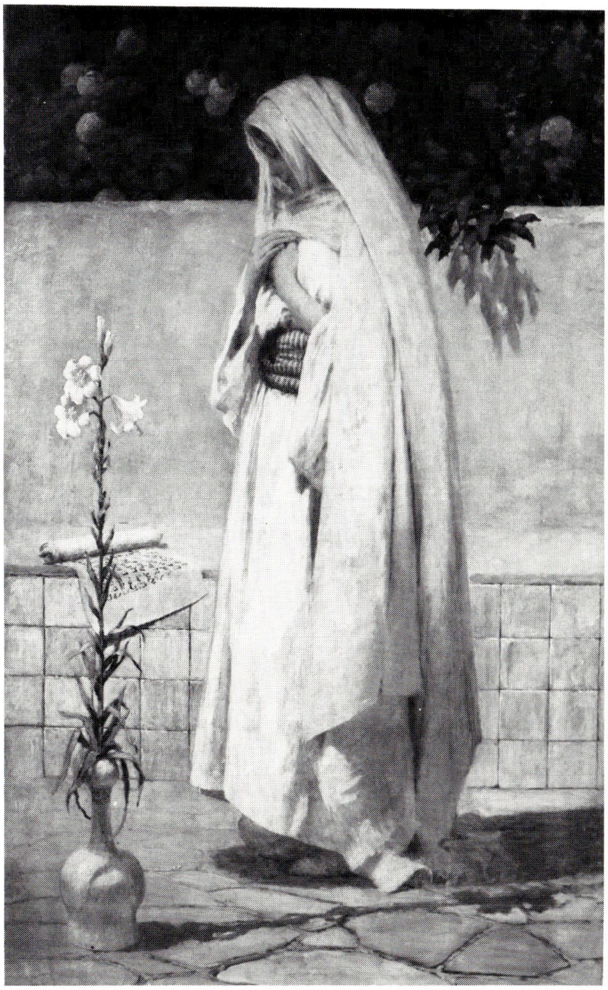

29. George Hitchcock, *The Annunciation,* cat. no. 30.

posed before a white wall; the pervasive blond tonalities and the presence of Mary's symbolic lily constitute the sole, very low-keyed reference to the miracle.

Similarly ambiguous is Hitchcock's *Blessed Mother,* also painted in Holland. Like the Breton peasants whom Lévy-Dhurmer posed against a rocky coastline as *Our Lady of Penmarc'h* in 1896, Hitchcock elevates to a religiously symbolic plane the rustic scene of maternity against a flower-filled and windmilled landscape. The hieratic pose and iconographical inclusions compete with the simple genre-like appeal of the scene to create an ambivalent image of considerable charm and power.

More generalized statements or symbols of feminine purity and virtue, without specific reference to Biblical sources, were also common in America at the turn of the century. While some observers quarreled with the identification of feminized culture as a peculiarly American trait, the phenomenon was certainly pronounced here, even if not limited to our shores.[1] The adulation of feminine purity in American womanhood reached its apogee in writings such as Henry Van Dyke's prescription for the training of females and his description of their role in modern culture. He detailed woman's "inevitable pilgrimage . . . from the places that are sweet and pleasant in their lowliness and tender bloom to the higher ranges of thought and feeling, with . . . an ever purer spiritual air to breathe . . . " For Van Dyck, assurance of woman's "progress, so reasonable, so beautiful, so triumphant" toward attainment of "the highest standard that is visible,—yes, and beyond that, to an ideal invisible save to the eyes of the heart," was nothing less than "one of the vital problems of civilization."[2] The subjects of such adulation did not universally enjoy the pedestal on which they found themselves placed. The Boston poet, Josephine Peabody, in 1895 confided to her journal: "What ever-lasting symbols women are! I know so well, when these beautiful moments happen, that it is none of it for me. I know so well that I am a symbol for somebody; I am a prism that catches the light a moment. It is the light that gladdens, not the prism. And yet for that moment, the prism, the symbol, the bringer of tidings, the accidental woman, becomes perforce . . . a messenger of God, an angel truly, wonderfully, most humbly . . . she must choose between the humbleness of real angelhood or the bitter pride of self-love that is bound to hurt."[3] Whether hurtful or not, the "accidental woman," symbolic of feminine purity, became a standard motif in the painting of the late nineteenth century both here and in Europe.

This generalized type is well known in the imagery of the period, ranging from Abbott Thayer's and William Closson's idealized angel-women to Charles Dana Gibson's fashionable girls. The graceful maidens who wander through the canvases of Maurice Denis and Alphonse Osbert, of Arthur B. Davies and J. Alden Weir, are all part of the large sisterhood of virginal purity. Among such subjects are the stylish women of Thomas Dewing's paintings, often posed in frozen attitudes with a disconcerting lack of communication between subjects. The peculiar charm of Dewing's figures derives as much from their pose and setting as from any specific symbolic

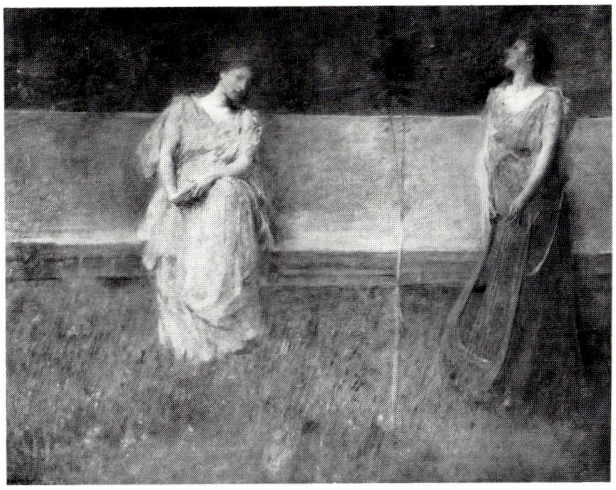

30. Thomas W. Dewing, *The Song*, 1891, Collection of Mr. Graham Williford. (Photo by Taylor & Dull)

roles played by his graceful subjects. His women are frequently accompanied by musical instruments, reflecting the general importance of music in late nineteenth-century culture. yet in many instances, particularly in his early works, Dewing's musicians seem distracted from their performances, as in *The Song* where the lyre stands silently at the woman's side; through such indirection the analogy suggested between feminine and musical sensibilities is more obliquely and paradoxically more potently stated than in the great number of pianists, harpists and other performers who crowded the canvases of the period. Instead of the communal enjoyment of music or of other's company, Dewing's multi-figure compositions developed an iconography of separation and detachment; for instance the three graces in *The Garden* are separated both posturally and, even more importantly, psychologically from each other, in a manner similar to certain paintings by Fernand Khnopff. Dewing's feminine isolates seem to relate only inwardly to their own states of mind, to their own reveries, in portrayals of introspection generally devoid of anecdote or specificity.

Similarly isolated is Weir's young woman in his painting of *The Open Book.* Posed against an indefinite landscape which is painted with the softened tones which generally excuse the artist's being grouped with the American Impressionists, the woman reflects upon the open pages couched in her lap. Her undress is similar to that found in many contemporaneous allegorical revelations of Truth and other meanings. While the symbolic meaning of Weir's figure and literary theme were more overt than anything encountered in Dewing's art, it still annoyed critics of the day for its lack of specificity; one reviewer complained that "the young woman's *deshabille* and the open volume on her lap are intended, between them, to convey some meaning seems clear, but it is not so clear what the meaning can be."[4] Like the older Dewing, Weir obliquely suggests rather than illustrates the possibility of the spirit's introspective journey inspired by art. "There is no frigate like a book," wrote Emily Dickinson, and from the volume's decorated pages, or carried upon musical strains, the sensitive feminine souls in Weir's and Dewing's paintings journey far into the realm of reverie and dream.

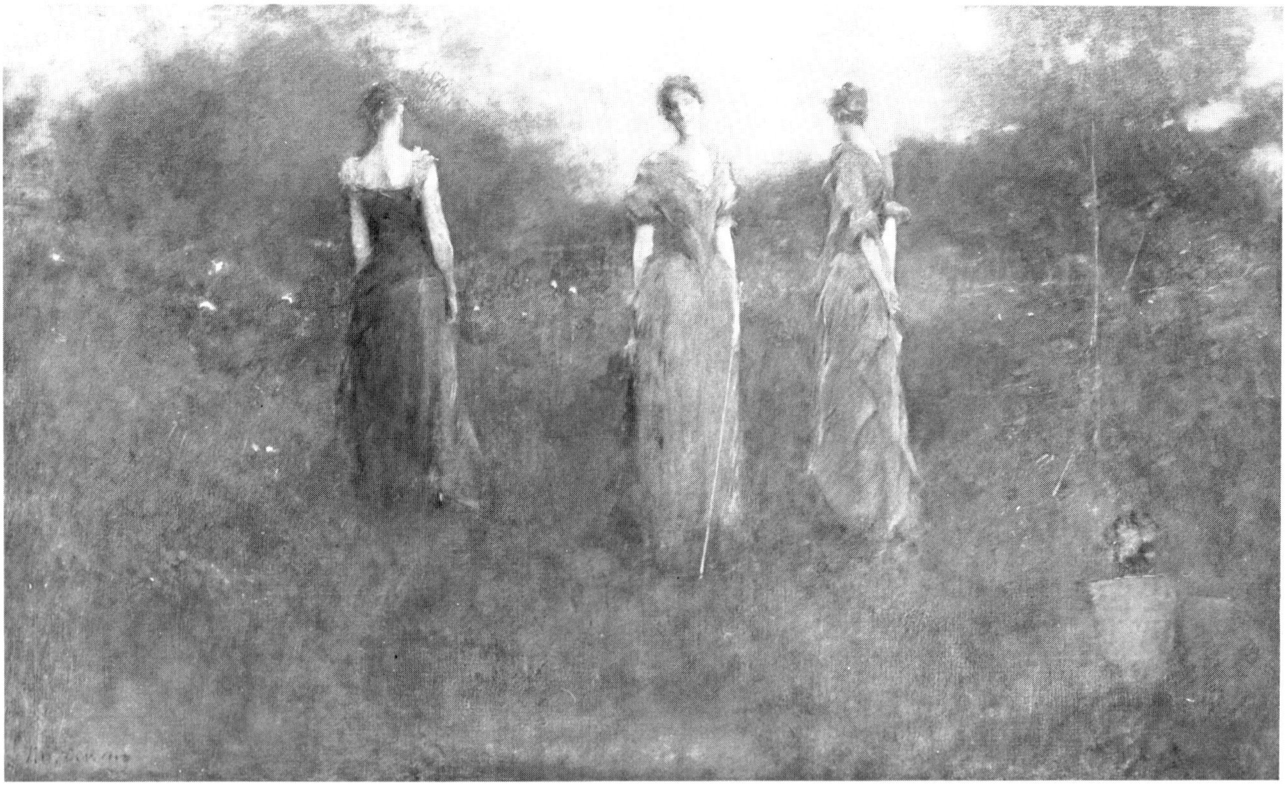

31. Thomas W. Dewing, *The Garden* (or *Spring Moonlight*), circa 1891, cat. no. 19.

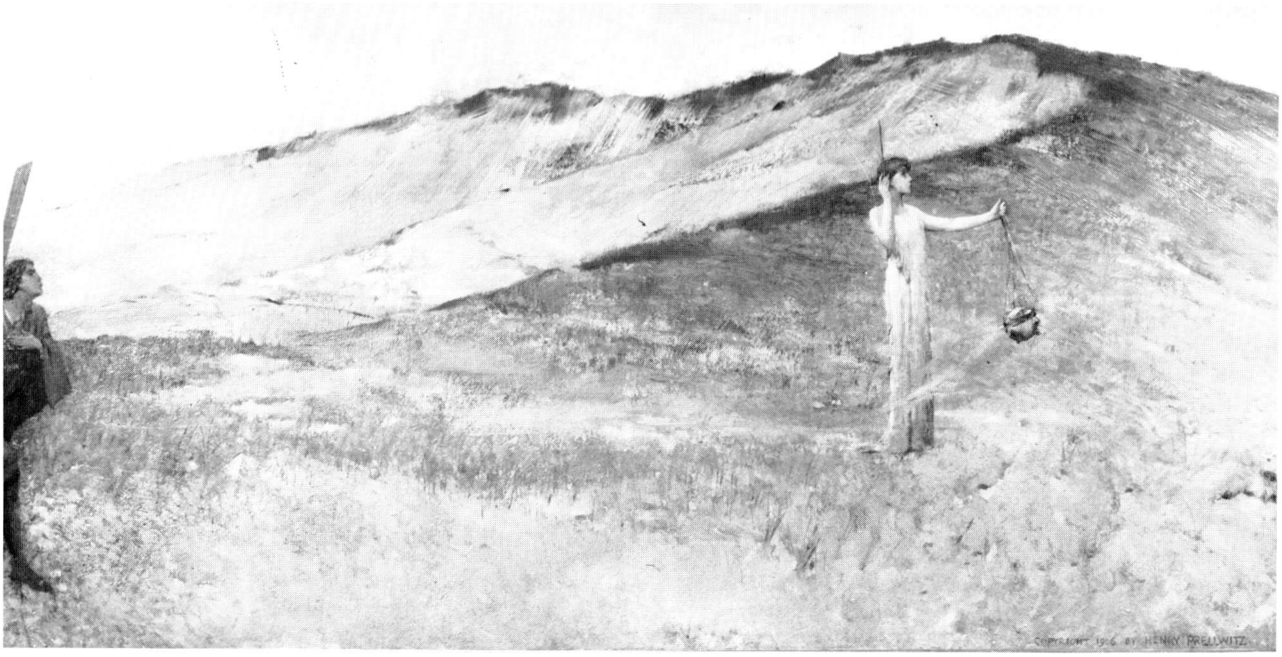

32. Henry Prellwitz, *Ariel Sings*, 1906, cat. no. 51.

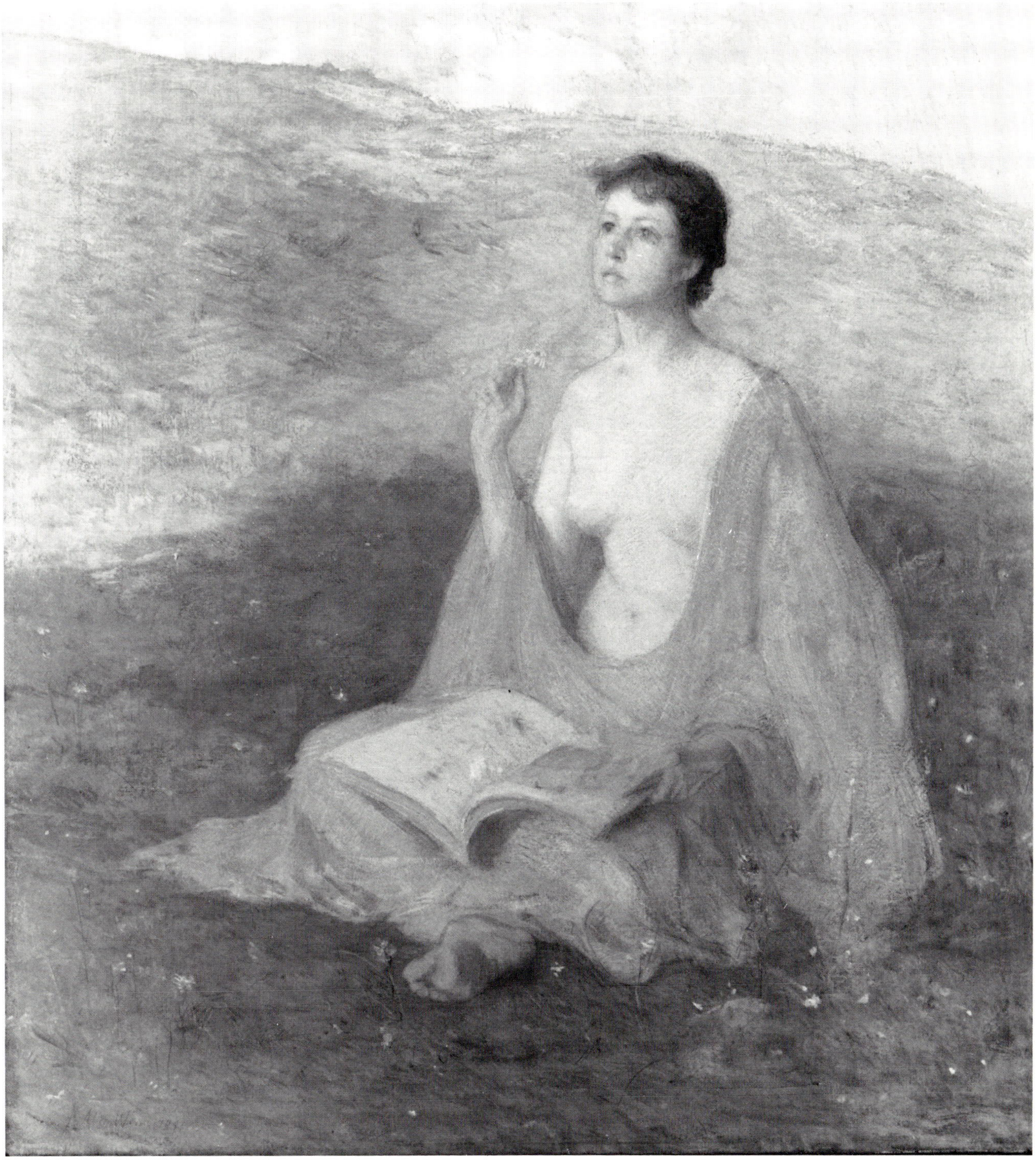

33. J. Alden Weir, *The Open Book,* 1891, cat. no. 66.

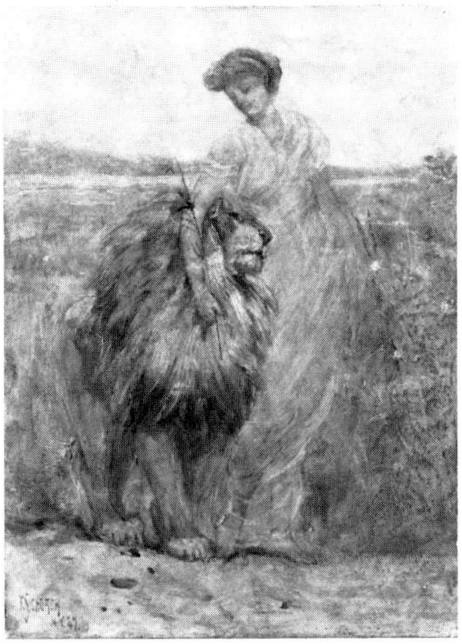

34. Frederick S. Church, *Supremacy*, 1887, National Collection of Fine Arts, Smithsonian Institution.

Woman's appeal for artists of the *fin de siècle* extended beyond meditative reverie. Her charms were equated or contrasted with numerous other animate and inanimate objects. One of the most familiar such contrasts was between the pure, slight form of the female and the brute, animalistic form of the bestial world—Beauty and the Beast. Frederick S. Church exploited such pairings of women and a whole menagerie of creatures in his fanciful paintings and illustrations of the 1870s onward. The woman's feminine dominance over the beast's brutal passions carried with it vaguely menacing but decidedly titillating erotic overtones, which helped to popularize Church's pairing of woman with, for instance, the King of the Jungle.

The animal world and the feminine realm intersected in artistic equivalencies as well as contrasts. Derived ultimately from a Symbolist concern for correspondences or equivalents between disparate objects, woman came to be seen as being like a bird, an angel, a flower, and other associative objects. Baudelaire's theory of correspondences, by which an idea out of one class of experience might be translated into the form or vocabulary of another, had an innate and long-lived appeal to Americans tutored on disputation by analogy as practiced by our thinkers from Edwards to Emerson. Baudelaire's correspondent vision easily took root in American art and literature, and as late as 1926 Allen Tate noted that it continued to "prosper here with an eager fecundity."[5]

Analogies to feminine grace and purity were particularly to be found in the bird world; swans and peacocks especially were paired with feminine subjects in equations of varied complexity. The white swans which floated through Mallarméan verse glided with equal muteness through the painted creations of Symbolist artists in Europe and America. An early canvas by Davies, called *Chalice*, is suggestive of ritual acts in its titling and imagery; diaphanously clad, lithesome women relax on the shore of a lake across which swans silently glide, in an idyllic equivalent to some of the contemporaneous inventions by Denis or Osbert. Later Bertram Hartman repeated the basic formula, only substituting flamingos for swans.

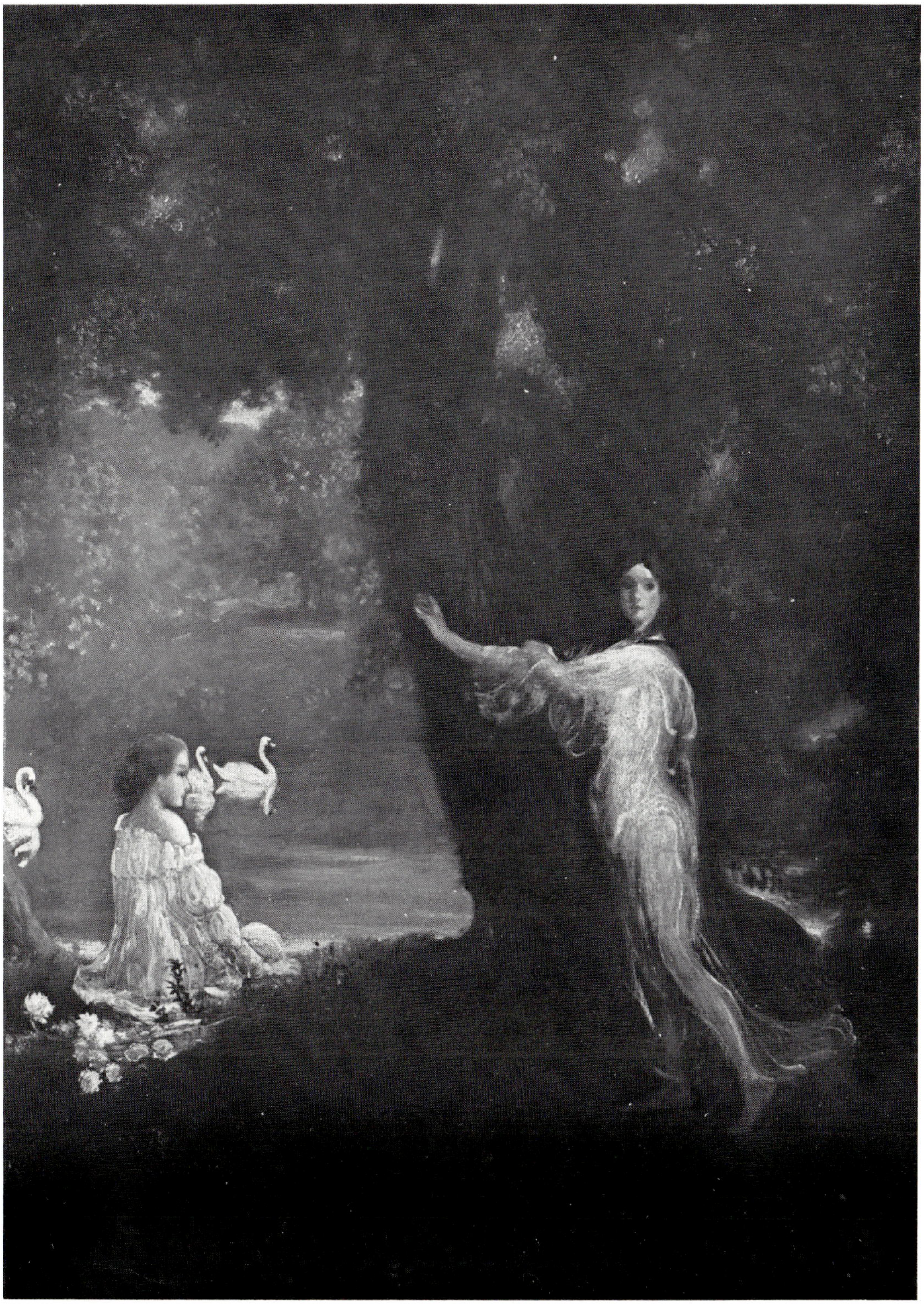

35. Arthur B. Davies, *Chalice,* 1897, cat. no. 15.

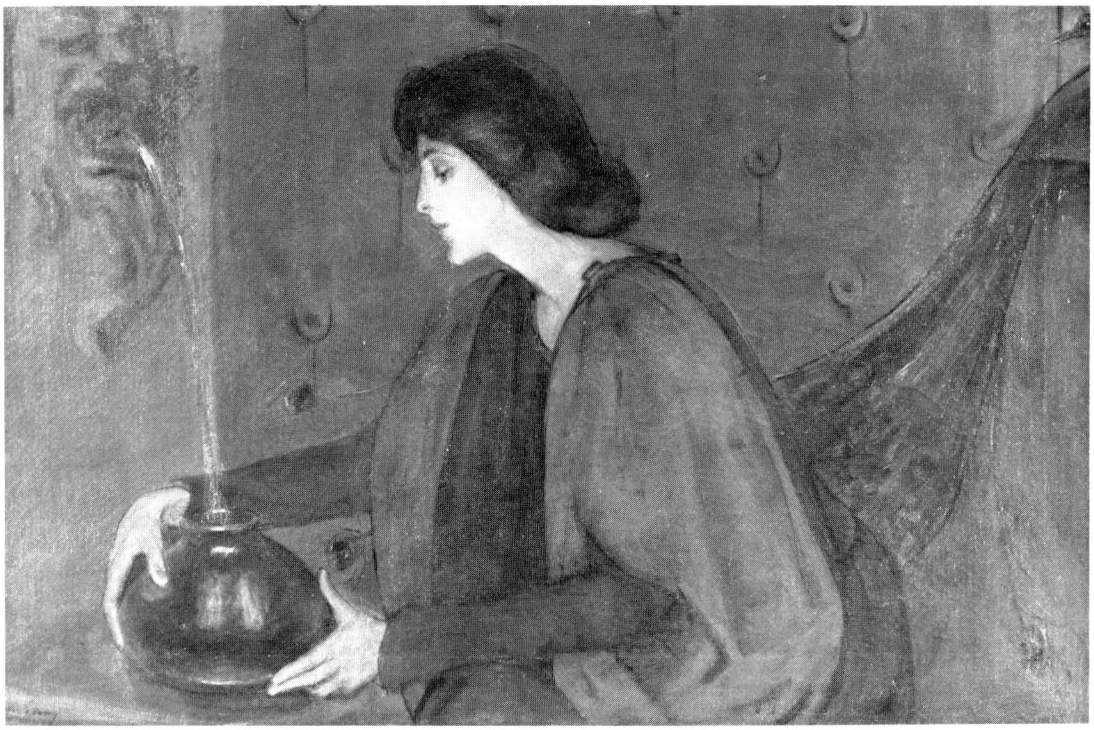

36. Alice Pike Barney, *Woman and Peacock*, cat. no. 2.

The peacock was an even more familiar image in late nineteenth-century art and decoration, appearing everywhere from illustrations to jewelry to the walls of Mr. Leyland's dining room, as decorated by Whistler. The peacock's decorative form also appeared in many easel paintings of the *fin de siècle* as an apt symbol for woman's sensual appeal, as for instance in the large canvas by Whistler's sometime protégée, Alice Barney. Painted with the same blue-green tonalities as the Peacock Room, Barney's *Woman with Peacock* also displays an interest in decorative patterning and gently curving forms defined by outline, concerns which characterized much avant-garde Parisian painting of the 1890s. Barney's close friend, the Symbolist painter Edmond Aman-Jean, had utilized a similar pairing of female subject and bird in his *Girl with Peacock*, suggesting yet another possible source for the American's interest in the motif. During the same period, other American painters, such as Charles Walter Stetson, William B. Closson and Alfred Maurer, were projecting comparable pictorial similes. Maurer exploited the subject for his painting of circa 1903 in which the woman's elaborate robe with its rich, varicolored patterns approximates the finery of the showbird after which the canvas is titled. In this instance, the equation of the showy peacock with feminine vanity is suggested, as the woman/peacock primps in the mirror. By 1905, the peacock-woman equation was so thoroughly ingrained in modern consciousness that in advertising for the Canfield Rubber Company the poor bird was put to work shilling for ladies' dress shields!

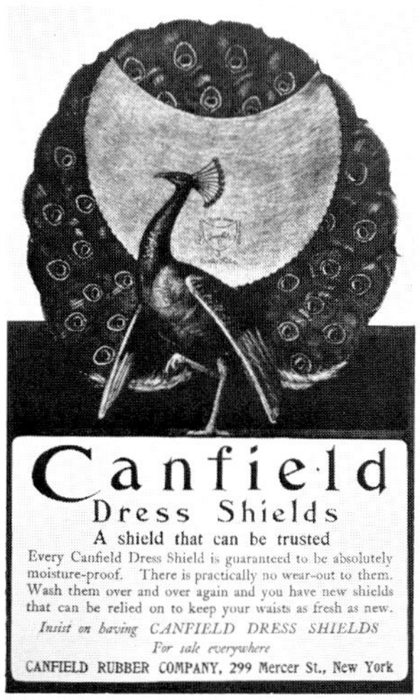

37. Advertisement for Canfield Dress Shields, from Harper's Bazar, 1905.

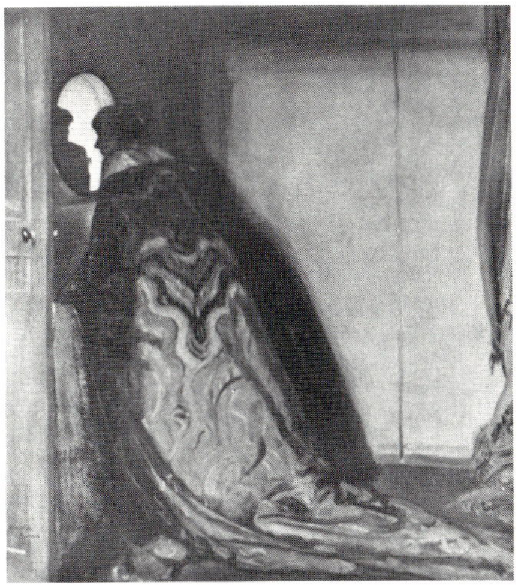

38. Alfred H. Maurer, *The Peacock*, 1903, Philadelphia Museum of Art.

In flora as well as fauna equivalents for woman's sensual charm and physical anatomy could be found. Such comparisons became a frequent occurrence in the waning years of the century, as many artists sought to capture woman's appeal in the evanescent charms of the flower in bud or blossom. The most famous of such combinations were perhaps the series of *Flora's Feast* by the English artist-illustrator, Walter Crane, but many of his contemporaries were simultaneously attracted to the pictorial analogy. Some focused upon a particular aspect of the blossom, such as its scent, as the excuse for synaesthetic exploration of similarities between flower and female. Aman-Jean's lithograph of *Perfume*, for instance, was inspired by such a linking, and in the appeal to the olfactory sense was also explored by Americans; Charles Curran's *Scent of the Roses*, like Aman-Jean's Symbolist print, focused upon this special aspect of the floral-female equivalency. Numerous as well were the paintings of women captured in the act of holding or smelling flowers, which through appeal to the olfactory senses extended the artist's realm beyond the merely retinal. As with the musical and auditory themes of Dewing, such subjects allowed Curran, Aman-Jean and others to suggest other sensory responses to their viewers.

One of the most striking late-century combinations is found in Vedder's *Morning Glory*. Here the unusual image resonates with meanings established through the juxtaposition of nude and blossom. The perfume suggested by Curran is present, but Vedder goes beyond the dual senses of sight and smell to suggest other complicated analogies between his two pictorial elements. The tactile appeal of soft flesh and soft petals is obvious; more startling is the erotic intent underlying the pairing. Unlike his earlier pencil drawings of petalled faces, such as the *Soul of the Sunflower* of 1868, which have been described as embodiments of a "'state of soul," the *Woman and Morning Glory* conveys a more sensual message, a "state of flesh" rather than a soulful meaning.[6] The sexual surrogate in floral guise has been discussed by Theodore Stebbins with regard to Martin Johnson Heade's magnificent magnolias of the same period[7]; in Vedder's case, the positioning of the nude woman in the deep-throated morning glory indicates a similar concern for ambivalent imagery fraught with sexual overtones. Poignancy is added to the artist's composition by the suggestion that the nude's abundant charms might be as fleeting as those of the short-lived morning glory. That this conjoined symbol had a potent appeal is attested to by the survival of the motif well into the present century; as late as 1940, Joseph Cornell re-used the basic analogy, albeit without Vedder's eroticism, in his collaged homage to Greta Garbo.[8]

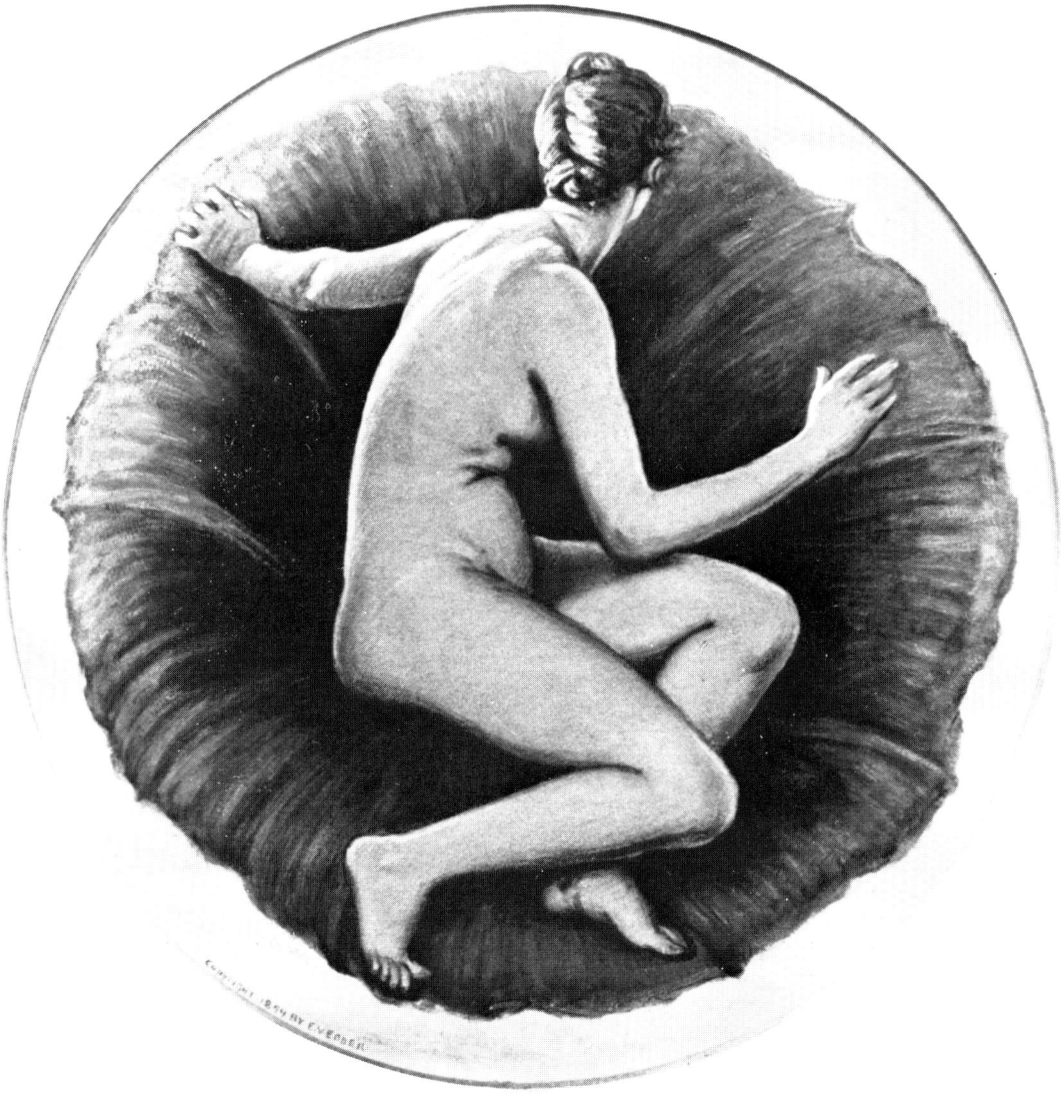

39. Elihu Vedder, *Morning Glory,* 1899, cat. no. 65.

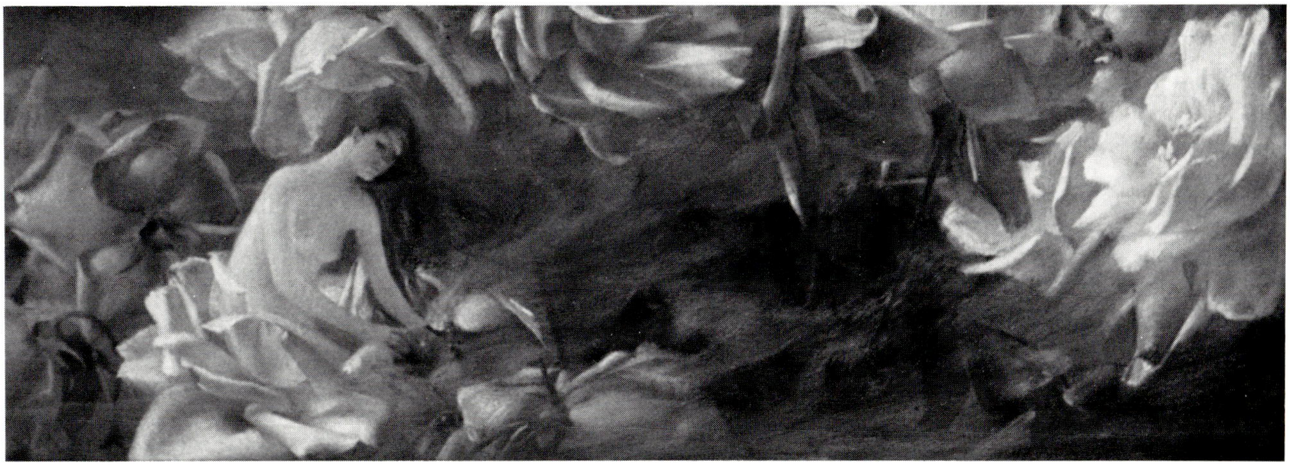

40. Charles C. Curran, *Scent of the Rose,* 1890, cat. no. 12.

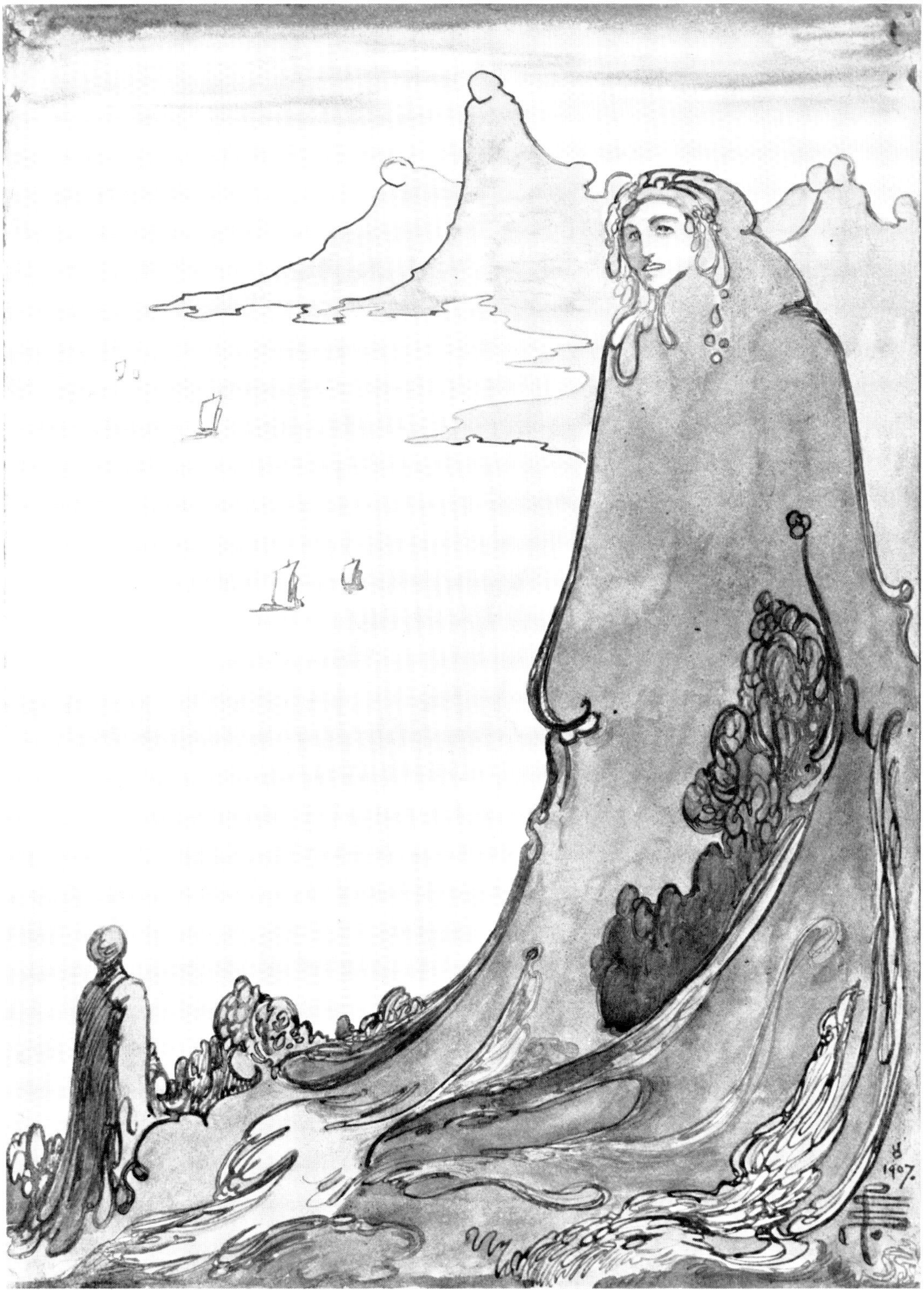

41. Pamela Colman Smith, *Beethoven Sonata No. II,* 1907, cat. no. 56.

American Visions and the American Dream

The lissome White Ladies of American painting were frequently shown in a meditative, dreamlike state. The dream, with its release from reason's strictures, encouraged the free associations dear to the imaginative spirit. The Symbolist aesthetic placed a premium upon such correspondences or equivalent states; while the Idea to which the painted Fact was related might vary with the artists involved, analogical relationships were generally a central concern in much Symbolist iconography.

Coupled with this approach to subject was an interest in synaesthesia, the appeal to multiple senses: Debussy's tone poems or Beethoven's harmonies could induce pictorial visions in some sensitive souls, like Pamela Coleman Smith's; for both painters and poets, color could evoke associative moods or states of mind, explaining the importance placed upon chromatic language in Symbolist verse and upon secondary and tertiary tones in Symbolist painting.

Although interest in such translated sensory responses extended well back into history, the synaesthetic state was first examined "scientifically" by Francis Galton in his *Inquiries Into Human Faculty,* published in 1883. His physiological investigations occasioned increased fascination with the phenomenon among both scientists and laymen; J.-K. Huysman's description of des Esseintes' liquor organ and Alexander Scriabin's experimentation with the color organ are two well-known instances of synaesthetic investigation outside the realm of painting which shortly followed Galton's publication. Painters, like writers and composers, were fond of the cultivation of synaesthetic response which advanced the analogical relationship between disparate things toward complete unity. Mallarmé's sonnet to *Le Cygne* represents the typical extreme to which the Symbolist poet was able to push Baudelairean simile or correspondence, finally achieving a complete and abstract union of image and effect. The painter's general intention is similar, and within the confines of his medium and his style he aspires toward the same convergence of image and effect, as in Curran's linking of women and floral scent.

Just as the synaesthetic state translates sensory stimuli into related but dissimilar images—Smith explained that her music pictures were "what I see when I hear music, thoughts loosened and set free by the spell of sound"[1]—so too could dream-life lend itself to the formation of symbolism. According to one early twentieth-century student of the phenomenon, "The very fact that we *sleep,* that is to say, that the avenues of sense which would normally supply the real image of corresponding order to the stimulus are more

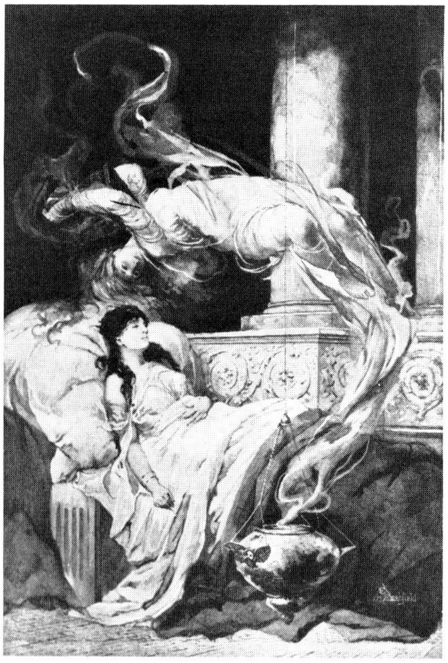

42. Edwin H. Blashfield,
Sleep and Poetry,
circa 1886, location unknown.

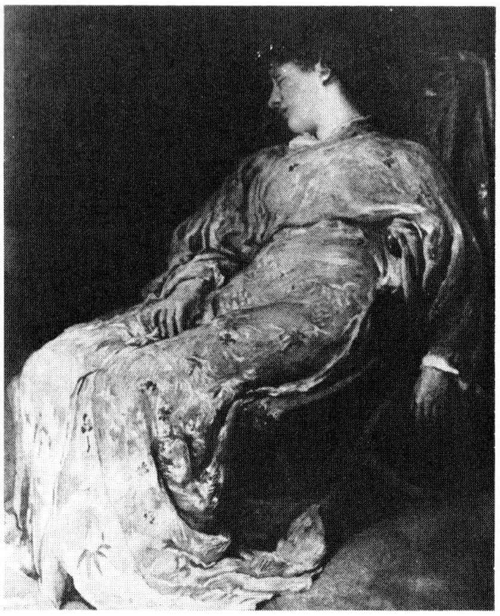

43. John La Farge,
Sleep, painting destroyed.

or less closed, renders symbolism inevitable. The direct channels being thus largely choked, other allied and parallel associations come into play, and since the control of attention and apperception is diminished, such play is often unimpeded. Symbolism is the natural and inevitable result of these conditions."[2]

Artists found one avenue of escape from their quotidian world in exploration of the dream. The sleeping mind and its visions had been of concern to earlier artists, such as Goya and Fuseli, and in fact constituted an important device for romantic painters well before them. Toward the conclusion of the nineteenth century, however, the interpretation of dreams came to have a new importance for artists and intellectuals throughout the western world.

The image of the sleeping figure, especially the sleeping woman, was of interest not only for the attractive languid pose which such a sitter presented, but as well for the fascination with the unseen activity which occupied the mind at rest. The newly important depiction of revery and sleep was certainly not confined to Symbolists nor to Europe; "Reveries" and "Sleeps" became standard subjects for Salon academicians and realist painters, as well as the more subjectively oriented, both here and abroad. The lowered glances and closed eyes of John Alexander's women in *Memories* are typical poses for such subjects and suggest the trance-like state into which such introspective subjects, and artists, were prone to fall.

Davies' image of *Sleep,* dating from about 1905, is a more curious conception; in the foreground of one of his typically vague and misty mountainous landscapes are scattered the recumbant forms of women covered with flowers. The arrangement of figures, and the subject itself, recall Ferdinand Hodler's shocking *Night* of 1890, although without the gruesome succubus which intrudes upon the Swiss artist's scene. A few years later, in a dramatic departure from his more familiar Barbizon-like landscapes and religious compositions, Elliott Daingerfield draped sleeping giants over the brim of the Grand Canyon in his *Sleepers* of 1914. As with the Davies, however, the Daingerfield painting lacks the suggestions of evil succubi, and would seem to illustrate that in America dreams were generally sweeter— and drier—, if no less fantastic, than in the Old World.

In 1933 Antoine Orliac postulated two basic tendencies within European Symbolist literature: Black Symbolism, replete with death-ridden chimera, which he saw as deriving from English and German romanticism, Goethe's satanism and Poe's tragic vision; and White Symbolism, with a more angelic cast of characters, descending from Swedenborg via Balzac, Wagner and the pre-Raphaelites. For Orliac, Huysmans and Barrès represented the Black pole, while Mallarmé, Maeterlinck, Rodenbach and Vielé-Griffin typified the White.[3] While Orliac himself admitted that the scheme was a simple one, it does have relevance for American visionary painters at the turn of the century; more of our artists, especially the interpreters of dreams, were drawn to the White Symbolism, without the dreadful phantasms which are common both to some types of European Symbolist painting and to American *Gothick* literature. The harmless, introspective

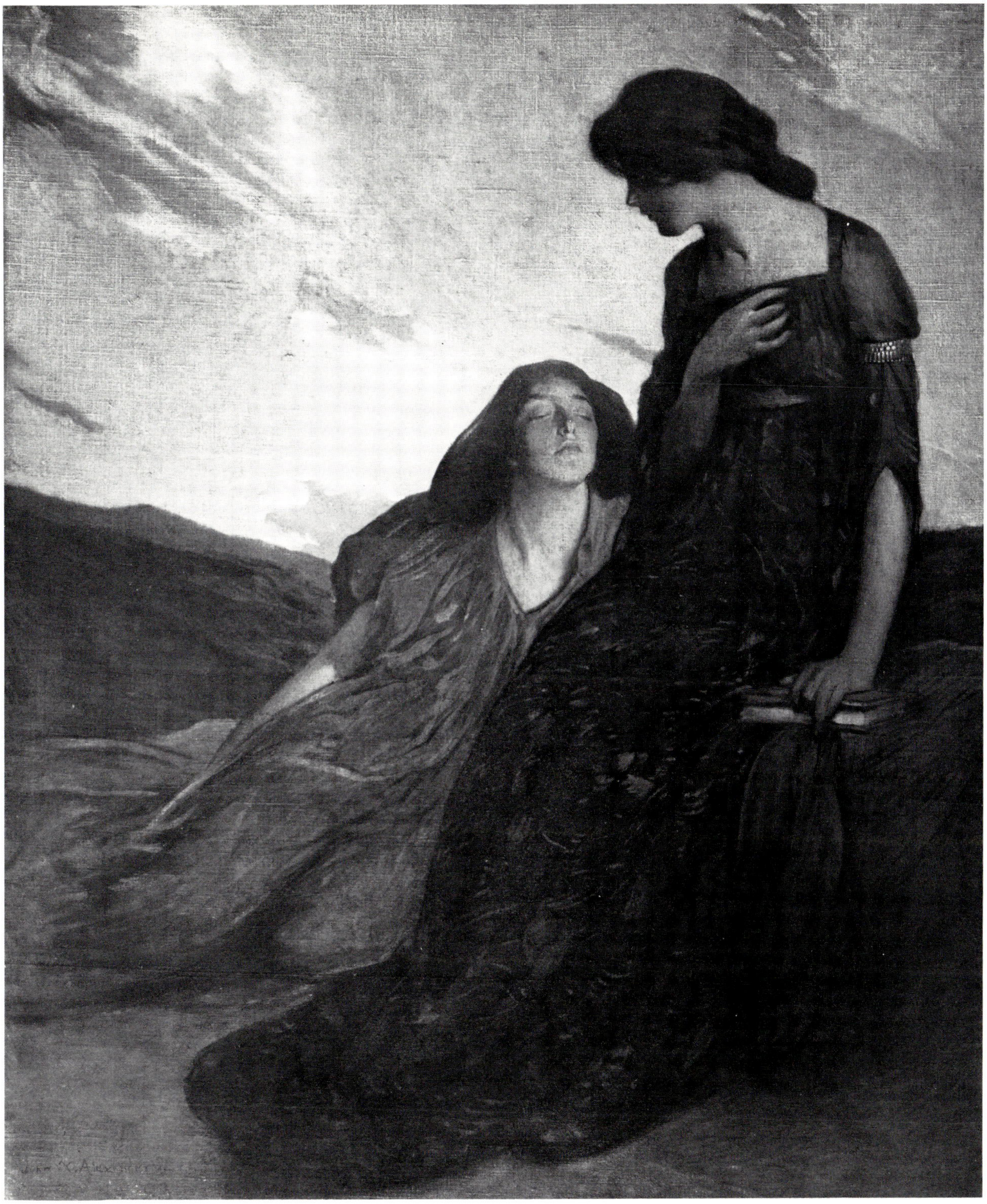

44. John W. Alexander, *Memories,* 1903, cat. no. 1.

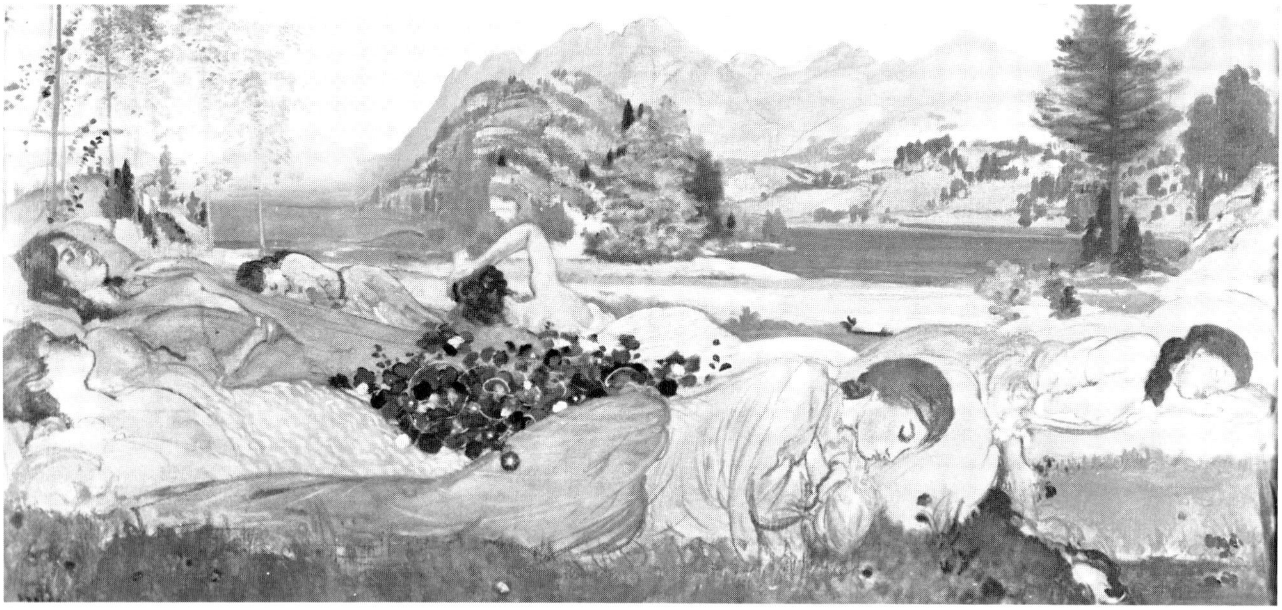

45. Arthur B. Davies, *Sleep*, circa 1905, cat. no. 16.

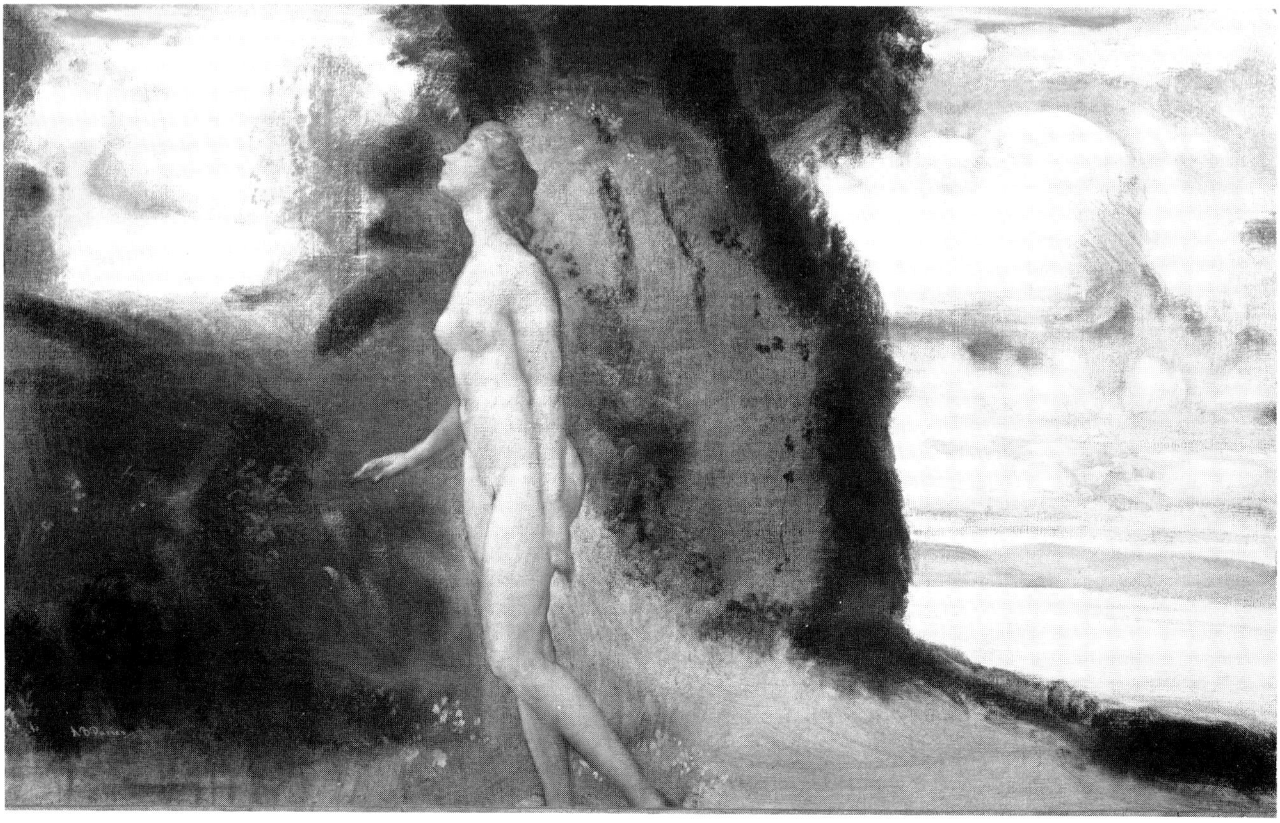

46. Arthur B. Davies, *Dream* (or *Measure of Dreams*), 1909, cat. no. 17.

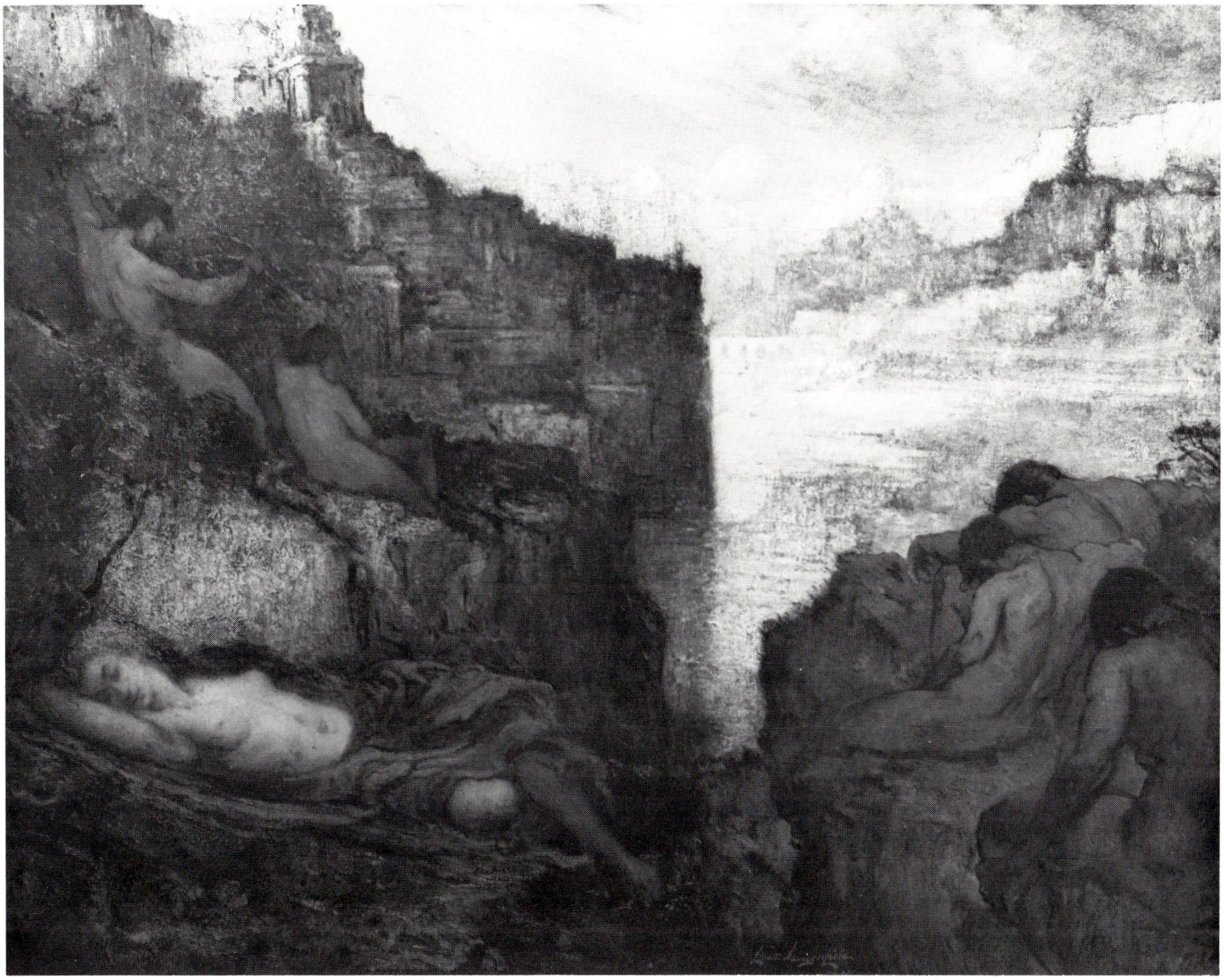

47. Elliott Daingerfield, *The Sleepers,* 1914, cat. no. 14.

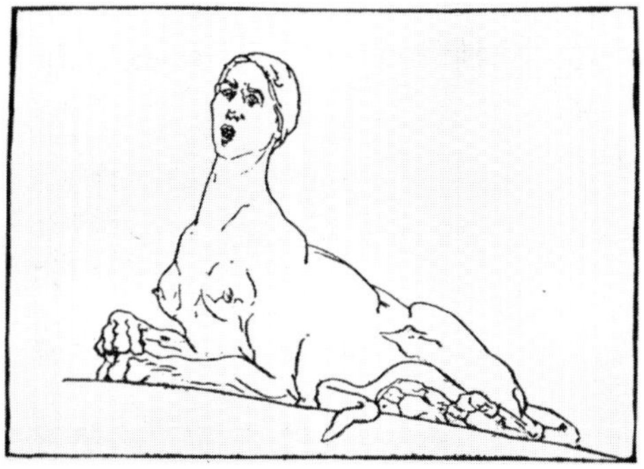

48. Alexander Séon,
La douleur de la chimera,
from The Chap-Book, II:9 (1895).

dreamers in Alexander's or Dewing's paintings, or Daingerfield's bizarre draping of canyons with Amazons, are at a far remove from the more extreme manifestations of Franco-Belgian Decadence in the same years, and are more typical of the American muse.

The fact that their dreams might have been sweeter or whiter does not, however, mitigate the importance of the visionary mode in American art; and although chimerae were less frequent here than in French and other continental exhibition halls or studios, they were not altogether unknown. Monstrous visions captured the imagination of the eccentric Louis Michael Eilshemius, as in his *Demon of the Rocks,* in which a fantastic triton bearer appears to frighten off the female nudes from his domain. In a similarly eccentric production, especially when considered in the light of the major portion of his work which dealt with American historical themes and genre incidents, Frank B. Mayer at the end of his life painted a gryphon reminiscent of the bizarre Rosicrucian creations of Alexandre Séon. Some have suggested that the Mayer painting may have been a symbolic statement with reference to the Spanish-American War, which did not occur until two years after its completion[4]; it seems more likely that it was a peculiarly private invention of the artist, of personal importance to him and not an allegorical statement on international diplomacy. The possibility even exists that Mayer may have known the Séon prototypes, to which his gryphon may be related, through their reproduction in *The Chap-Book* only a year before his painting was done.[5] Smith's *Blue Cat* of 1907 is more

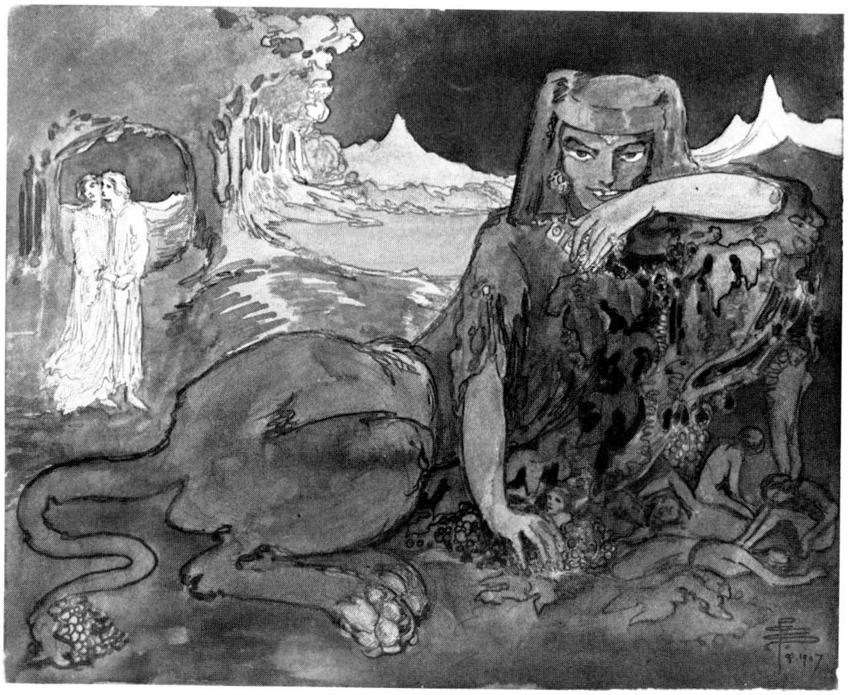

49. Pamela Colman Smith, *The Blue Cat,* 1907, cat. no. 57.

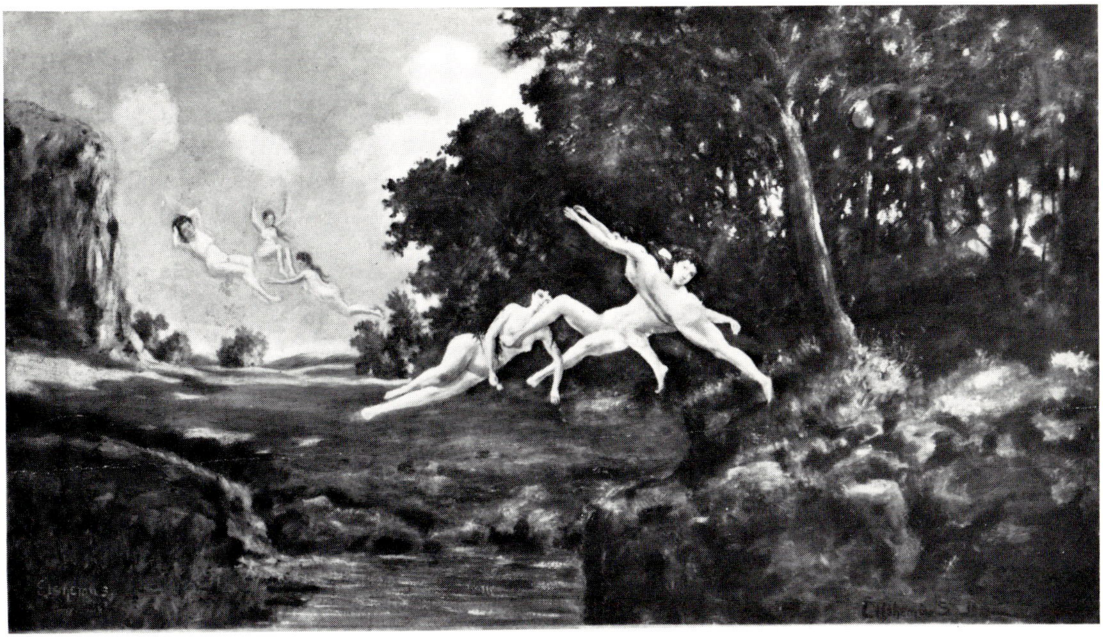

50. Louis M. Eilshemius, *Afternoon Wind,* 1899, cat. no. 22. (Collection, The Museum of Modern Art, New York.)

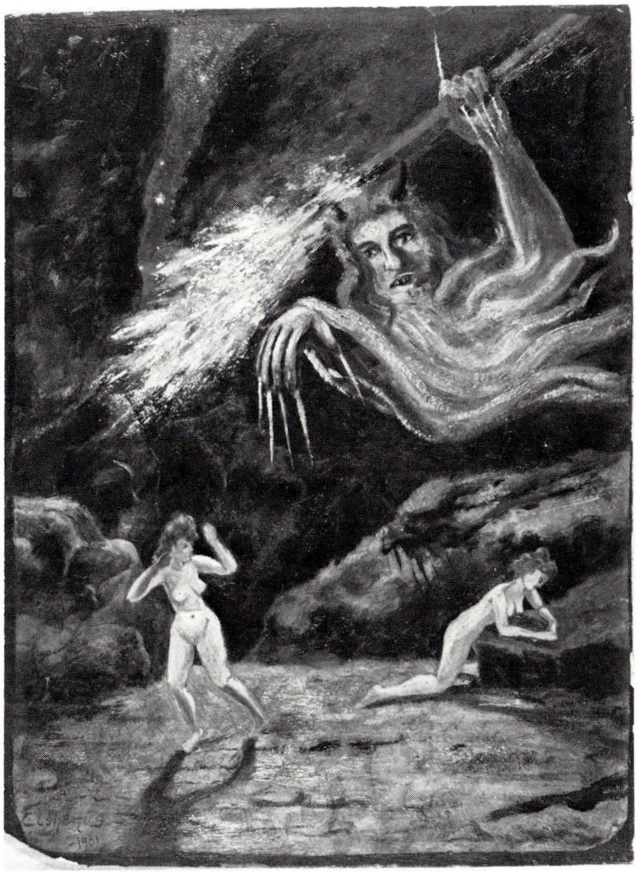

51. Louis M. Eilshemius, *The Demon of the Rocks,* 1901, cat. no. 23. (Collection, The Museum of Modern Art, New York.)

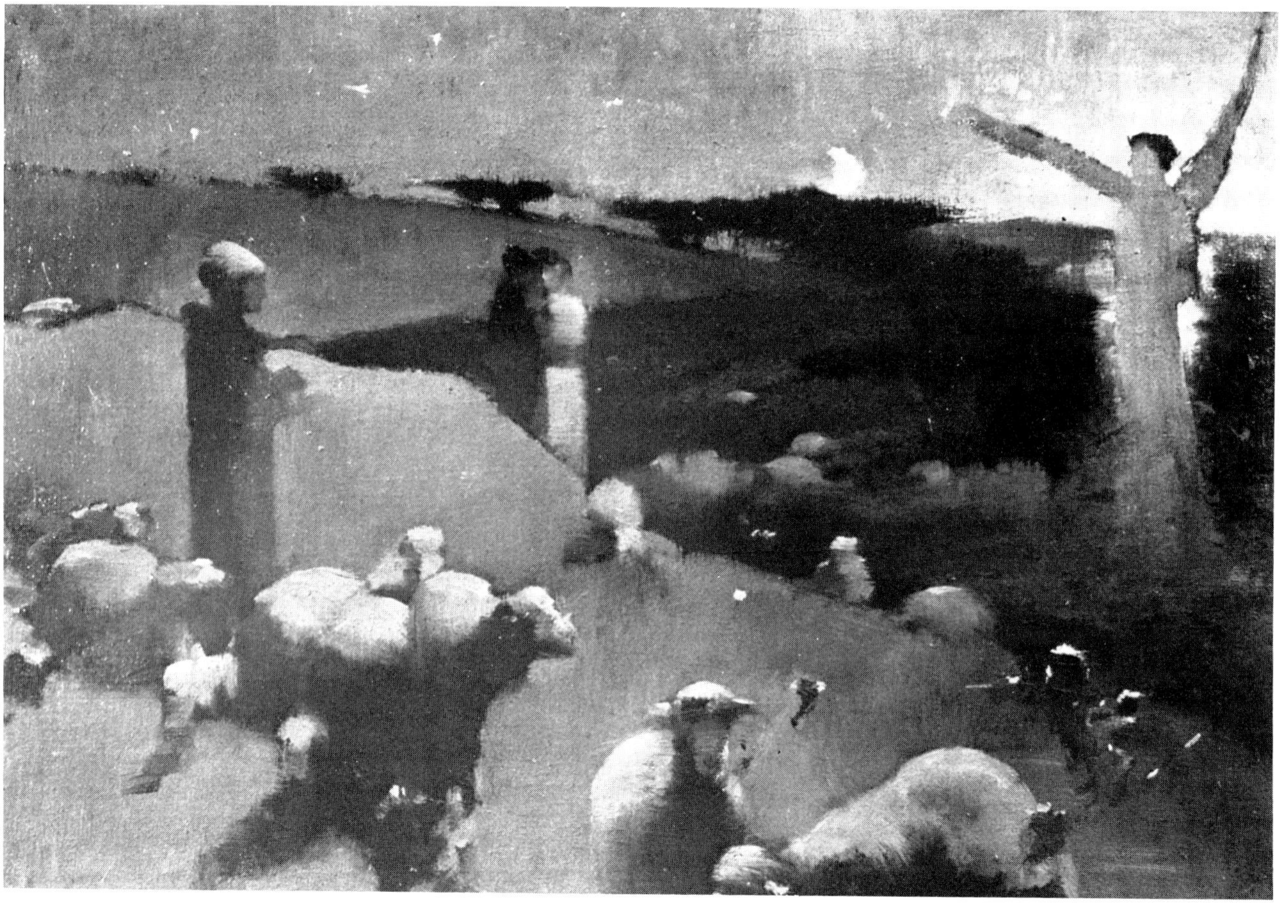

52. Charles R. Peters, *Visitation (Angels Appearing to the Shepherds)*, cat. no. 49.

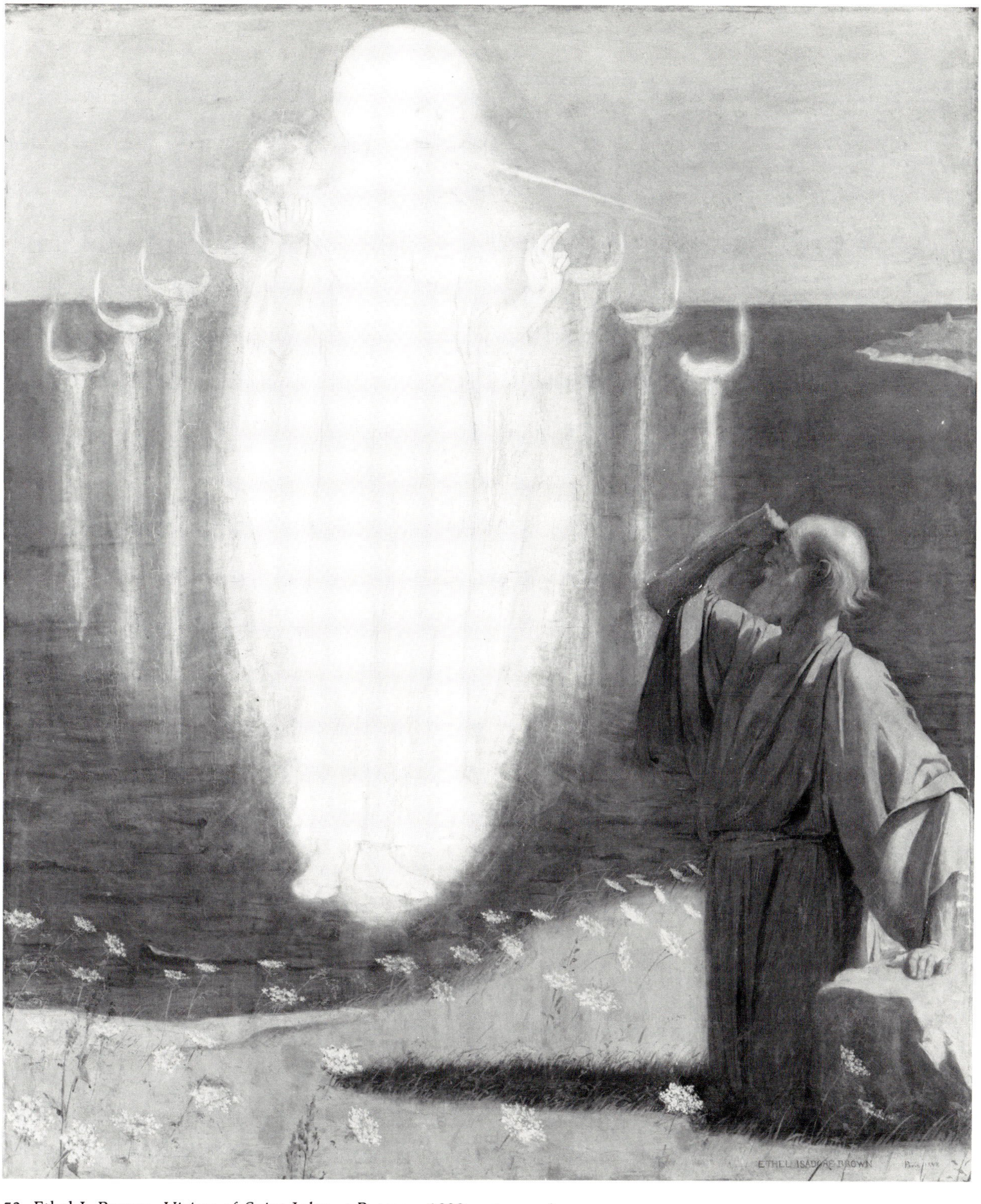

53. Ethel I. Brown, *Vision of Saint John at Patmos,* 1898, cat. no. 6.

characteristic of her visionary work, which often involved themes drawn from her private imagination; the mystical artist has imbued her creature with more frightful characteristics, as occurred in the contemporary continental productions by Redon, Khnoppf, Klinger and others.

Just as it had for painters of angelic or demonic women, so too did the Bible offer late nineteenth-century artists visionary themes which were of appeal to the introspective age. The Annunciation motif, mentioned above, was scarcely the sole example of such divine apparitions. The angelic Visitation to the Shepherds, for instance, provided another such subject which, like the Annunciation, was well rooted within western painting tradition. As interpreted by Charles Rollo Peters at the end of the century, the painting displays a generalized reliance upon Puvis de Chavannes' style, especially in the simplified notations of human and animal forms and the cool, crespuscular palette of blue-greys and muted browns. The moonlit setting for Peter's apparition was a favorite device of the artist's, although he generally used it for more mundane subjects, such as his Cazin-like nighttime views of landscape and adobes in his native California. While in Paris in the 1880s, Peters work had been admired by both Whistler and Alexander Harrison, and the latter urged the artist to specialize in the evocative nocturnal views by which he is best remembered today. Whistler's influence, as well as Puvis', is to be found in this interest in night-lighted, mysteriously evocative scenes; so pronounced was Peters' success in this vein that Whistler once exclaimed, "That man is the only one besides myself who can paint nocturnes!"[6]

The visionary theme of Peters' *Visitation* was echoed in a large canvas by the little-known Boston painter, Ethel Isadore Brown. Her *Vision of St. John at Patmos* was painted in Paris in 1898. The Biblical subject was of the type frequently assigned to students in French ateliers. Drawing upon the *Book of Revelations,* the artist depicted the saint's vision of "seven golden lampstands; and in the middle of the lampstands one like a son of man, clothed in a robe reaching to the feet, and girded across His breast with a golden girdle. And His head and His hair were white like white wool, like snow; and His eyes were like a flame of fire; and His feet were like burnished bronze . . . And in His right hand He held seven stars; and out of His mouth came a sharp two edged sword, and His face was like the sunshining in its strength . . . " (*Rev.,* I:12-16). The apparition hovers above a landscape dotted with Queen Anne's lace blossoms totalling the Scripturally significant number of forty. The artist's careful translation of John's narrative echoes earlier compositions also based upon apparitional motifs, such as Carolus-Duran's *Vision* which was exhibited in the Salon of 1883. However, the patterning with which her scene is composed and the flat application of paint suggest not Carolus-Duran's bravura technique but rather the influence of Puvis again. The predominant clear blue tones of the painting and the whiteness of the vision also recall Puvis, in works such as his *Dream* of 1883. That major example of the French master's art had been sold from the collection of the important critic, Theodore Duret, in 1894 and Brown may well have known Puvis' *Dream* or other of his works like it.

Her style and her visionary subject may even have been intended as a tribute to the well-loved dean of French artists who died in the same year as the *Vision of St. John Patmos* was painted.

The fascination with medieval Christianity was demonstrated by the pre-Raphaelites, and also made an impact on other American painters at the end of the century. The works of Mary L. Macomber and Sarah Dodson particularly display that British influence. The former's *Memory Comforting Sorrow* is typical of her work in the last decades of the century, which first occasioned acclaim from her American patrons. The pathetic subject, handled with linear grace and delicacy, recalls the enormous popularity of Edmund Burne-Jones and his fellow members of the pre-Raphaelite Brotherhood during the *fin de siècle.*

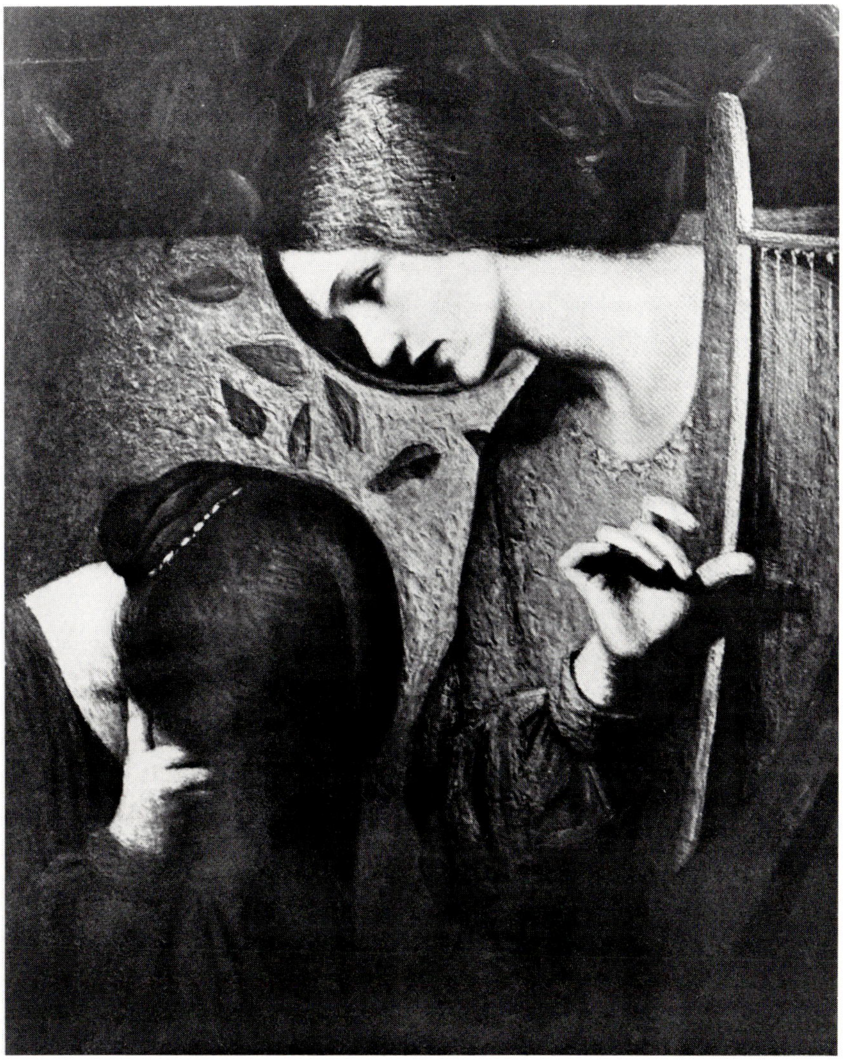

54. Mary L. Macomber, *Memory Comforting Sorrow*, 1905, cat. no. 35.

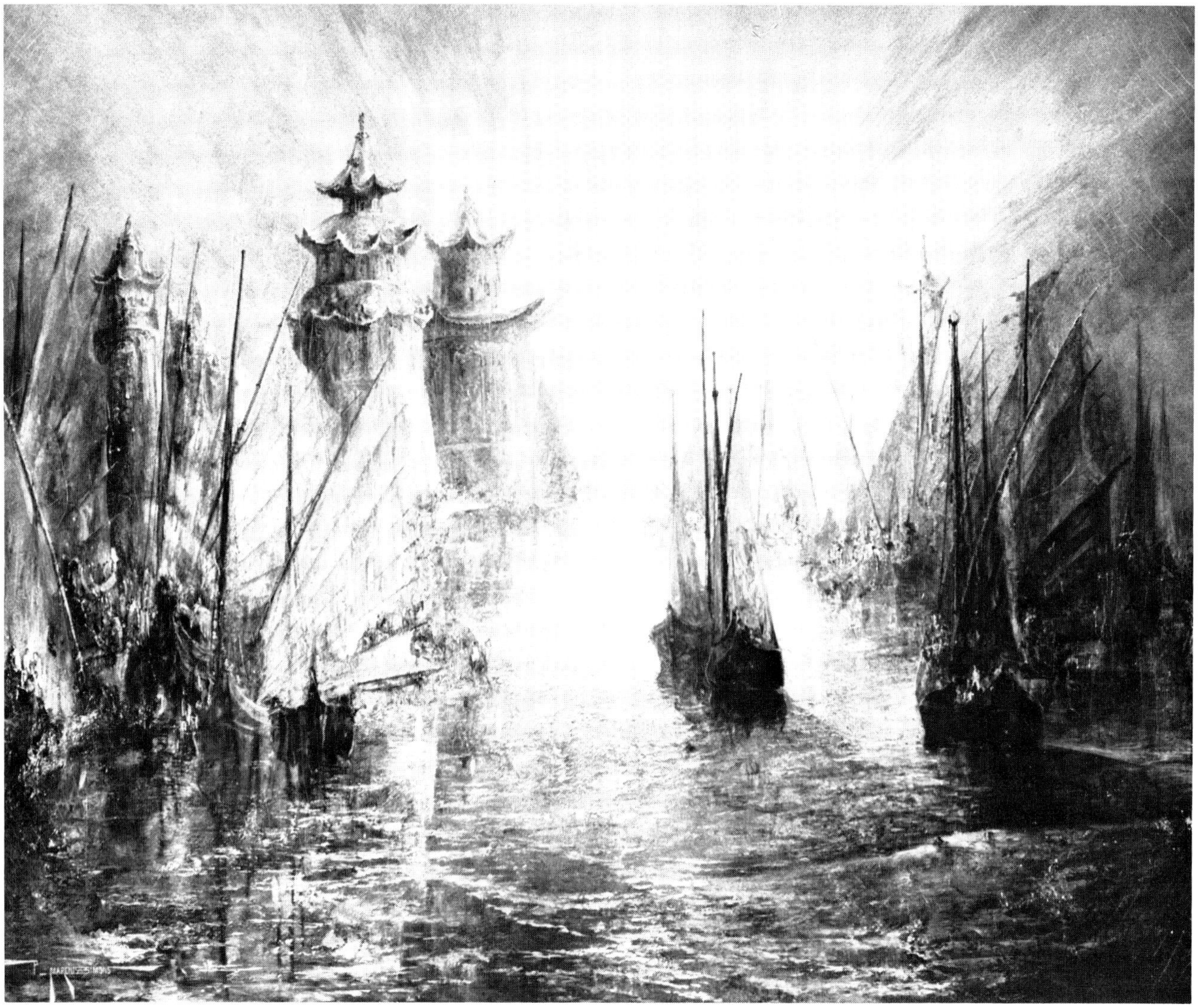

55. Pinckney Marcius-Simons, *Porcelain Towers,* cat. no. 38.

The most obsessive interest in esoteric Christian imagery was demonstrated by Sâr Peladan and the members of his Ordre de la Rose+Croix. The lone American to show in the Salons organized by Peladan was Pinckney Marcius-Simons, whose paintings on occasion included motifs drawn from cabalistic Rosicrucianism, such as angels and visions. In the Rosicrucian Salons and elsewhere Marcius-Simons also showed a strong predilection for Wagnerian subjects, from about 1894 onwards, he was involved with the realization of a great series of paintings illustrating operatic themes. From this cycle Roland Knoedler selected for exhibition in New York in 1904 a series of eight large works and related oil sketches based upon Wagner's *Parsifal.* The *Parsifal Tone Pictures* sought to give not so much presentations of the Bayreuth performances, but rather "a lasting memento of how Wagner himself saw the stage pictures and wished them to be seen." In seeking to explain the curious images to an American audience, the catalogue noted that "the painter, like the musician, claims to be but a poet, using his art merely as a means of expressing ideas. . . . Marcius-Simons believes that . . . the palette and brush can also give to the present generation what it demands as a condition of greatness in every art—food for thought. Painting, like music, should commence when all other arts purporting to express an idea of vision fail."[7]

Marcius-Simons' rich colorism characterized his technique, whether applied to Wagnerian, Christian or secular themes. The jewel-like color has occasioned comparisons of his work to both Turner and Moreau.[8] The dreamlike subject and visions, such as the angel's apparition in *Cupid and the Flowers,* relate the artist to the Symbolist movement; Peladan praised Marcius-Simons as "the Rosicrucian standard bearer in America," and the artist himself termed his works "symbolistic paintings."[9]

Although acclaimed by Peladan, Marcius-Simons, like many of the Rosicrucian exhibitors, was not as ardent in his beliefs nor as doctrinal in his imagery as the colorful leader of the order; after the collapse of Peladan's Salons in 1897, Marcius-Simons left the Rosicrucian circle and spent his last years as a scene designer in Bayreuth, where he died in 1909. While the dogmatic pronouncements of Sâr Peladan and his visionary concerns had some impact on the American's work, Marcius-Simons displayed an independence in his *oeuvre* and a generalized predilection for the mystical which transgressed the narrow limitations which the Rosicrucian leader tried to impose upon his band of followers.

Visions of Life and Death

Like Mary Macomber, Elihu Vedder was also enamored of English art, and this interest found occasional reflection in his varied works of the 1880s and 1890s. The enormous project of "accompaniments" for Edward Fitzgerald's translation of the *Rubáiyát of Omar Khayyám* which occupied Vedder from 1883 to 1884 was marked at many points by stylistic affinities with the work of his friend, Walter Crane, and other late nineteenth-century artists in Britain. The *Rubáiyát* drawings provided Vedder with abundant materials for subsequent translation into painted form. His *Cup of Death* evolved from one such design, and like Macomber's *Memory Comforting Sorrow,* reflects some of the decorative intent of contemporaneous English art. Vedder's conception is, however, richer in invention than Macomber's and not so narrowly dependent upon pre-Raphealite sources; also dissimilar from her work is Vedder's derivation of his subject from the poetic imagery of a Persian mystic. This fascination with the East, both of the Levant and Persia and of the Far East, was notable in America and Europe in the last years of the century. Through his *Rubáiyát* accompaniments, Vedder was both instigator and participant in the Persian revival of the *fin de siècle.*

William Morris Hunt was the first American to employ Persian legends in his work, notably in the mural scheme for the Albany State House which included his famed *Flight of Anahita.* Despite the abundance of oriental motifs in the decorative arts of mid-century onwards, the literature and legends of Persia, India and the Far East remained within the purview of but a few specialists. With Vedder's drawings based upon the most accessible of eastern authors, a new enthusiasm for such sources was born. The vogue reached perhaps its highest point in John Singer Sargent's murals for the Boston Public Library, begun in 1890 but not fully installed until 1919, which included among various allegorical themes one striking departure from traditional mural iconography—the panel of Astarte, part of his representation of pagan deities.

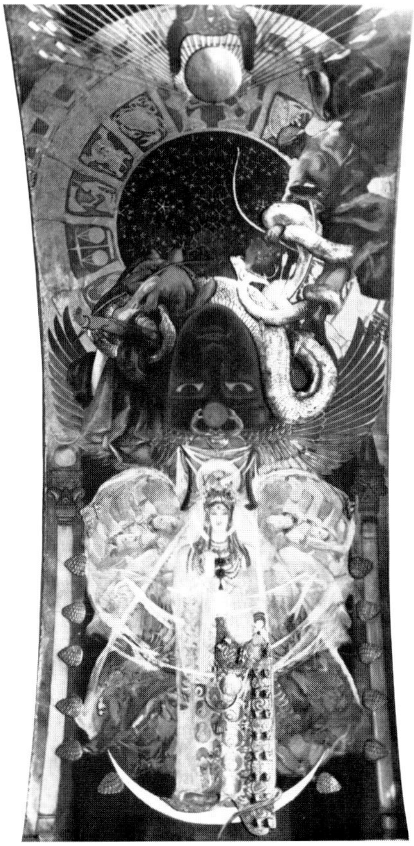

56. John S. Sargent, *Astarte: The Pagan Gods,* 1890-1895, Boston Public Library.

Astarte was the Babylonian goddess of love and fertility, the queen of heaven, whose exoticism allured a number of western artists and writers of the *fin de siècle.* Sargent's selection of the motif for the Boston murals accorded with the general revival of interest in her regenerative powers as detailed by archaeologists and historians of the day. The first important modern representation of her came in 1877, with Rossetti's *Astarte Syriaca.* Hunt's mural of the same period treats Astarte's Persian counterpart, Anahita; in 1882 Frederick Freer exhibited an Astarte at the Salamagundi Club's exhibition in New York. However, the strongest affinities to Sargent's conception reside not in English or American paintings but in the Symbolist environment of France and Belgium. Recently Doreen Burke has

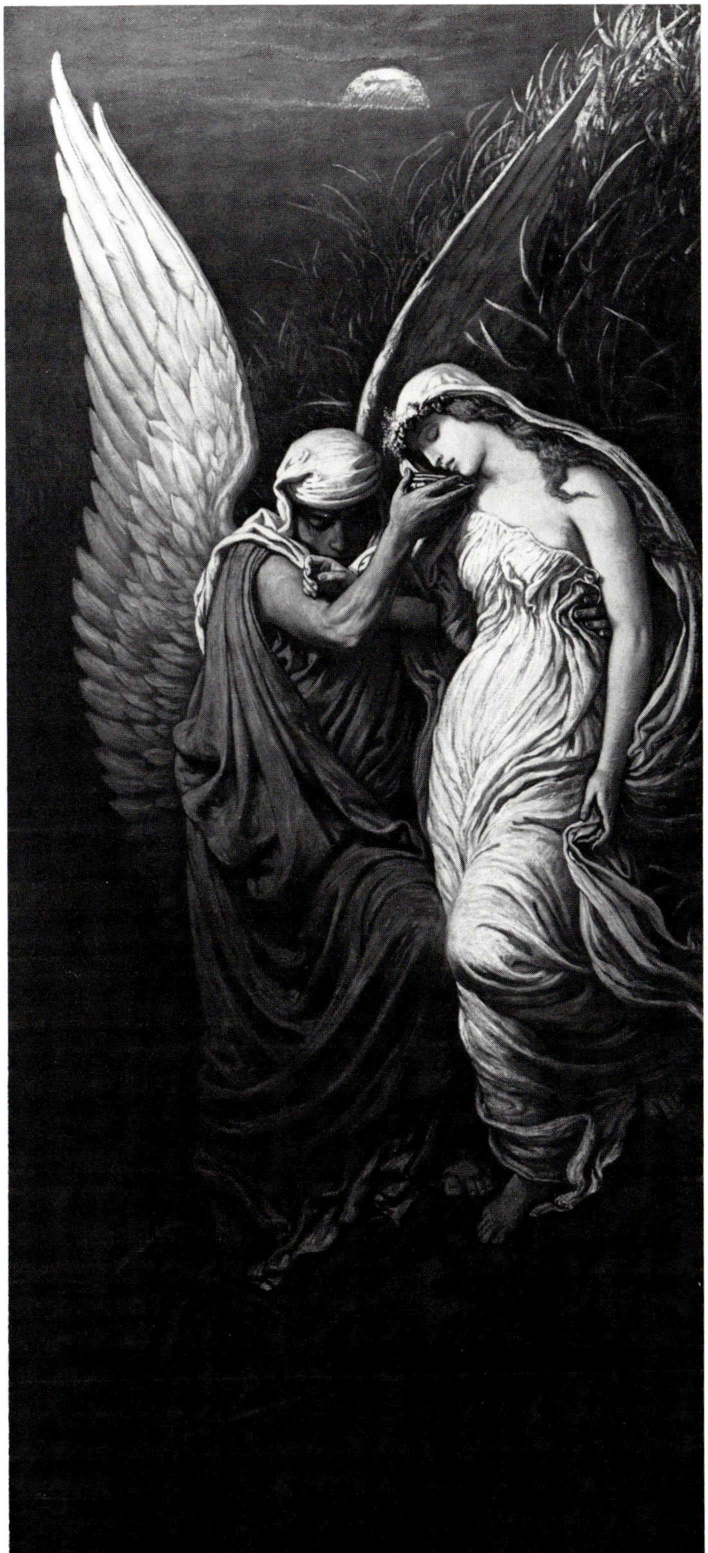

57. Elihu Vedder, *The Cup of Death,* 1885, cat. no. 63.

thoroughly examined the importance of the Sargent mural in the Symbolist context, tracing its sources to the historicism of Flaubert and Moreau, and more specifically, to the treatments of the goddess by both Khnoppf and Peladan in 1888, and to Ernest Reyer's and Camille du Locle's operatic translation of Flaubert's *Salammbô* in 1890.[1]

Sargent's treatment of the Babylonian goddessas a *femme fatale* relates his attitude to the pervasive concern for Dark Ladies which ran through the turn of the century. Despite the influences from the Symbolist milieu of the 1890s, Sargent's primary concern in the Boston Public Library murals appears to have been with their success as decoration rather than their symbolism. When the Boston lunettes were exhibited at London's Royal Academy prior to their shipment to America, the artist expressed pleasure that a friend had been stimulated visually by the paintings. "I was delighted to find that you got some pleasure out of it through your eyes," he wrote to Lady Lewis, "and were not fidgeting about the obscurity of those old symbols. What a tiresome thing a perfectly clear symbol would be."[2] Burke ends her investigation of the affinities between Sargent's *Astarte* and Peladan, Khnoppf, *et al.*, with the recognition that "if he borrowed his theme from symbolist art and literature, he simply drew upon them as another treasury of imagery and detail without concern for their complex philosophical and aesthetic intentions."[3] Thus while the Symbolist ambiance lent a strong flavor to the mural conception, it was ultimately not the overriding concern of the artist in the development of the Boston Public Library project.

Sargent's historicism, however, is typical of his period. In an era of archaeological excavation and scientific exploration, interest in ancient civilizations and aboriginal cultures was inevitably revived. For imaginative spirits of the *fin de siècle,* the quest for experience beyond the daily routine of Paris, Boston or New York became an obsession; wanderlust marked the closing of the century, although significantly the Grand Tour itinerary of an earlier generation was replaced by more remote or evocative destinations. The hegiras of John La Farge and Henry Adams to Japan and the South Seas, of Paul Gauguin to Tahiti, of Emile Bernard to Egypt and the Levant, and of Ralph Blakelock to the American West are all part of this reaching outward; and often the object of such artistic quests was not simply ever more grandiose scenes and novel experiences but a search for more personally meaningful images and incidents.

The primitive culture and faith of the Breton peasant had early captured the imagination of French and American artists alike, whose summer treks to the rugged peninsula of Brittany became something of a mass migration by the early 1880s. The primal appeal of the people and the place was compelling for an artist like Gauguin. "I find there the wild, the primitive," he wrote from Pont-Aven to his friend, Emile Schuffenecker. "When my clogs resound on that stony soil, I hear the dull, muffled powerful tone I am trying to find in painting."[4] Even the electrification of the village could not spoil its allure; a later visitor to Pont-Aven wrote that "Brittany is one of the few places that never seem to lose their artistic seduction. It grows civilized, philistinized . . . [but] Brittany seems to be the only part of the world which can support electric light and yet not lose its character."[5] The journals and written accounts of travelers to the region are nearly unanimous in such comments on the landscape and especially on its inhabitants, whose rugged individualism and enduring, mystical faith drew admiring reactions from tourists and artists alike.

Tantalizing parallels exist between the commentary of travelers to Pont-Aven, Le Pouldu and Finisterre and the slightly later narratives of tourists in the American Southwest, responding to the savage landscape and the exotic faiths and mores of the Indian. Blakelock's life-long concern with the American Indian, whom he had encountered on his Western journey in the 1860s, is evinced in a late painting which Elliott Daingerfield romantically retitled *The Vision of Life.* Originally exhibited as *The Ghost Dance,* the unfinished painting suggests the teepees and Indian settlements which often occur in more complete form in his landscape paintings. From his Western experiences Blakelock returned with a profound interest and respect for the primeval life of the Indian immersed in a wilderness setting. The resulting paintings exist somewhere between the archaeological exactitude practiced by academicians treating similar aboriginal themes, such as Emmanuel Fremiet or Malvina Hoffmann, and the carefully posed *tableaux vivants* drawn from Southwestern subjects as painted by E. I. Couse, Oscar Blumenschein and other pioneers of the New Mexico school. In that regard Blakelock's use of primitive subjects is closer to Gauguin's treatment of Breton peasants or Tahitian natives: although the painter's works are vastly different in appearance, each has used the native subject as an impetus to imaginative and symbolic treatments which transcend both realist reportage and romantic stagecraft.

The vision of life which Blakelock located in the primitive American wilderness relates to other Indian dance themes which the artist painted in the 1890s. Blakelock's contemporaries, however, were not content with the descriptive image implied by the original *Ghost Dance* title. One viewer wrote that the painting depicted "a joyous group from the twilight world. . . , " while Daingerfield analyzed the image as a procession of life around the Madonna and Child.[6] It was Daingerfield who thought that *The Vision of Life* would be a "fairer title," and who "had the pleasure of re-naming" the painting while it hung in Chicago in Joseph Snydacker's collection.[7] Whether as ghost dance or life's procession, Blakelock's image does suggest analogies with another predominant concern of the period, the cycle of life. His amorphic white shapes, which most observers read as humans, seem to grow from the humus of the forest floor and suggest the genesis of being, of growth.

This hint of organic principle in the vision of life/ghost dance parallels the curious works of two later, and unfortunately little known, artists of the pre-World War I era, George Alfred Williams and Rex Slinkard. Williams' series of *The Drama of Life,* executed in the mid-1910s, similarly shows figures emerging out of land forms. *The Drama of Life—The Marginal Way,* completed in 1914, was the first of the large figure compositions which marked Williams' departure from his earlier landscape imagery; his

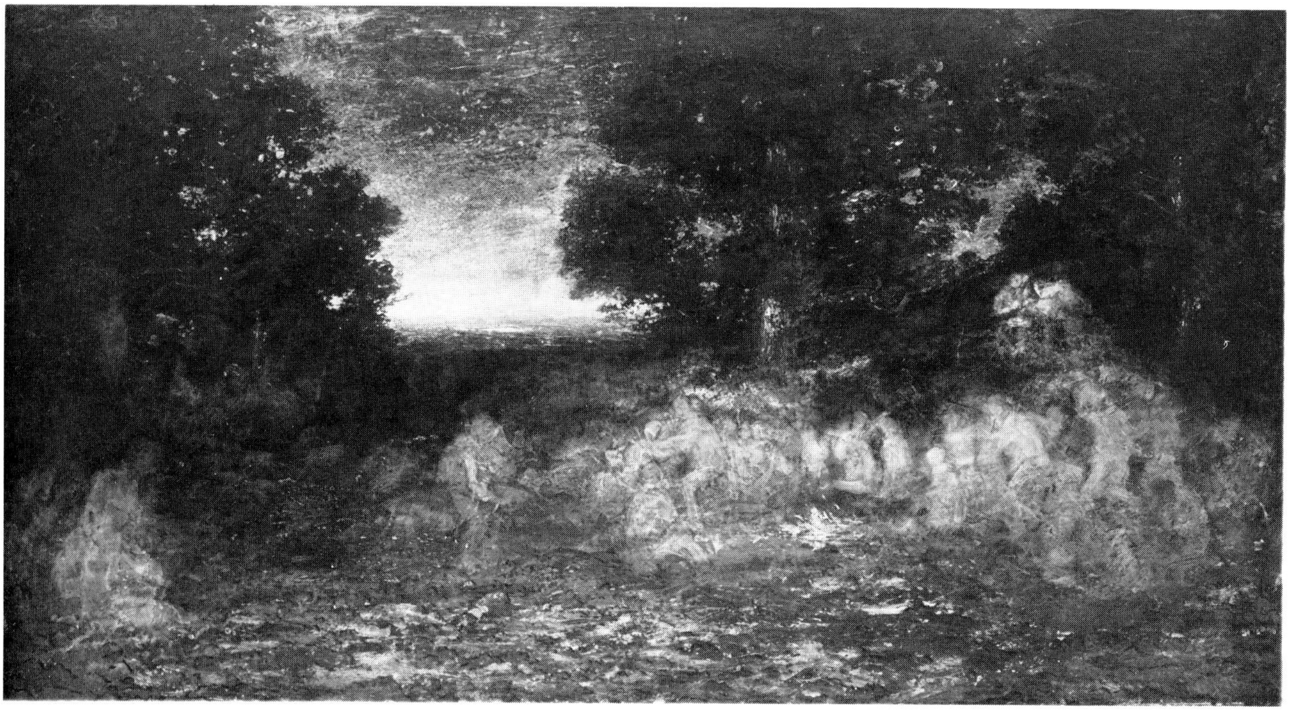

58. Albert Blakelock, *The Vision of Life* (or *The Ghost Dance*), circa 1895, cat. no. 4.

human topography of emergent forms depicts various types ranging from fashionable girls to haggard crones to a bare- breasted satanic woman darkly painted at the center of the composition. Like Redon, Williams strove to "render tangible the hallucinations of dreams. . . . Great art," he wrote," is born subjectively and idealistically in the far reaches of the mind." Williams believed that if the painting "conforms to the laws of rhythm that exist in the life movement of the organically sensed spirit" and if the work is "true intuitively, the vision [will] live naturally."[8]

Williams' ambivalent evocation of the organic spirit is echoed in Slinkard's *My Song*, painted the following year. The pervasive blue tonalities of his canvas, which synaesthetically establish a strong mood in the viewer, unite his simplified forms into a tableau of revery imbued with a more elegaic quality than *The Drama of Life*. The musical title of the painting also helps to strengthen this note of revery, typical of the California mystic who was posthumously acclaimed by Marsden Hartley and William Carlos Williams, both artists of a similar temperament.[9] As did George Williams, Slinkard worked outward from his private imagination, whose dreams and visions he sought to materialize on the canvas. "It's wonderful to work. To work with the inside of oneself."[10] "Imagination— that's the one thing I can paint with. I am lost without it."[11] Throughout his letters run references to the artists he admired, Puvis de Chavannes, Botticelli, Arthur B. Davies, and Giotto, whom he praised for having "a reason, a moving reason, back of all. A before and after. A belief in something."[12] In their cosmic view of the world, in their rooting of figures to earth forms, just as Augustus Tack did with his *Madonna of the Everlasting Hills*, painters like

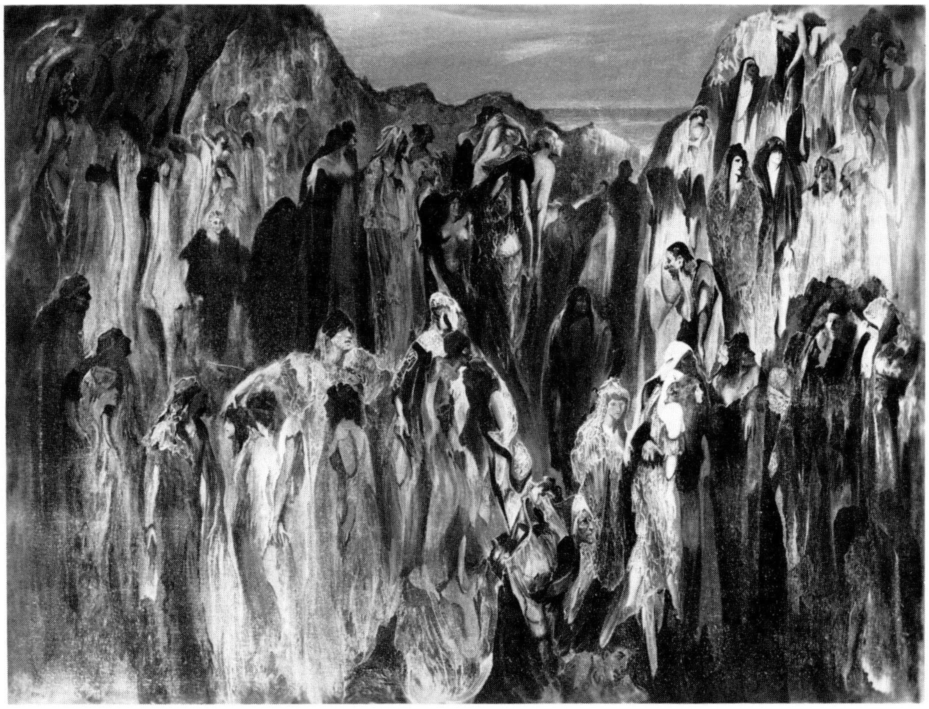

59. George Alfred Williams, *The Drama of Life— The Marginal Way,* 1913, cat. no. 67.

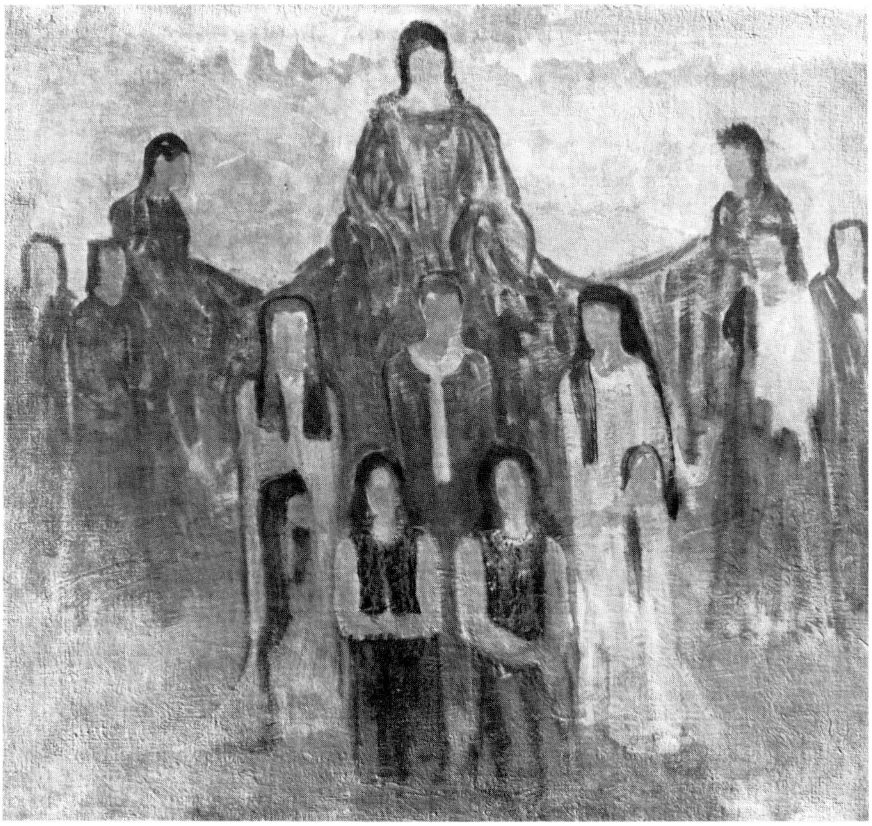

60. Rex Slinkard, *My Song,* 1915-1916, cat. no. 54. (Photo by Stanford University Photographic Division)

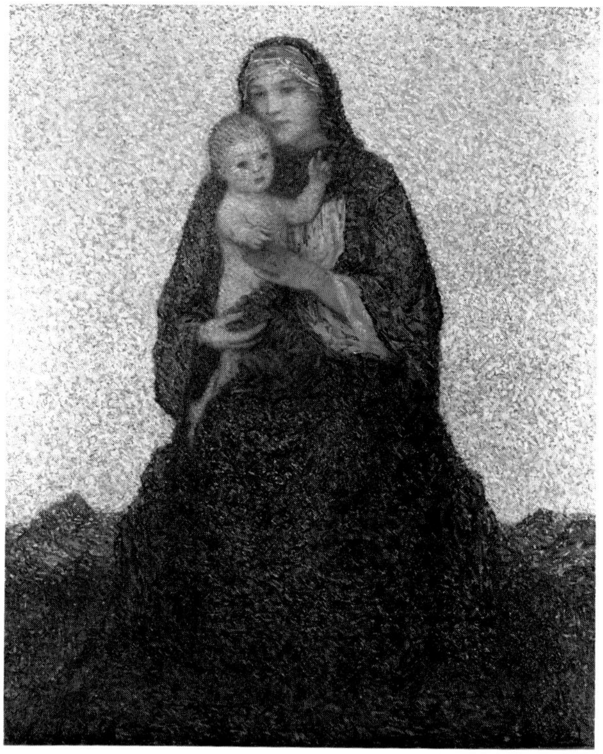

61. Augustus Vincent Tack, *Madonna of the Everlasting Hills,* circa 1914, cat. no. 60.

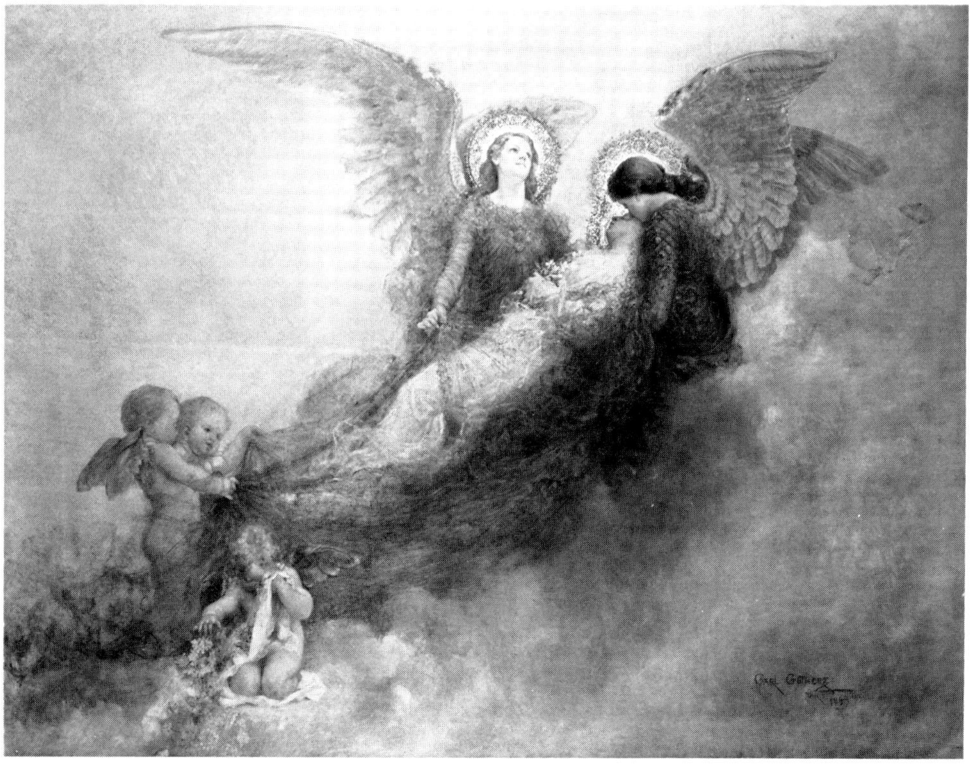

62. Carl Gutherz, *Arcessita ab Angelus,* 1889, cat. no. 25.

Blakelock, Williams and Slinkard suggest the primacy of regenerative organicism over both metaphysical transcendance and mechanistic principles.

It was the charm of a more primitive faith dealing with elementals which attracted these artists of the turn of the century and caused them to pose questions pictorially of life's meaning, of existence. " . . . [T]he instincts presently teach that the problem of essence must take precedence of all others," wrote Emerson in 1876; "—the questions of Whence? What? and Whither? and the solution of these must be in a life . . . "[13] His challenge was answered artistically by painters in Europe and America. Just as Edvard Munch explored life's passages, and as Gauguin in Tahiti queried *Whence Come We? What Are We? Whither Go We?,* so too were Americans probing for the meaning of existence in their visions of the drama of life. Thereby they are related to the international spirit of doubt which characterized Symbolist thought at the turn of the century.

Other painters examined life's cycle in a more traditional mode than did Gauguin or Slinkard, Munch or Blakelock. Generations of artists had coped with the problem of how to represent the ultimate terror of death. In this country a native tradition of funerary art, replete with death's heads, weeping willows and similar devices, was well developed by the nineteenth century. Such iconography was not, however, the favored motif of American imaginatives at the end of the nineteenth century; by its very ubiquity, it had formularized and depersonalized both the question and the artist's personal, visual response. Traditional Christian concepts were still applicable, however, if suitably re-worked to suit the mood sought by the painter. Carl Gutherz's large picture, *Arcessita ab Angelis,* painted in Paris in 1889, relies upon rather traditional imagery as angels bear the ethereal body to realms of light; yet, as in all his ideal compositions, the artist employed a symbolic program which affected choice of subject and its handling. Mortality as a passage was also explored by Daingerfield in his *Mystic Brim* of 1893, in which mother and child stand, attended by an angel, at the brink of the unknown, while about them swirl blond forms suggestive of angels and spirits.

Less conventional were the handlings of the death theme by Edith Nagler and Romaine Brooks. Nagler's *Vivitur Ingenio Caetera Mortis Erunt* recombines accepted funerary symbols—mourning veils, silenced violin, lavendar chrysanthemums—in a ritualistic evocation of mortality. More startling yet is Brooks' singular body of work, which includes images of death quite unrelated to the generalized metaphorical statements of Daingerfield or Gutherz. Brooks' painting, *Le Trajet,* focuses upon the air-borne corpse, symbolically launched across an infinite field of grey. The artist's distinctive mannerisms in anatomical handling are here especially evident. The morbid spectre painted by the expatriate Brooks owes less to any natively American tradition than it does to French sources which she encountered in Paris. Slightly later than Brooks, Philip Leslie Hale idealized his floating woman in the *Moonlit Pool,* where Whistlerian effects and the reference to a tradition of Ophelia-like victims, softens the impact of the deathly theme.

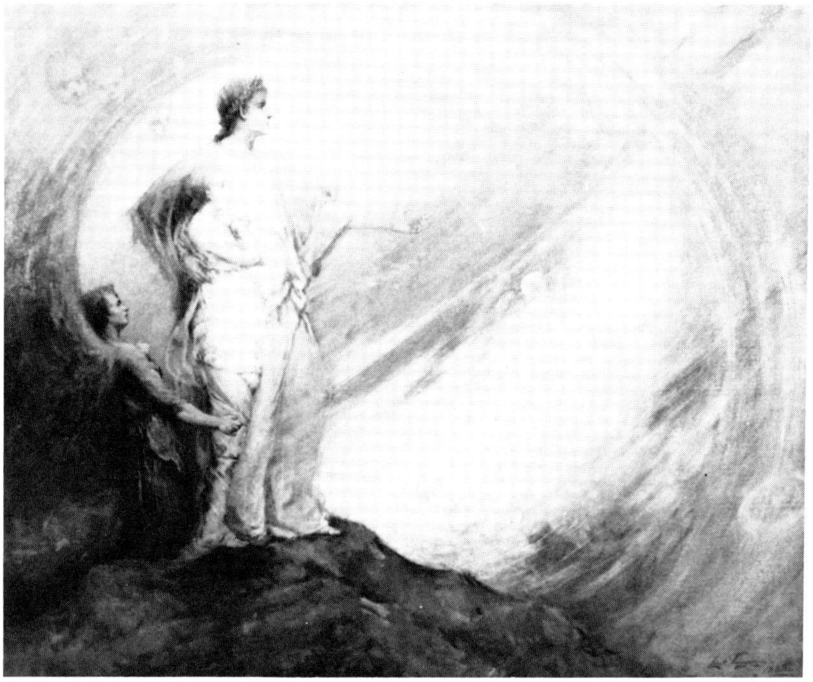

63. Elliott Daingerfield, *The Mystic Brim*, 1893, cat. no. 13.

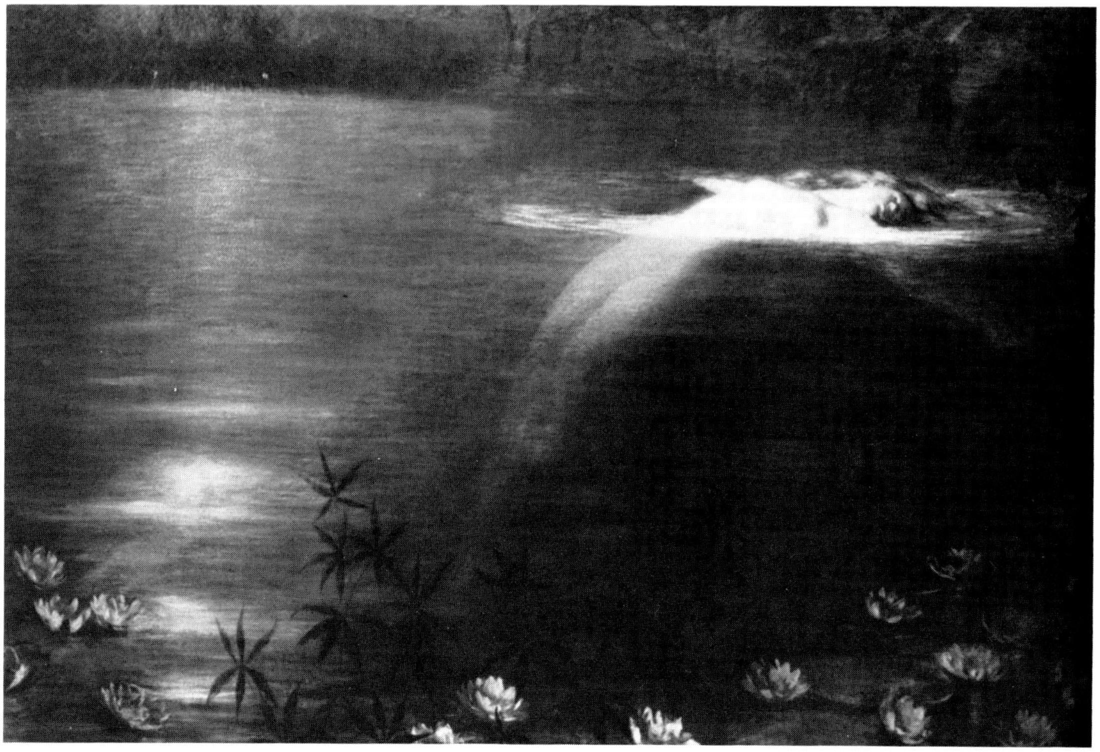

64. Philip L. Hale, *Moonlit Pool*, circa 1918, cat. no. 26.

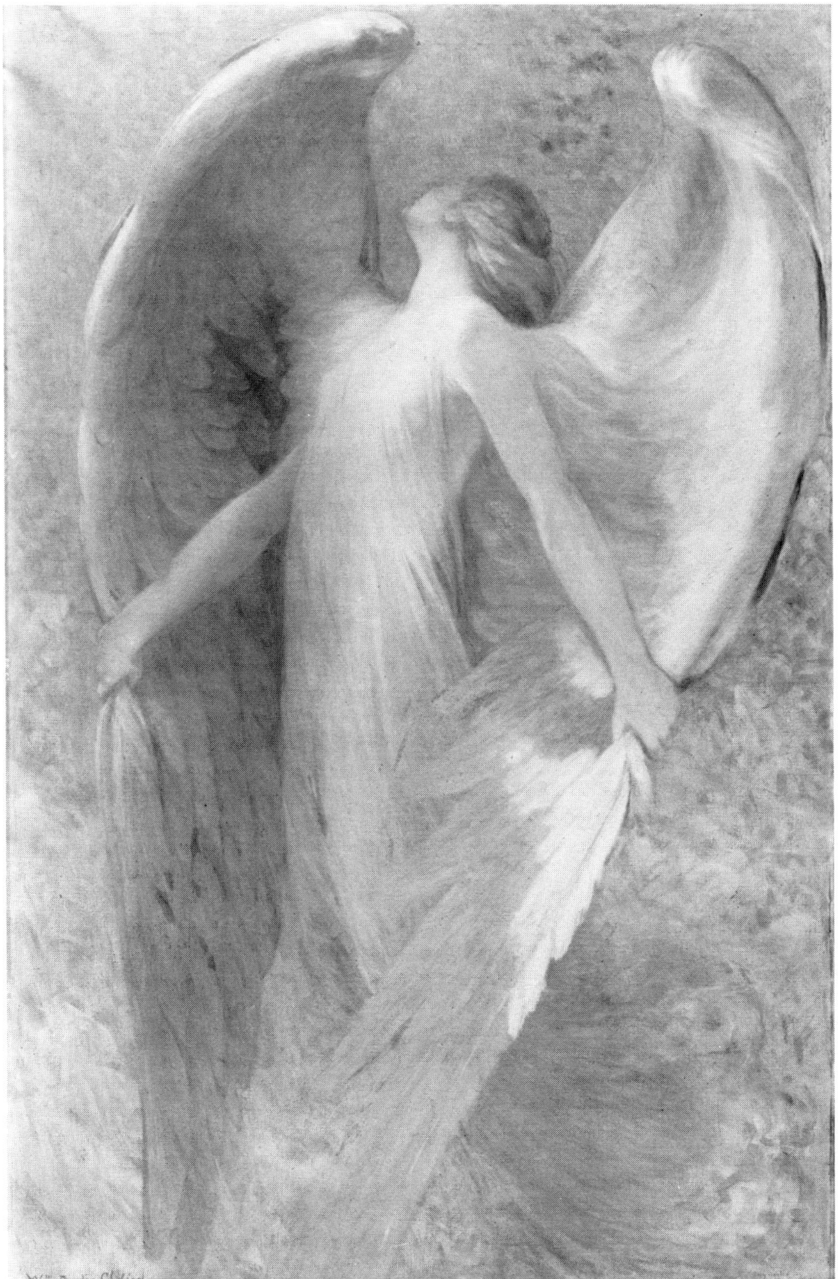

65. William B. Closson, *The Angel,* 1912, cat. no. 10.

Sense and Sensuality: Neo-Paganism in America

The instinctual life of the senses cultivated by the Symbolists was the basis for a revived paganism at the turn of the century. Turning away from the perceptual world of haystacks, cathedral fronts and boat basins, imaginative painters in Europe and America resorted to more distant subjects, remote in both time and place from their own. The antique world had, of course, constituted a traditional source of imagery for artists of an earlier generation. Yet a neo-classicist like Horatio Greenough was attracted to classical form and intellect, and contended for Greek principles, not Greek things. For the subjectivist painters of the later period, the appeal of the pagan past was to the life of the senses, as symbolized to them by Dionysus or Bacchus. In lieu of the Apollonian perfection sought early in the century, the *fin-de-siècle* artists painted paeans "in praise of Dionysus", as Charles Stetson had titled one of his canvases. Stetson's attitude represented that of an international group of artists whose resort to the instinctual life of the imagination found reflection in varied pagan rites, arcadian idylls and bacchic revels.

As the sensual concerns of the neo-pagans at the end of the century grew, dryads and nymphs, centaurs and an entire antique bestiary came to populate Symbolist paintings in Europe and America. The centaur in particular became a popular motif of the period for both writers and painters. De Guérin's romantic prose poem (1840) of the man/beast was translated in Stuart Merrill's *Pastels in Prose,* where it drew considerable attention from American readers. Even before the 1890 publication of Merrill's volume, however, La Farge, Ryder and other Americans had included the mythical creature in their paintings. In 1881 a version by La Farge was praised as being the most successful realization of the theme "since the days of the Greeks. . . . It has much of the poetic insight of Maurice de Guérin's prose poem 'The Centaur,' which may possibly have suggested it."[1] In an era marked by Darwinian concerns for man's evolution from lower forms of life, the hybrid centaur exercised a compelling fascination. Theologians as well as artists were drawn to the centaur analogy; The Reverend Lyman Abbott explained that "We carry the animal with us. When we indulge our appetites, or our greed, or our covetousness, or our pride, or our vainglory, or our selfishness, we are falling back into the animal. . . . Every man is two men,—a centaur, part animal, part man."[2] The centaur permitted the artist to explore the baser, more bestial aspects of man's nature; in some cases, the most extreme perhaps being the works of Arnold Boecklin, centaurs engaged in brutal conflict and struggle, activities perhaps inappropriate to more "civilized" man with his fully evolved intellect. One reviewer of the

Paris Salon of 1881 noted this tendency on the part of the "legendary painters" represented there: "In their works of imagination the ancients took as much pains to gloss over as we to enhance the inherent ugliness of human nature, and delighted as earnestly in raising mortal existence above its mean earthly level as we in plodding through the mire of baser commonplace."[3]

Other treatments of the centaur and similar imaginary creatures stress a different aspect; instead of plodding through commonplace activities, such creatures amble as surrogate humans through idealized dreamscapes, revelling in sensual idylls denied to proper Victorian society. Ryder's centaur and La Farge's centauress, the unicorns of Moreau, Davies and Armand Point, Blakelock's Pegasus, the piping Marsyas by Vedder and other such imaginative creations invite our sympathy and vicarious participation in the sensual and reflective activities which they are privileged to pursue.

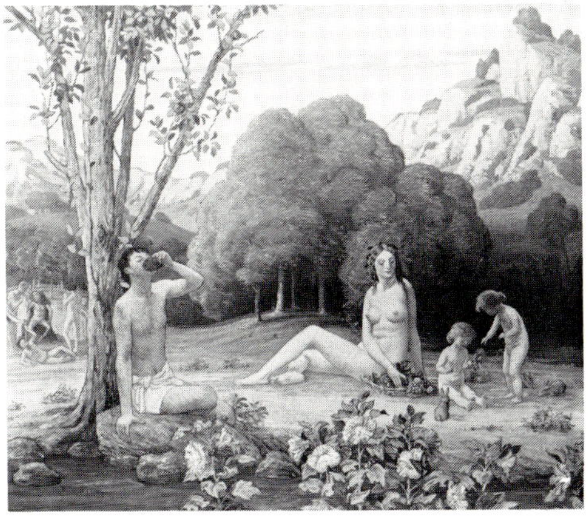

66. Bryson Burroughs, *The Age of Gold*, 1913, The Newark Museum.

Where such landscapes are populated by humans, the figures are generally nude or clothed in non-specific but vaguely antique robes and garments. Frank DuMond's women in a landscape appear like priestesses performing a ritual exercise in nature, particularly the standing figure who seems to invoke some power from above. Bryson Burroughs, one of Puvis de Chavannes' most faithful supporters and slavish imitators among American painters, titled a 1913 canvas *The Age of Gold;* the verbal play on the "Gilded Age" served to distinguish the antique and humanistic concerns of the Burroughs conception from the prevalent mechanism and materialism of modern culture on the eve of the First World War. The painting's message of idealized pagan culture is conveyed by a handsome family of nudes seated at a fountain of youth; their perfect physiques are contrasted with a Silenus-like figure surrounded by young inebriates. Many observers have noted the fascination with physical culture in turn-of-the-century America, and our "profound admiration of 'looks,'—physical beauty considered after a pagan sort of way."[4] The obvious metaphor of healthy sexuality painted by Burroughs found more subtle variants among other American painters. For instance, Bertram Hartman's female nudes relax like pearls—the title of the painting—beside the calm waters of his suggestively Alpine lake; his is an evocation of the Golden Age comparable to those ranging from Davies' to the early works of Henri Matisse.

Other reversions to ancient motifs made more specific reference to the bacchic rites and pagan poets popularly associated with the vanished cultures of Greece and Rome. Charles Stetson painted a series of Dionysian revels in the late 1880s and 1890s, of which his *Pagan Procession* is an outstanding example. Stetson's parade, with frolicking young maidens at the head, is painted in the high-keyed palette characteristic of the artist's work; his pronounced colorism and his painterly technique earned him comparisons with Whistler and especially with the Venetian Old Masters.[5] In Paris, Charles Curran similarly exploited bacchic subjects, as in his *Bacchanal* of 1890, one of several paintings on the theme; the agitated forms of the nymphs are hastily rendered in a sketchy style more reminiscent of Hans Makart than of the slavish antiquarianism with which similar Salon subjects were often handled.

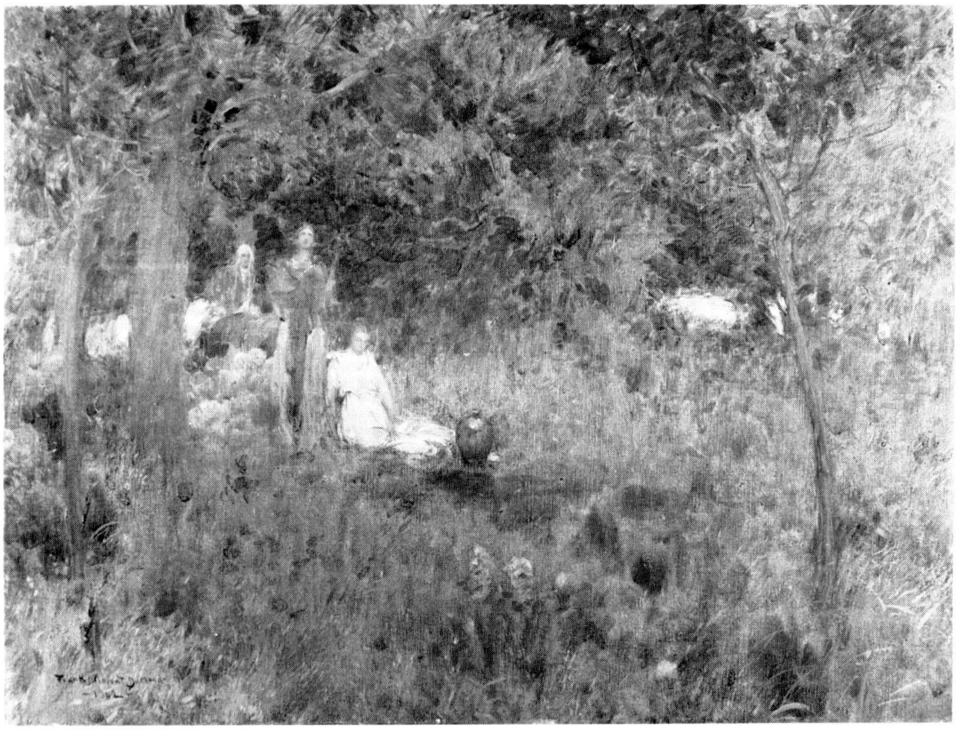

67. Frank V. DuMond, *Figures in Landscape,* 1902, cat. no. 21.

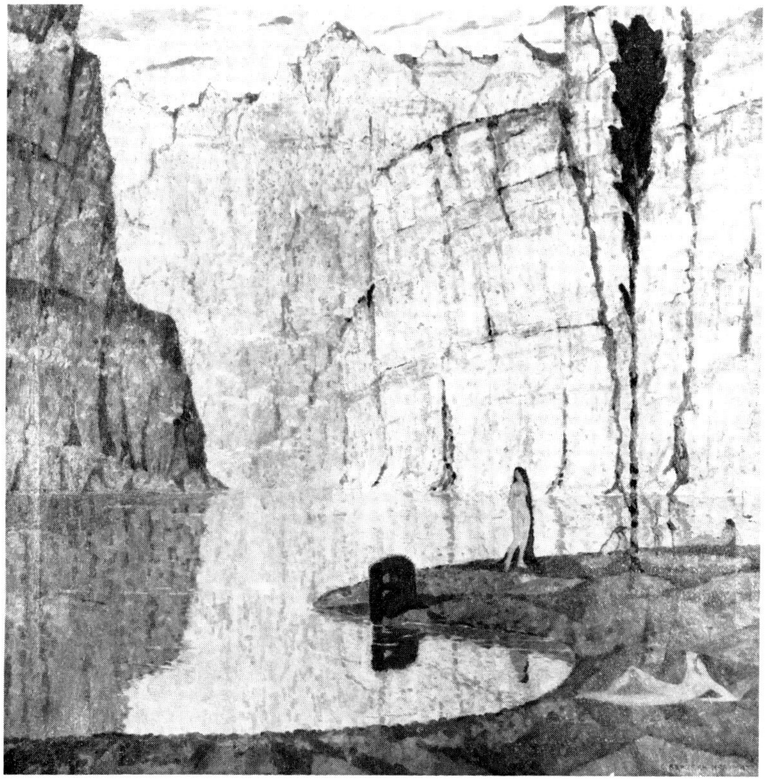

68. C. Bertram Hartman, *Pearls,* 1911, cat. no. 28.

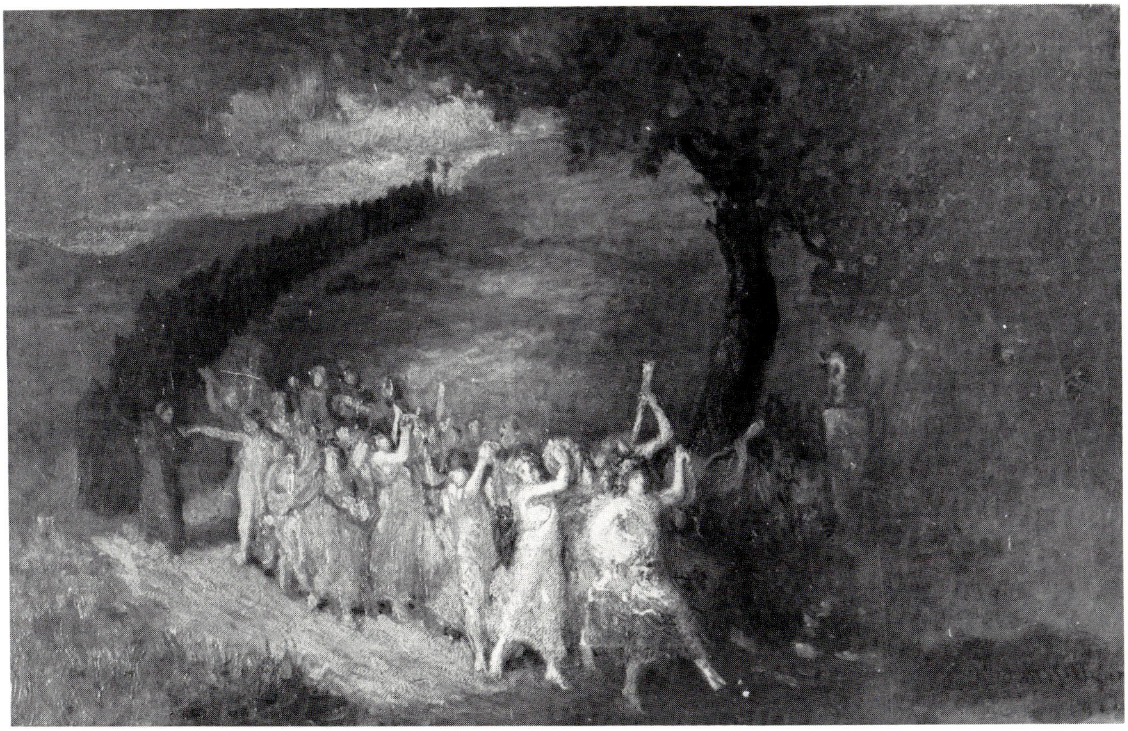

69. Charles W. Stetson, *A Pagan Procession,* 1892, cat. no. 59.

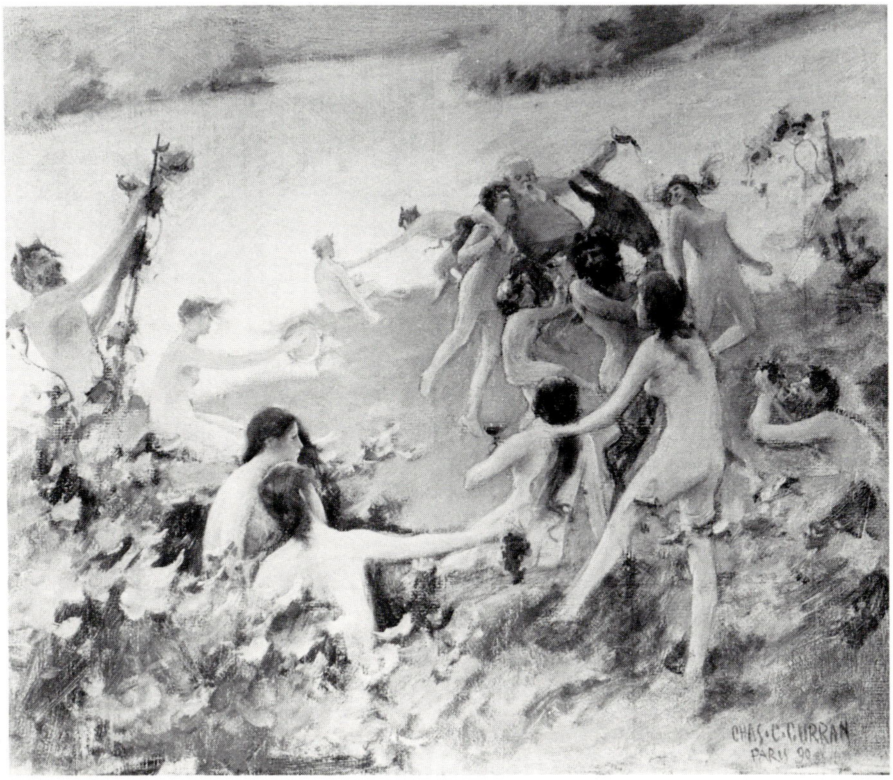

70. Charles C. Curran, *Bacchanal,* 1890, cat. no. 11. (Photo by Hugh Poisson)

Other Americans evoked the rich sensual life of the ancients through poetic themes. Sappho was a subject particularly favored by painters and sculptors in the last half of the nineteenth century, during which period she was almost universally regarded as the greatest of the ancient female poets. From the fourth century B. C. onwards, commentators on Sappho's verses acclaimed her lyric talent as evinced in her descriptions of private passions; so notable was her poetic achievement that the later Greeks classed her as the tenth of the Muses. The revulsion with which the ancients greeted the problem of female homosexuality caused them to disavow allegations of Sappho's own lesbianism; as late as the tenth century A. D., the lexicon known as the Suda simply stated that "she was slanderously accused of shameful intimacy with certain of her female pupils."[6]

It was at the end of the nineteenth century that Sappho's role began to change markedly. Many artists and writers persisted in their adulation of the poet and her lyrical love poetry, without consideration of her sexual preferences. Some journalists defended Sappho's physical beauty, basing their conclusions on ancient Greek vase painting and Mytilenaean coinage, without reference to her sexual practices. Rebutting allegations that Sappho was short of stature and darkly complexioned, qualities which would have been at odds with Greek ideals of beauty, one writer concluded that "the comic poets traduced her in this allegation as in other matters."[7] George Maynard's painting of Sappho was praised by another writer as "possessing great beauty of tone and refined in sentiment . . . , " qualities appropriate to the traditional conception of the poet.[8]

At the same time Maynard was painting his "beautiful and refined" Sappho, Alphonse Daudet was penning quite another version. His novel, *Sappho,* was first published in 1884, and featured the sexual adventures of Fanny, a model and mistress to many artists, who had once posed for a bronze statue of the Greek poet, from whence comes the tale's title. The moralistic subtitle of Daudet's book—*Or, Lured by a Bad Woman's Fatal Beauty!*[9]—reiterated the period's fascination with the *femme fatale.* While Fanny appeared enthusiastically heterosexual, Daudet suggested the possibility of a homoerotic liaison in her past, and her character clearly drew upon the sensual legacy of "the name that had come drifting down the centuries, picking up all the mud of infamous legend, until all its primal grace was lost, just as a goddess's name had become the name of a disease."[10] The term "Sapphism" first appeared in Billing's *National Medical Dictionary* in 1890, and within a few years achieved general usage as a synonym for lesbianism.[11] French fascination with Sappho as a lesbian was further developed in Pierre Louys's *Songs of Bilitis,* published in 1895, which continued the decade's amplification of her sensual legacy and its complication with homosexual overtones.

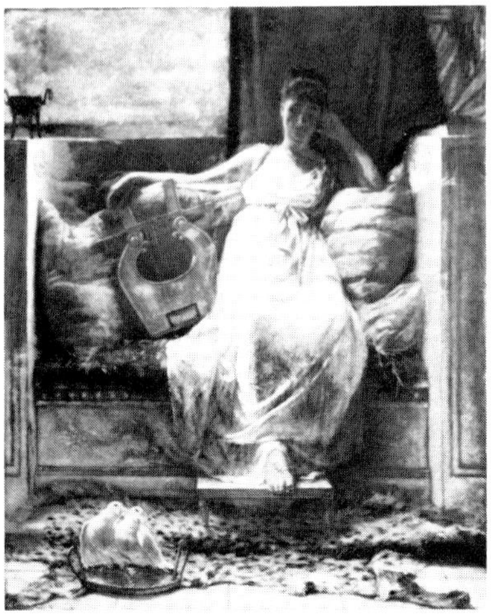

71. George W. Maynard, *Sappho,* circa 1887, Pennsylvania Academy of the Fine Arts.

Whether as lyrical poet or practicing lesbian, Sappho's appeal to the *fin de siècle* grew commensurately with her notoriety. Robert Newman's conception of the poet adheres more closely to the traditional romantic conception rather than to the modern erotic view. His *Sappho* is poised with her lyre on the brink of the cliff from which she made her suicidal leap into the

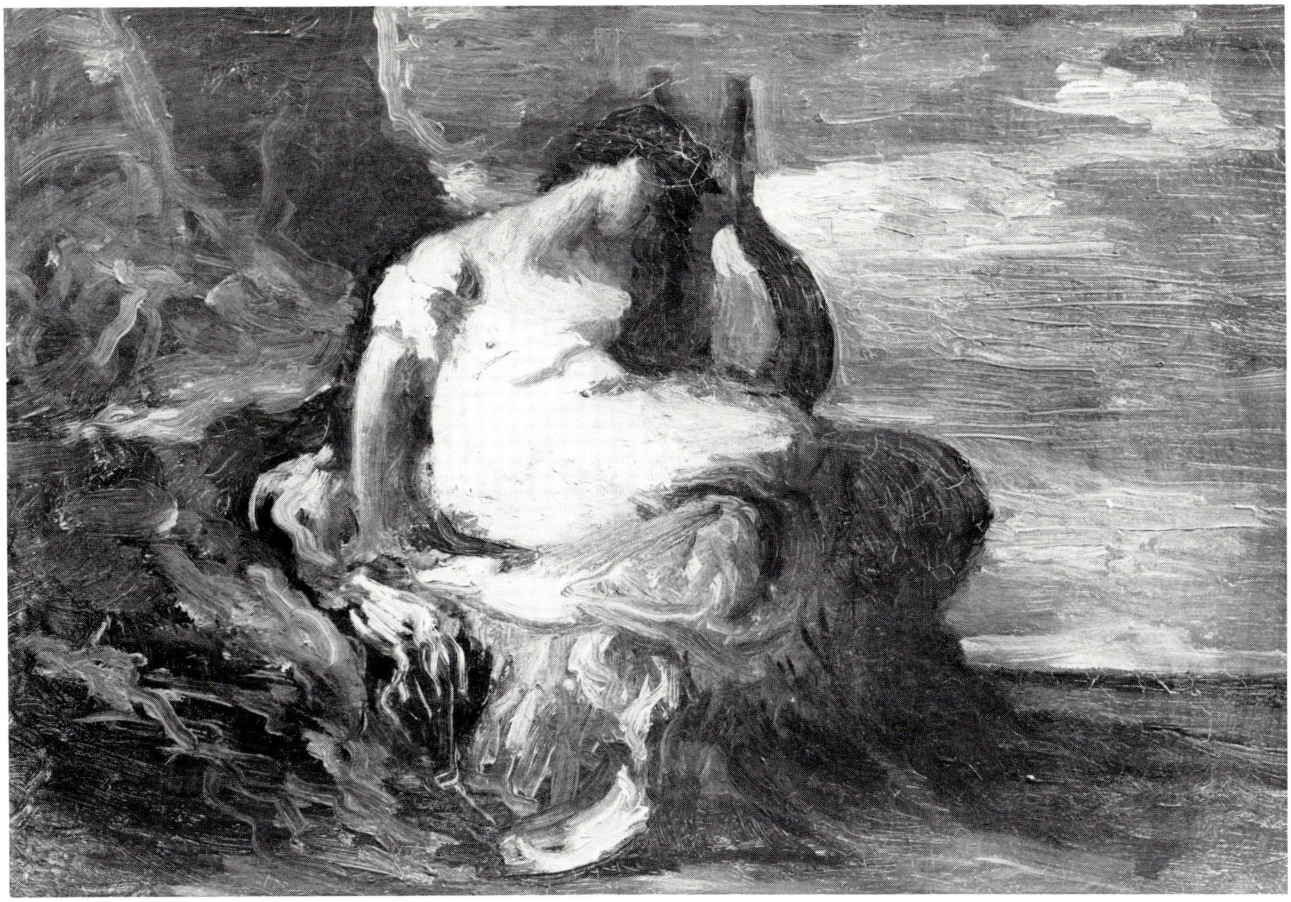

72. Robert L. Newman, *Sappho,* cat. no. 44.

sea, despairing over the unrequited love of Phaon. The loose brushwork is typical of Newman's manner as found especially in the religious paintings for which he is best remembered. In its pose and its painterliness, the American work bears striking similarities to Theodore Chasseriau's *Sappho* of 1849, a work which Newman might have known while studying in the French capital in the 1850s. The Newman painting lacks the more specifically homoerotic references of some of the French Decadents' examples of the 1890s. Instead, the American artist exalts pictorially the sensual appeal of the poet and her verses, an attraction which is echoed in the vigor and looseness of the brushstrokes and the sensuosity of the paint surface.

Nature and Imagination: The American Landscape

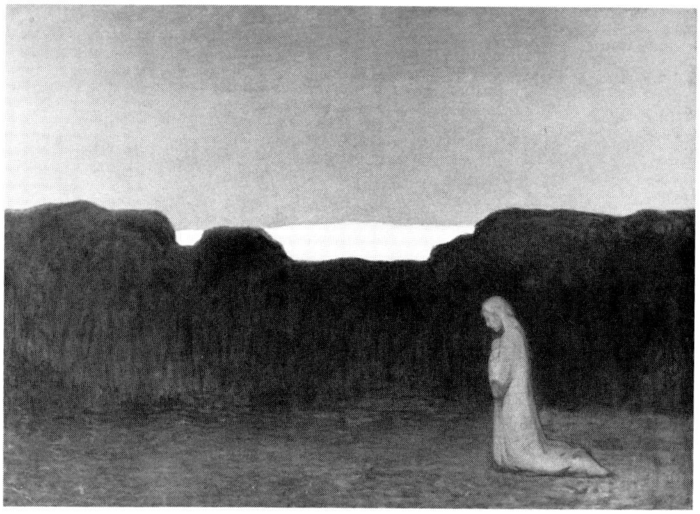

73. Gottardo Piazzoni, *Lux Eterna,* 1914, cat. no. 50.

European Symbolists focused primarily upon the figurative subject, as did many American painters of a similar temperament. Yet the importance of landscape as a support for such figurative concerns, as with Ryder or Blakelock, for instance, cannot be overlooked. Even among the French Symbolists there were a few painters who turned to the unpopulated landscape as a means of conveying their mood and meaning, as with the Breton views of Maurice Chabas and Charles Filiger. The strong landscape tradition in American art insured the survival of the motif into the early years of the twentieth century, but the tradition did not continue unaltered.

Returning to Washington in April 1895, after a western trek of "at least 20,000 miles," Henry Adams "was beginning to think . . . that he knew enough about the edges of life—tropical islands, mountain solitudes, archaic law, and retrograde types. Infinitely more amusing and incomparably more picturesque than civilization, they educated only artists. . . . one was driven from beauty to beauty as though art were a trotting-match."[1] Even the surviving limners of the American landscape were reconsidering the education obtained on the picturesque edges of life. "There is no denying the fact that the early landscape painters of America were too strongly affected by the prevailing idea that we had the greatest country in the world for *scenery,*" confessed the aged Worthington Whittredge; " . . . the artists thought the only way to get along was to paint *scenery.* . . . Simplicity of subject was not in demand."[2] Dating from the years immediately after the Civil War was the emergence of an alternative to the "brown-tree" tradition of the "Hudson River school," which stressed simpler subjects and a landscape of mood and subjective response quite dissimilar from that practiced by Cole or Durand, Church or Bierstadt. In his contributions to the National Academy exhibitions of the 1860s, George Inness clearly announced his departure from Ruskinian principles of exactitude in renditions of nature's forms. In an often-quoted definition of the artist's purpose, Inness claimed that "a work of art does not appeal to the intellect. It does not appeal to the moral sense. Its aim is not to instruct, not to edify, but to awaken an emotion." For Inness, "the civilized landscape can communicate human sentiment; and therefore I love it more and think it more worthy of reproduction than that which is savage and untamed. It is more significant."[3] Later in his life, and especially in his last decade, his "signature years," the subjective aspect of Inness' landscape style came to the fore and excited great acclaim from among his contemporaries. Inness was a Swedenborgian convert, and the principles of correspondent realities preached by the Swedish mystic came to affect the artist's view of the world. The qualities of light, as evidence of divine presence in the world, and the generalizations of landscape elements to achieve a religious and poetic mood, were particularly noted in his canvases after about 1884. Inness' emotion and imagination compromised a slavish dedication to the copying of natural forms. In this he exemplified the principle of at least one critic of the period: "It is well to begin with nature; but one should go on with art."[4]

The artful combination of natural subject and personal spirit which Inness effected was reflected in the work of many younger painters at the turn of the century. The use of particularlized light, be it slanting sunrays or moonlight, and simplified, unified elements in the natural setting became an obsession for the tonalists, who were recently the subject of perceptive examination by Wanda Corn. Related in spirit are the works of other younger artists who complicated the iconography of the subjective landscape through the prominent introduction of figures which evoked a more complex response to pictorial stimuli. The early works of Edward Steichen, for example, are characterized by a Maeterlinckean subtlety in which landscape and figure jointly support the gently stated mood; his *Shrouded Figure in Moonlight* translates into paint the mood and the meaning of Maeterlinck's essay on silence. Similarly, in California the Swiss emigre Gottardo Piazzoni posed a kneeling figure before a simplified and mysterious landscape in his *Lux Aeterna* of 1914, in an evocation of a generalized religious mood.

In each of these instances—Inness, Steichen, Piazzoni—the artist was painting not with an eye toward his natural model, but "away from nature." It was not the perceived world which concerned them, but rather their internal and personal responses to their environment. The introspective landscape sought not mimesis, but a subjective translation of the subject. Such a conception would affirm Inness' assertion that "knowledge must bow to spirit."[5] As did Paul Gauguin, these Americans believed that the painter should be wary of imitation and should direct his attention away from nature, not toward her. "The oft-repeated phrase, 'Paint from Nature,' is a good one is properly understood," warned Elliott Daingerfield; "Paint from—in the sense of away—not by her, lest she has her way with you and not you with her."[6]

American Introspectives After 1900

In March 1878, the New England Psychological Society heard a report that warned of "certain conditions incident to, and drawing out of, a high state of civilization, which in some degree tend to explain both the development and increase of insanity."[1] While the plague of dementia feared by some psychologists never materialized, the rapidly changing social conditions of late nineteenth-century life did serve to alter radically the cultural ambience for younger American artists. The painters who matured after about 1900 inherited a world which would have been unrecognizable to an earlier generation. Whereas their parents and grandparents had had to cope personally with the assaults to tradition dealt by Darwin, warfare, robber barons, modern science and the like, the younger artists worked in a world in which change was understood as a given. That is not to say that it was universally accepted or favored, but the flux of *fin-de-siècle* culture was more generally recognized and its impact was evidenced in various ways after the turn of the twentieth century.

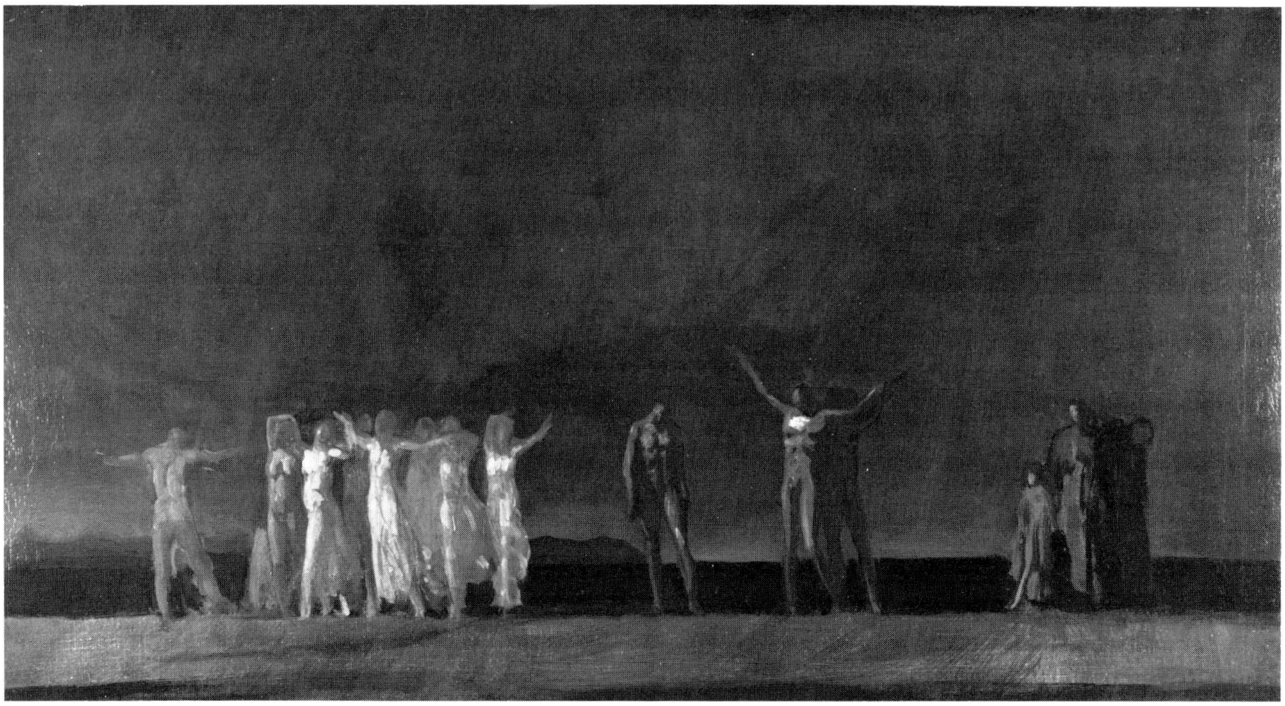

74. Rockwell Kent, *Nocturnal Dance,* circa 1905, cat. no. 32.

In 1913, the Armory Show introduced American audiences for the first time to large numbers of European modernists. Although the impact of the International Exhibition of Modern Art, as it is properly called, has been sometimes overestimated in subsequent accounts of the event, it does nevertheless provide one important landmark in histories of American modernism. The show's large representation of Redon, Gauguin and other European Symbolists, particularly from the French school, made available to artists and laymen in this country examples of their work which had never previously been available in such numbers. From such encounters Americans might have drawn a general iconography of Symbolist painting. The reliance upon figurative themes, often focusing upon the feminine subject, the preponderant concern for topics of mortality and life's cycles, an interest in analogical relationships between figures and a variety of nonhuman subjects—in short, an entire vocabulary of subjectivist responses to man's condition in the modern world came to be recognized among our younger artists in the years before World War I. Edward Manigault's *Procession* of 1911 evokes parallels with Denis' ritualistic marches of figures across decoratively patterned landscapes; in Manigault's case, however, he excepts himself from the general Symbolist aversion to modern imagery with the inclusion of motor cars in his Prendergast-like patterned forest. Rockwell Kent's *Night Dance* and Manierre Dawson's *Figures on Pale Blue* similarly parallel decorative arrangements of figures by French or American masters included at the Armory show.

The effort to codify the subjectivist view of the world reached its logical conclusion in the 1917 debut of a group of young New York painters who called themselves the Introspectives. Centered around Claude Buck and his brother-in-law, Benjamin Kopman, their initial exhibitions at the Whitney Studio and the Knoedler Gallery excited considerable interest among art patrons and critics of the day. The introspective stance of the group was outlined by Jennings Tofel in the closest thing to a Symbolist manifesto that exists in American art history. Tofel declared that modernism had served its purpose in revitalizing art, but faulted the modernists for being sensational and not profound. He lamented the backsliding of art into "the hands of intellectual blacksmiths . . . whose art is the art of illustration—the journalism of art, the occurrences of the day, the things of the day. . . . We have no dearth of prose painters painting prose stories, histories and newspapers. We now want poet painters, painters of lyrics and epics." The Introspectives' credo drew heavily upon the precedent of French Symbolist thought. "There are no rules laid down for the constituents of this group to obey. They agree, however, on the principles of beauty, order and the faculties of imagination and fancy." In the best tradition of Baudelaire and Mallarmé, Introspective art "shall suggest more than relate, for suggestion is the depth beyond the depth—the gauntlet to the imagination of the observer, that disturbs and quickens his sensibilities."[2]

Claude Buck's contributions to the Introspective aesthetic are of particular interest. American intervention in World War I, which nearly coincided with the opening of the Introspectives' exhibitions, irrevocably altered

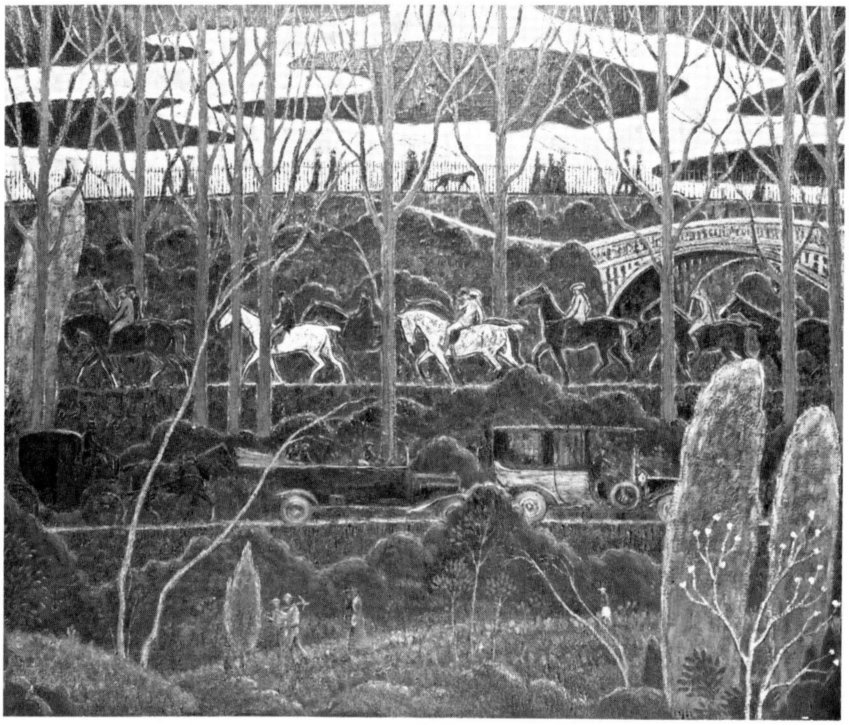

75. Edward M. Manigault,
Procession, 1911, cat. no. 36.

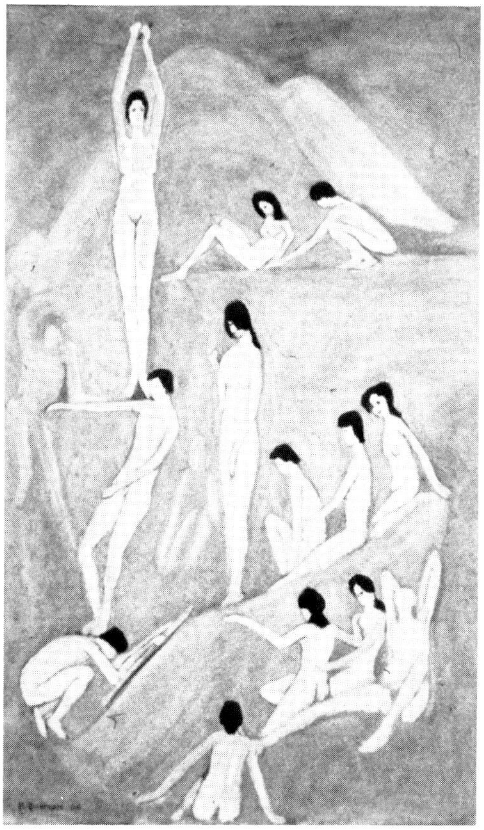

76. Manierre Dawson,
Figures on Pale Blue, 1906,
cat. no. 18.

patterns of American taste and artistic production, and today the Introspectives are nearly unknown. Buck, born in 1890, typifies the predicament of the younger imaginative artists in the second decade of this century. In his youthful works he was drawn to themes similar to those which had preoccupied French Symbolist painters a generation earlier. Like his Introspective colleagues he believed in art as "an echo of the human voice within, an intensification of the spiritual and physical life of nature"; their art sought to "reconcile the individual with the universal."[3] Such expressions led critics to characterize Buck and his fellow artists as "leaning toward the transcendental."[4] Of particular fascination in his early years were the writings of Edgar Allen Poe, whose *Raven* and *City in the Sea* Buck illustrated. He also painted literary themes from Poe's *Ulalume, Lenore, Eldorado,* and *The Conqueror Worm,* among others; these were generally small canvases painted with a jewel-like color and rich impasto. Buck admired Poe as "the first human being to play great emotional symphonies on the full keyboard of human sensations. He did not reject any sensation a human being could feel, but found them all valuable to better reveal his conception of beauty."[5] As had the poet, so too did the painter seek to "perform a spiritual as well as a physical service . . . [by] giv[ing] one a vision of life or nature that is much nobler than one has had before."[6] Buck's morbid themes derived from Poe or elsewhere were pictorialized in imaginative forms which demonstrate close affinities with the European Symbolist vocabulary. His *Death and the Maiden* provides nearly an anthology of such Symbolist devices—a dead, nude female, beside a body of water, with peacocks and blossoms prominently featured. The interest in coloristic effects and the paint application, as well as the subject itself, suggest parallels with a number of European precursors ranging from Moreau to Redon to Delville.

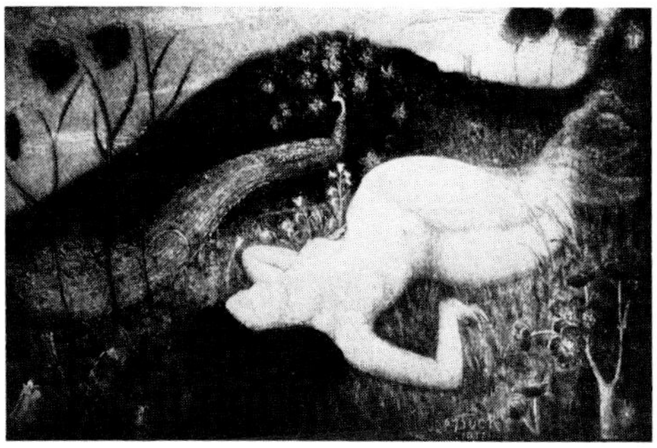

77. Claude Buck,
Death and the Maiden, 1917,
location unknown.

The early imaginative paintings by Claude Buck and his Introspective colleagues indicate how thoroughly aspects of European Symbolist iconography and mood had become merged with American artistic production. Unfortunately for Buck, the national experience of world war, the artist's move from New York to Chicago, and his subsequent turn to more socially oriented and topical subjects all have contributed to the general neglect which the highly imaginative compositions of his youth have received. But if the Symbolist concerns of the Introspectives were frustrated by a changing climate in the United States about 1917, there were other ways in which those concerns continued to affect and enrich American painting of the early twentieth century.

Abstract Symbolism

Late in 1915, Anita Pollitzer received a roll of drawings and watercolors from her former classmate at Columbia Teachers College, Georgia O'Keeffe. The works which O'Keeffe mailed were part of the correspondence the two friends carried on between New York and O'Keeffe's various teaching positions in South Carolina and Texas in the years immediately preceding the First World War. O'Keeffe's parcel was dispatched with the specific instructions that her friend show the works to no one, indicating the personal quality of the communication they shared. From her admonition and her reaction to Pollitzer's disobedience of it, it is clear that these early works on paper, by which she first came to the attention of a New York audience, carried with them a meaning of great personal importance to the artist. As a form of non-verbal communication between close friends, the drawings conveyed a private sense which O'Keeffe was unable to verbalize. Recognizing the striking importance of the drawings and watercolors, Pollitzer hastened with them to Alfred Stieglitz's "291" Gallery; there the impresario uttered his legendary evaluation—"Finally, a woman on paper."[1] Stieglitz's exhibition of the works in May, 1916, shocked the New York critics, who were unprepared for the radically simplified and abstracted imagery contained in them. The 1916 showing was followed by a second the next year, this time mounted with the painter's permission.

To the reviewers of the two O'Keeffe exhibitions at 291 Fifth Avenue, her work appeared miraculous, as something developed *sui generis* on the barren plains of North Texas remote from the New York art center, and inexplicable, save by acclaim of O'Keeffe's innate genius. Comparable explanations had, of course, served to explain the earlier imaginative imagery of Ryder and other similarly isolated "geniuses." Subsequent critics have linked O'Keeffe's early abstract designs with the Japanese-derived aesthetic theory of her last mentor, Arthur Wesley Dow. He had preached a formalist system based upon the synthetic massing of dark and light masses in flat relationships on the picture plane. For Dow, the successful work of art had a formal "beauty entirely independent of meaning."[2] Today, when her early work is discussed, it is generally the relationship to Dow which is used to explain the unexpected eruption of O'Keeffe's innovative talent about 1915.

While Dow's tutelage had an indubitable impact upon his talented student, the circumstances surrounding the creation of the works sent to Anita Pollitzer suggest another possible interpretation for O'Keeffe's early paintings and drawings. As with many of her contemporaries, O'Keeffe's initial training was at the hands of teachers like Frank DuMond, John Vanderpoel and F. Luis Mora, artists who were of the generation most deeply affected by the subjectivist strains of late nineteenth-century painting. For these artist-teachers, the role of the painter was to convey some aspect of personal meaning or mood, however decoratively or sentimentally treated. From such instructors O'Keeffe and others of her generation were early imbued with a sense of art as personal expression and with the primacy of meaning or content in their creations. Insofar as the nineteenth-century artist was tied to recognizable subjects, however inventively he might have treated them, he was hampered by tangibilities which prevented the complete union of image and sensual effect which Symbolist poets or musicians could achieve. With the move toward abstraction and the ultimate abandonment of the object in their most radical paintings from about 1911 to 1917, artists like O'Keeffe and Arthur Dove and Marsden Hartley could finally achieve the equivalent merger of image and sensual effect or meaning as Mallarmé had earlier accomplished in his verse.

Recently Françoise Meltzer has studied the role of color in Symbolist poetry. In comparing Baudelaire's *Albatross* to Mallarmé's sonnet to the swan, she noted that the earlier poet's "extended simile, forceful though it is, has the same limitations as Poe's *Raven;* there is still a distance between the poet and the image of the bird. As soon as a simile is used, analogy appears, in itself a parallel but not an embodiment of a concept. Mallarmé, on the other hand, manages the union of effect and image through the use of color. All three realms of the poem, landscape, 'poet,' and feeling . . . become inextricable and synonymous—precisely the intent of the Symbolist poem."[3] Although the standards of poetic and artistic criticism are different, O'Keeffe in her early work achieved a comparable merger of painted image and evoked meaning, realized in her case through the devaluation of the realistically depicted object in her artwork. To Mallarmé's language there is a dual quality, according to Meltzer: "words without nominata, and sense or image without words."[4] Similarly in the early abstractions of Georgia O'Keeffe we encounter forms without concrete reference, and sense or meaning without objects.

By making the Mallarméan break-through to non-mimetic, anti-illusionistic evocation of image or meaning, O'Keeffe drew upon the significant heritage of late nineteenth-century Symbolism to achieve her decidedly twentieth-century abstraction. Her innovations, and those simultaneously made by Dove and Hartley, establish a mode of "Abstract Symbolism" by which the aesthetic formulated by an earlier generation becomes the basis for a modernist revolution. According to one historian, the Stieglitz coterie, to which all three painters were related, reflected in their art and their dialogue "the continuing aura of Symbolism with its predilection for circumlocution, intuitive communication and evocation"; their style, both verbally and pictorially, betrayed "a kind of Mallarméan fear of specificity."[5] As important as the avoidance of specificity is the sense of nature's vitalism which O'Keeffe in her Texas works and Dove in his organic abstractions were able to convey, while resorting neither to naturalist verisimilitude nor tonalist fog. Freed of the representational imperative, their pioneering efforts in the mid-1910s re-established the vitality of Symbolist *corréspondance* and subjectivist aesthetics for a new generation.

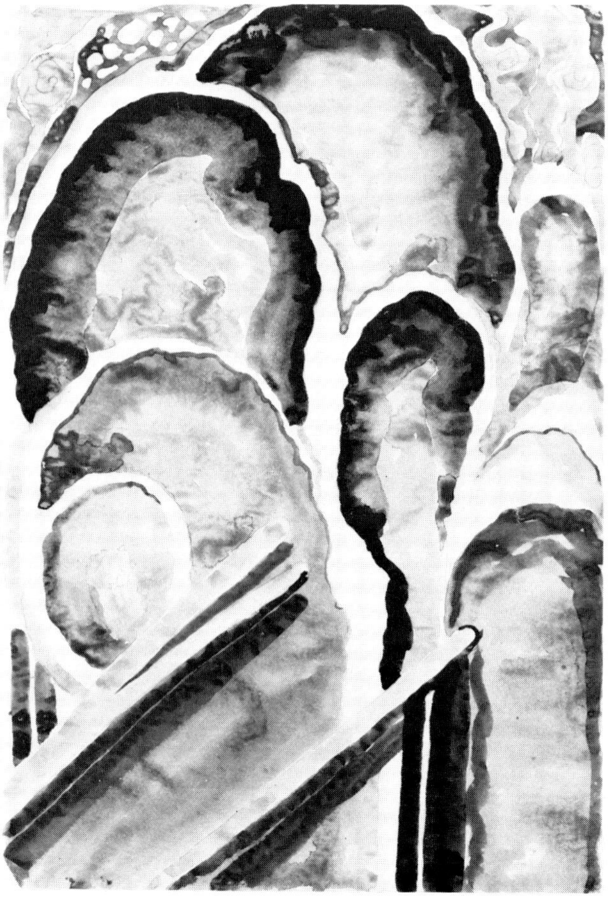

78. Georgia O'Keeffe, *Blue No. I,* 1916, cat. no. 45.

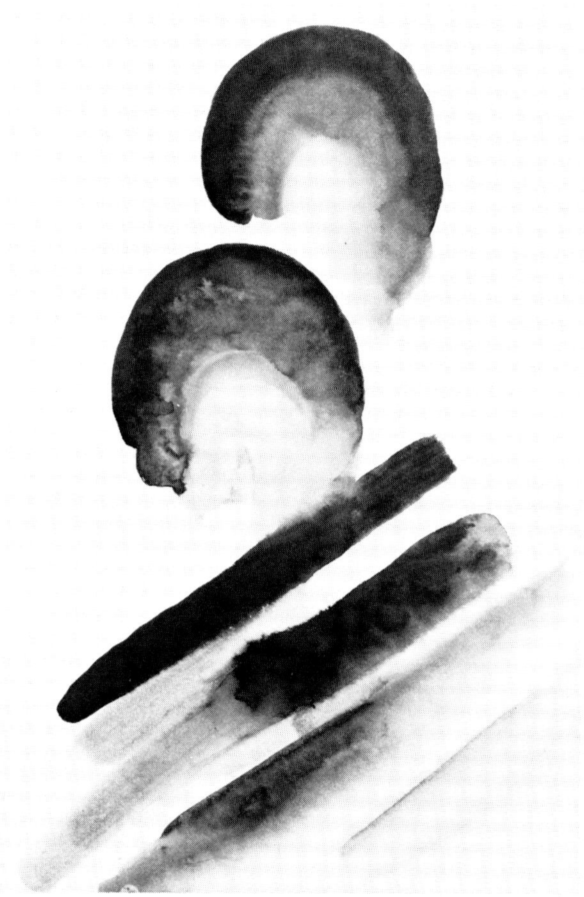

79. Georgia O'Keeffe, *Blue No. II,* 1916, cat. no. 46.

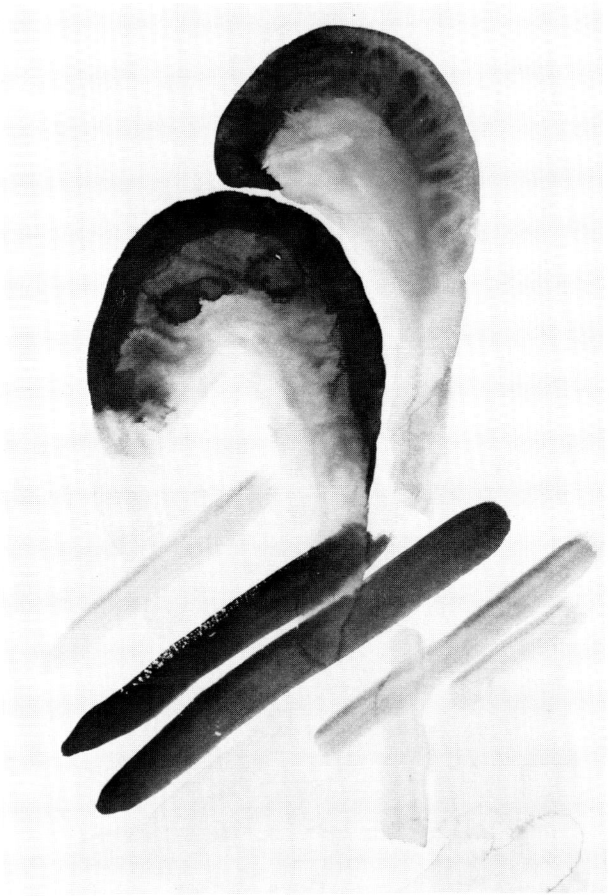

80. Georgia O'Keeffe, *Blue No. III,* 1916, cat. no. 47.

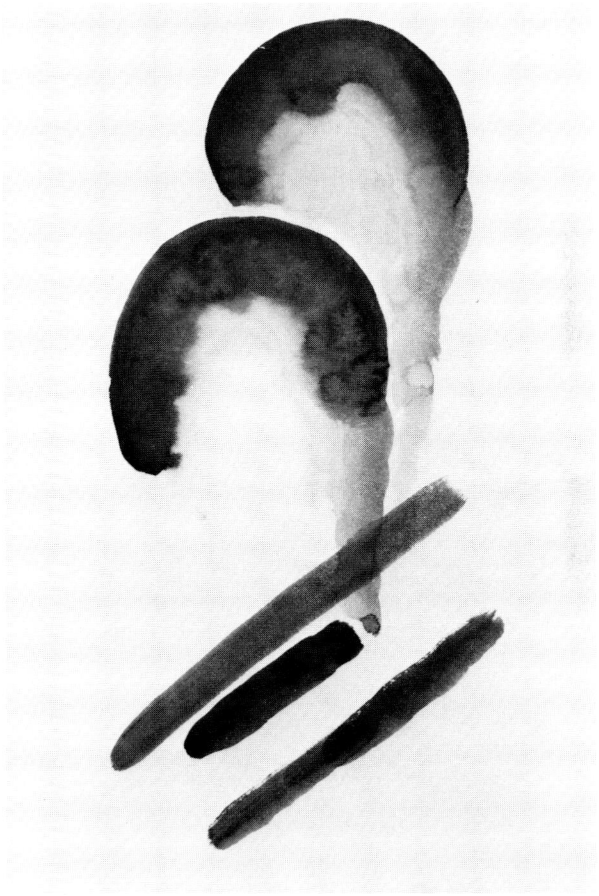

81. Georgia O'Keeffe, *Blue No. IV,* 1916, cat. no. 48.

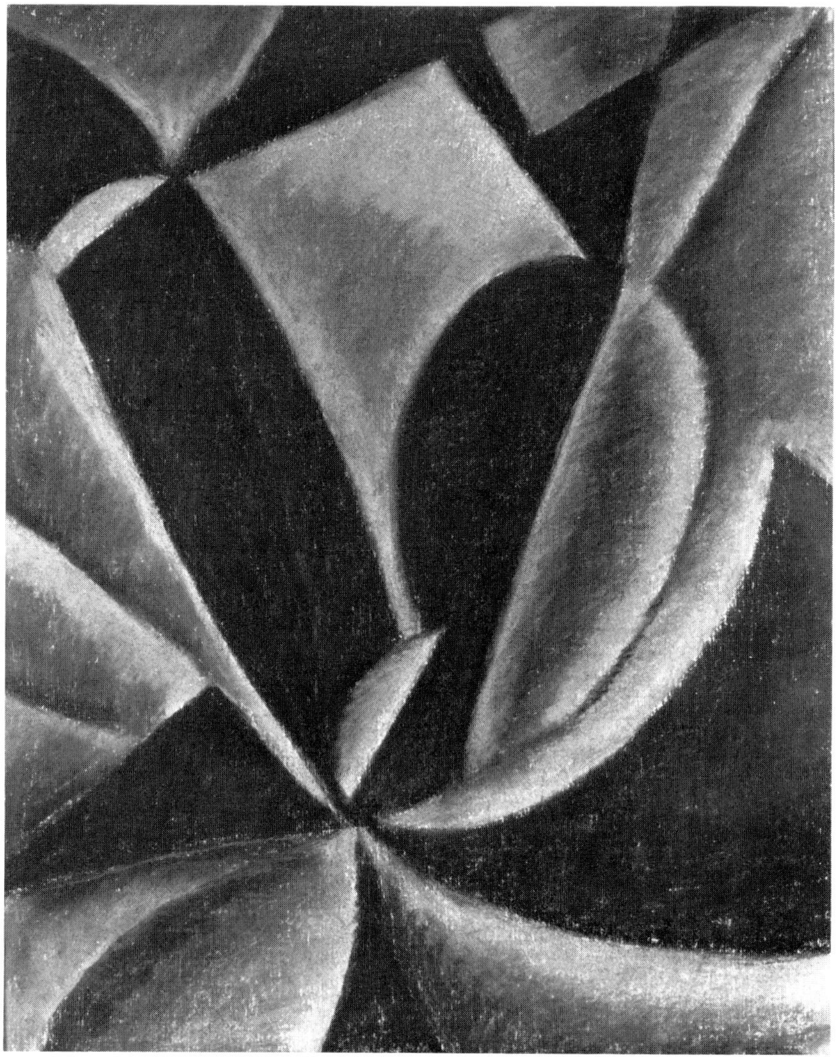

82. Arthur G. Dove, *Movement No. 1*, 1911, cat. no. 20.

Marsden Hartley, who was naturally drawn to the imaginative imagery of Ryder, similarly invested his paintings with personal sense or content, as had the older painter whom he worshipped. Hartley's musical abstractions of 1912-1913 sought, as did the music from which he drew his inspiration, to move the viewer (or listener) directly, without first passing through the referential language of forms traditionally the concern of the visual artist. Hartley was not content with synaesthetic visions, such as had occurred to Pamela Smith; rather, he sought an immediacy of effect which he translated through his abstract symbols, heralding yet another bridge between the aesthetic preoccupations of an earlier generation and the abstraction of the twentieth century. The Abstract Symbolists' emphasis upon content and sense provides a seldom-recognized source for the genesis of American modernism. This link parallels the often-examined and well-documented formalist tie between American modernism and European postimpressionism, and helps to place the exceptional "genius" of an O'Keeffe, a Dove or a Hartley in context.

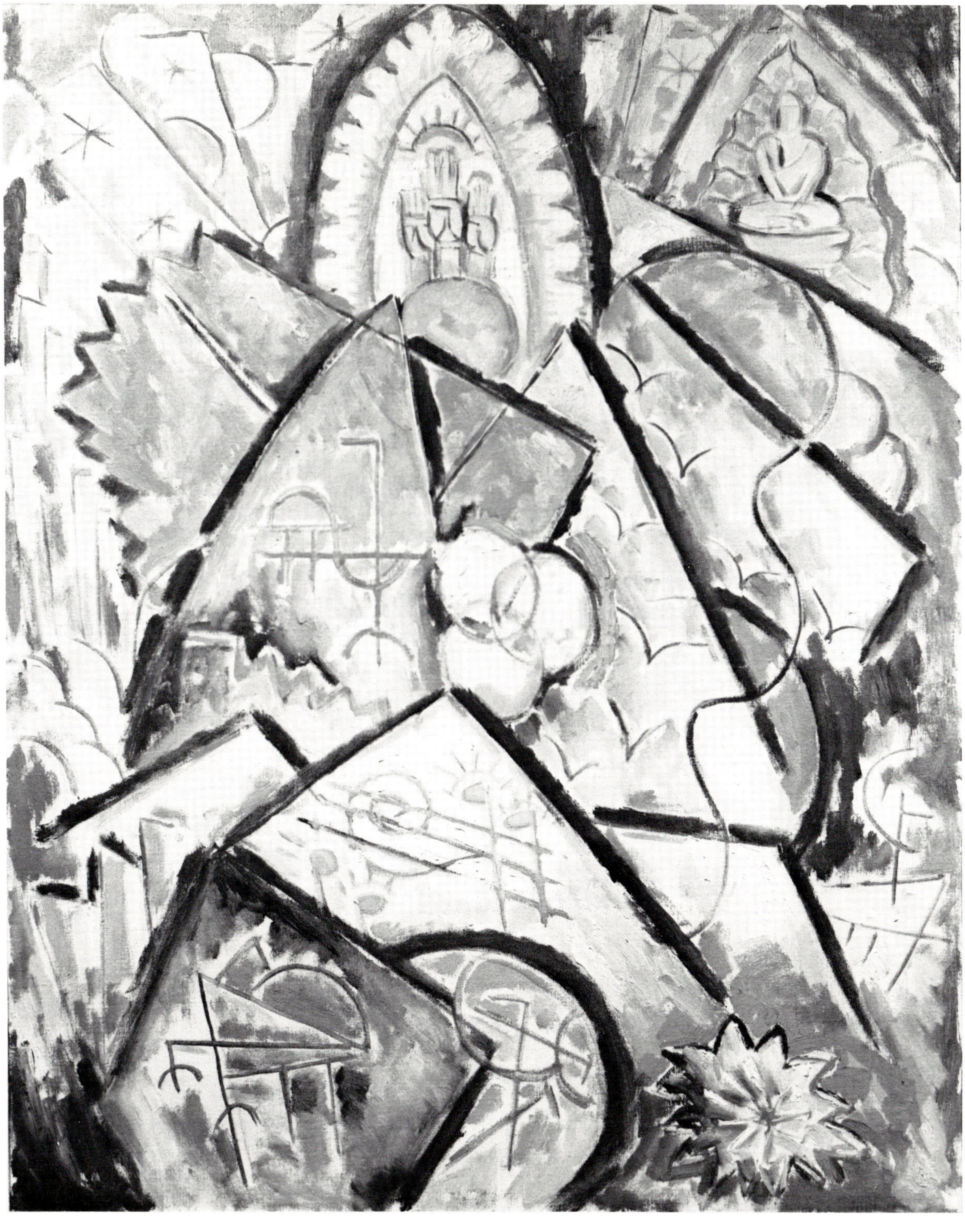

83. Marsden Hartley, *Musical Theme (Oriental Symphony),* 1912-1913, cat. no. 27.

That the symbolic and intuitive conceptions of our turn-of-the-century introspective artists have, with only a few exceptions, been so neglected for so long is a tribute to the hegemony of formalist criticism and historiography in the twentieth century. The quest for "symbolic form" has blinded many critics and historians to the equally important search for "significant content" which obsessed so many American artists of the period. As Robert Goldwater correctly noted, "the reflexive procedure of such formalist analyses—pre-occupied as it is with the painters *how,* and finding in that how the meaning of the work—tends to minimize the importance of *what* it is that the artist renders."[6] In seeking to illuminate the importance of cubes, cones and spheres, of grids and facets, of paint surfaces, and of the picture plane, we have consciously or unconsciously denigrated the Symbolists' "essential aim . . . to objectify the subjective (the externalization of the Idea) instead of subjectifying the objective (nature seen through the eyes of a temperament)."[7] Paradoxically, but significantly, it was not until the mid-twentieth-century rise of Abstract Expressionism and its abolition of the objective reference that artists and critics began to apply language concerned with meaning and content to the subjectless paintings.

In 1931 Edmund Wilson noted that "the literary history of our time is to a great extent that of the development of Symbolism and of its fusion or conflict with Naturalism."[8] Perhaps only now, as we near another *fin de siècle,* can we in a more balanced fashion appreciate the similar development, conflict and fusion of Symbolist and realist, perceptual aesthetics in the visual arts of the late nineteenth and early twentieth centuries. When that revisionary history of the period is finally written, the American temple of the mind and imagination should assume its rightful place alongside the monuments to facts and formalism, and the long-deferred recognition will be awarded at last to our artists' contributions to the *fin de siècle's* international flourishing of the imaginative life and the Symbolist mood.

Notes

Temples of the Mind

1. Ryder, "Temple of the Mind," oil on panel, 17-¾ x 16 inches. The painting is in the collection of the Albright-Knox Art Gallery, Buffalo, N.Y. As with many of the artist's works, the heavily impastoed painting on its fragile support is in perilous condition, due to the working methods and materials utilized by the painter. After considerable discussion with conservators and curators, Robert Buck, Director of the Gallery, made the curatorially responsible decision that the fragile panel should not travel. As a consequence the painting, regrettably but correctly, could not be included in the present exhibition. I am grateful to Mr. Buck for his careful consideration of the matter, and his helpful responses to multiple inquiries regarding the painting.
2. Ryder to John Pickard, New York, November 3, 1907, in Allan Weller, "An Unpublished Letter by Albert P. Ryder," *Art in America,* 27:2 (April 1939), 102.

Seduction in America

1. Leslie Fiedler, *Love and Death in the American Novel* (New York: Stein and Day, 1975).
2. ". . . though evil is dealt with in American literature of the late nineteenth century, it was not a viable concept for American artists, being rarely a part of imagery in painting or sculpture." Lois Marie Fink, "American Participation in the Paris Salons, 1870-1900," address to the International Art Congress, Bologna, Italy, September 1979, typescript p. 4. See also, Lois Marie Fink, "19th Century Evolutionary Art," *The American Art Journal,* X:2 (November 1978), 81, 105.
3. Saint Louis Exposition, *Thirteenth Annual Exhibition: Catalogue of the Art Department* (St. Louis, 1896), 11, 114-115. I am grateful to Doreen B. Burke for calling this reference to my attention.
4. Charles Henry Meltzer, "Ethics and 'The Ring of the Nibelung'," *The Craftsman,* XI:1 (October 1906), 6.
5. John P. Jackson, "The Ring of the Nibelung," *The Cosmopolitan,* VI:5 (March 1889), 416.
6. Jackson, 416.
7. Kirschner, *Wagner Jahrbuck,* 1886, quoted in Jackson, 418.

From Sea to Shining Sea: Submarine Fantasies in American Art

1. "Wagner's 'Rheingold'," *The Critic,* 14:263 (January 12, 1889), 21.
2. For a typical appreciation of Boecklin, see Claude Phillips, "Arnold Boecklin," *The Magazine of Art* (London), VIII (1885), 441-447. For the French reaction to Boecklin, see Valérie Brière, "Boecklin et la critique française," in *Arnold Boecklin, 1827-1901: Gemalde, Zeichnungen, Plastiken* (Basel: Schwabe & Co., 1977), 121-122.

The Virgin and the virgins: The White Lady in American Painting

1. In commenting on Paul Bourget's description of the American cult of virginity, Mark Twain argued that "purity of woman may fairly be called universal with us, but that is the case in some other countries. We have no monopoly of it; it cannot be named American." Mark Twain, "What Paul Bourget Thinks of Us," *The North American Review,* CLX (January 1895), 56. See also Paul Bourget, *Outre-Mer, passim.*
2. Henry Van Dyke, "The Way to Womanhood," *Harper's Bazar,* XXXIX:4 (April 1905), 336-337.
3. Josephine Peabody Journal, October 1895, quoted in Gibran and Gibran, 100.
4. "The Fine Arts: The Society of American Artists," *The Critic,* 18 n.s. 15:383 (May 2, 1891), 243.
5. Allen Tate, "One Escape from the Dilemma," *The Fugitive* (September 1926), 35.
6. Jane Dillenberger, "Between Faith and Doubt: Subjects for Meditation," in Joshua C. Taylor, Jane Dillenberger and Richard Murray, *Perceptions and Evocations: The Art of Elihu Vedder* (Washington: National Collection of Fine Arts, 1979), *passim.*
7. Theodore Stebbins, *The Life and Works of Martin Johnson Heade* (New Haven: Yale University Press, 1975), 176.
8. The unfinished Garbo collage is in the collection of the Joseph Cornell Study Center at the National Collection of Fine Arts, Washington, D.C. I am grateful to Lynda Hartigan, Curator, for calling this work to my attention.

American Visions and the American Dream

1. Smith quoted in "Pictures in Music," *The Strand Magazine,* 35:210 (June 1908), 635.
2. Havelock Ellis, "The Symbolism of Dreams," *The Popular Science Monthly,* 77 (1910), 47.
3. Antoine Orliac, *La Cathédrale Symboliste: Délivrance de Reve* (Paris: Mercure de France, 1933), 288-289.
4. Sale catalogue, Adam A. Weschler & Son, Washington, D.C., October 3-6, 1974, lot 1310.
5. Alexandre Séon, "La douleur de la chimère," reproduced in *The Chap-Book,* II:9 (1895), 384.
6. Whistler quoted in Betty Lochrie Hoag, *The Gifted Peters Family* (Carmel, Cal: Carmel Museum of Art, 1968), [1].
7. *The Parsifal Tone-Pictures* (New York: M. Knoedler, 1904), 15, 12.
8. ". . . we are involuntarily reminded of Turner. . . . Like Turner, he [Marcius-Simons] is a remarkable colorist . . . " Frances Keyser, "Some American Artists in Paris," *International Studio,* 4:16 (June 1898), 250; " . . . not since Turner has there been another man on whose canvas glowed so much of that unearthly 'light that never was on land or sea' . . . " Theodore Roosevelt, "An Art Exhibition," in his *History as Literature and Other Essays* (New York: Scribner's, 1913), 309; Joseph Mashek described Marcius-Simon's "Victory," 1904, as "in a very Moreauean vein . . . " Mashek, "Teddy's Taste: Theodore Roosevelt and the Armory Show," *Art Forum,* IX:3 (November 1970), 71.
9. Peladan quoted in *French Symbolist Painters: Moreau, Puvis de Chavannes, Redon and Their Followers* (London: Arts Council of Great Britain, 1972), 71; *Symbolistic Paintings by P. Marcius-Simons at the Gallery of Doll & Richards* (New York: Republic Press, 1896).

Visions of Life and Death

1. Doreen Bolger Burke, *"Astarte:* Sargent's Study for *The Pagan Gods," Fenway Court* (Boston: Gardner Museum, 1976), 9-19.
2. Sargent quoted in Richard Ormond, *John Singer Sargent, Paintings, Drawings, Watercolors* (London: Phaidon Press, 1970), 90.
3. Burke, 14.
4. Gauguin to Schuffenecker, Pont-Aven, February 1888, quoted in Delevoy, *Symbolists and Symbolism,* 80.
5. Katherine De Forest, "A Little Trip in Brittany," *Harper's Bazar,* 33:43 (October 27, 1900), 1654.
6. Anderson Galleries, *Illustrated Catalogue of Valuable Paintings by American and European Masters, The Collection of the Late Joseph G. Snydacker* (sale #1638) (New York, 1922), lot 35; Elliott Daingerfield, *Ralph Albert Blakelock* (New York: privately printed, 1914), 25.
7. Daingerfield, *Blakelock,* 25; Daingerfield to Woodruff J. Parker, New York, April 5, 1922, Art Institute of Chicago, Blakelock object folder #1947.55.
8. George Alfred Williams, "Principles," *American Magazine of Art,* 8:5 (March 1917), 198.
9. See Marsden Hartley, "Rex Slinkard, Ranchman and Poet-Painter," in *Rex Slinkard, 1887-1918: Memorial Exhibition* (New York: M. Knoedler, 1920), n.p.; also, "Letters of Rex Slinkard," in *Contact* (New York), edited by William Carlos Williams and Robert McAlmon , no. 1 (December 1920), 2-4, no. 2 (January 1921), 2, and no. 3 (Spring 1921), 1-8.
10. *Contact,* no. 3 (Spring 1921), 2.
11. *Contact,* no. 3 (Spring 1921), 4.
12. *Contact,* no. 1 (December 1920), 3.
13. Emerson, "Swedenborg," in *Representative Men,* 92.

Sense and Sensuality: Neo-Paganism in America

1. George Parsons Lathrop, "John La Farge," *Scribner's Magazine,* XXI:4 (February 1881), 410.
2. Lyman Abbott, *The Theology of an Evolutionist* (Boston, 1897), 48.
3. Gaston Schefer, "The Antique," in Charles Carroll, ed., *The Salon* (New York: Samuel L. Hall, 1881), 58.
4. Bourget, *Outre-Mer,* 60-61.
5. George Whitaker quoted in George Leland Miner, *Angell's Lane* (Providence: Akerman-Standard Press, 1948), 133.
6. Quoted in Judith P. Hallett, "Sappho and Her Social Context: Sense and Sensuality," *Signs: Journal of Women in Culture and Society,* 4:3 (Spring 1979) 448. Hallett's article (pp. 447-464) rebuts the claims for Sappho's lesbianism, and gives a good background for the development of such allegations. See also a contrary point of view in Eva Stehle Stigers, "Romantic Sensuality, Poetic Sense: A Response to Hallett on Sappho," *Signs,* 4:3 (Spring 1979), 465-471.
7. "Morning Room: Sappho's Beauty," *The Art Interchange,* II:11 (May 28, 1879), 90.
8. "Fine Arts: The American Art Association," *The Nation,* 44:1143 (May 26, 1887), 45-46.
9. The subtitle is given by Bourget, *Outre-Mer,* 40.
10. Alphonse Daudet, *Sappho* (New York: Pantheon Books, 1951), 41.
11. Hallett, "Sappho and Her Social Context," 451.

Nature and Imagination: The American Landscape

1. Adams, *The Education of Henry Adams,* 350-351.
2. Whittredge quoted in *Worthington Whittredge* (Utica, N.Y.: Munson-Williams-Proctor Institute, 1969), 16-17.
3. Inness quoted in Montgomery Schuyler, "George Inness: The Man and His Work," *Forum,* 18 (November 1894), 310.
4. "The Fine Arts: The Society of American Artists," *The Critic,* i8, n.s. 15: 383 (May 2, 1891), 243.
5. Inness quoted in Carole A. Taynton, "Idyllic Landscapes," *Museum News* (Toledo Museum of Art), ser. 2, vol. 8 (Summer 1965), 36.
6. Elliott Daingerfield, "Nature Versus Art," *Scribner's Magazine,* XLIX (February 1911), 255.

American Introspectives after 1900

1. "The Relations of Insanity to Modern Civilization," *Scribner's Monthly,* XVII:4 (February 1879), 582.
2. Toffel quoted in Edith W. Powell, "The Introspectives," *International Studio,* 61:242 (April 1917), xcii. Portions of the statement were incorporated into Claude Buck's "Foreword" to the catalogue for his one-man show at the Thurber Art Galleries, Chicago, 1920.
3. Unidentified newspaper clipping, Chicago, *circa* 1921, from Claude Buck Scrapbook, in possession of Mrs. Claude Buck. I am grateful to Mrs. Buck for her generous help in assembling and sharing information on her husband's career.
4. "Chicago" (review of Introspectives' exhibition at Chicago Arts Club), *American Art News,* XIX:31 (May 14, 1921), 10.
5. Buck quoted in untitled clipping from Chicago *Post,* 1924, in Buck Scrapbook.
6. Buck quoted in "Palos in Autumn," Chicago *Post,* undated clipping in Buck Scrapbook.

Abstract Symbolism

1. Stieglitz quoted in Anita Pollitzer, "That's Georgia," *The Saturday Review of Literature,* XXXIII (November 4, 1950), 42.
2. Arthur Wesley Dow, *Composition* (New York: Baker and Taylor, 1903; 5th edition), 37.
3. Francoise Meltzer, "Color as Cognition in Symbolist Verse," *Critical Inquiry,* 5:2 (Winter 1978), 263-264.
4. Meltzer, 260.
5. Ann Lee Morgan, "Toward the Definition of Early Modernism in America: A Study of Arthur Dove," unpublished Ph.D. dissertation, University of Iowa, 1973, 207.
6. Robert Goldwater, "Symbolic Form: Symbolic Content," in *Acts of the Twentieth International Congress of the History of Art: Problems of the 19th & 20th Centuries* (Princeton, N.J.: Princeton University Press, 1963), vol. IV, 111.
7. Gustave Kahn quoted in Henri Dorra, "Symbolist and Other Visionaries," in *Visionaries and Dreamers* (Washington: Corcoran Gallery, 1956), 11.
8. Wilson, *Axel's Castle,* 25.

III: Color Plates

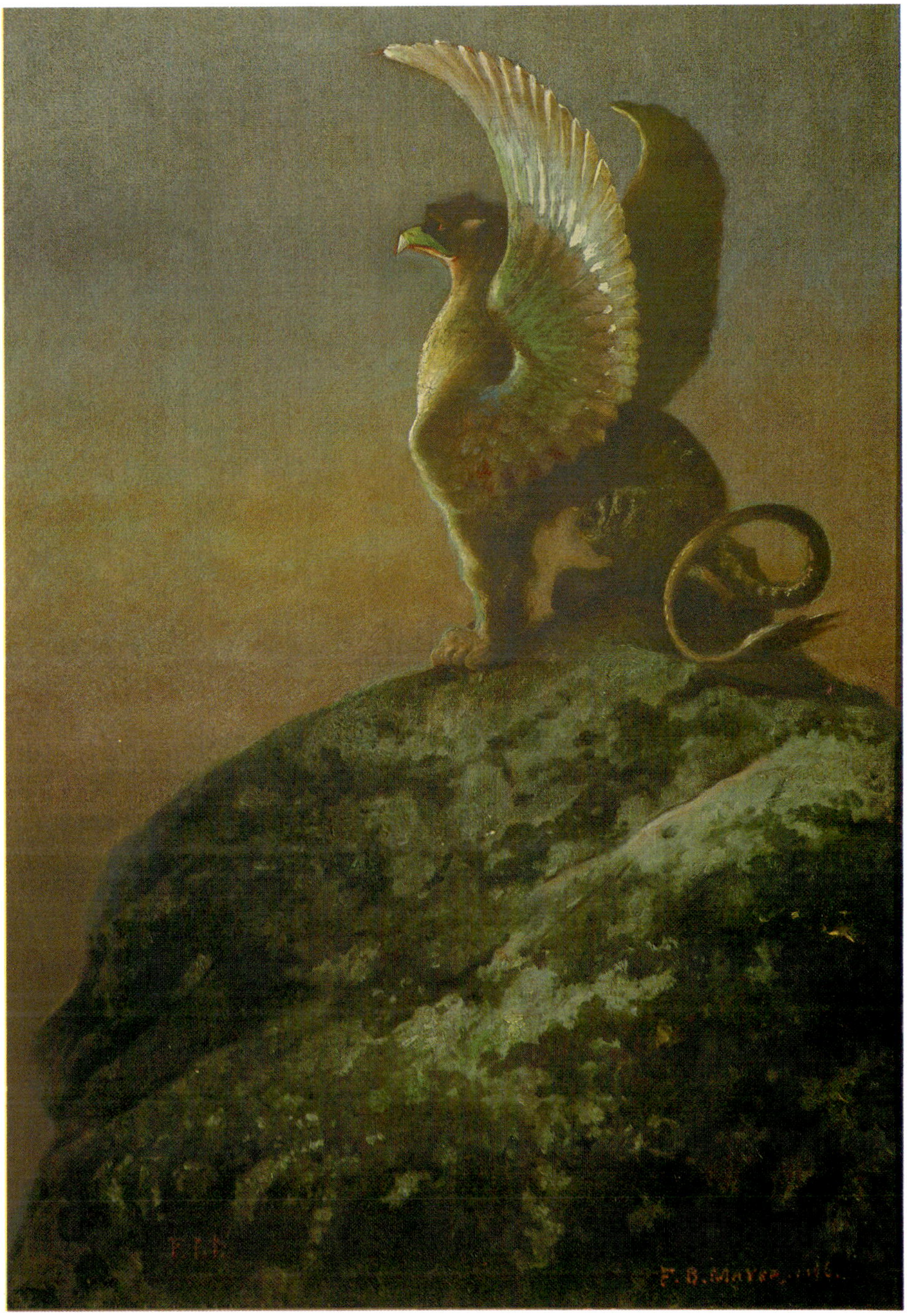

I. Frank B. Mayer, *Vigilance, The Gryphon,* cat. no. 42. (Photo by Eddie Owen.)

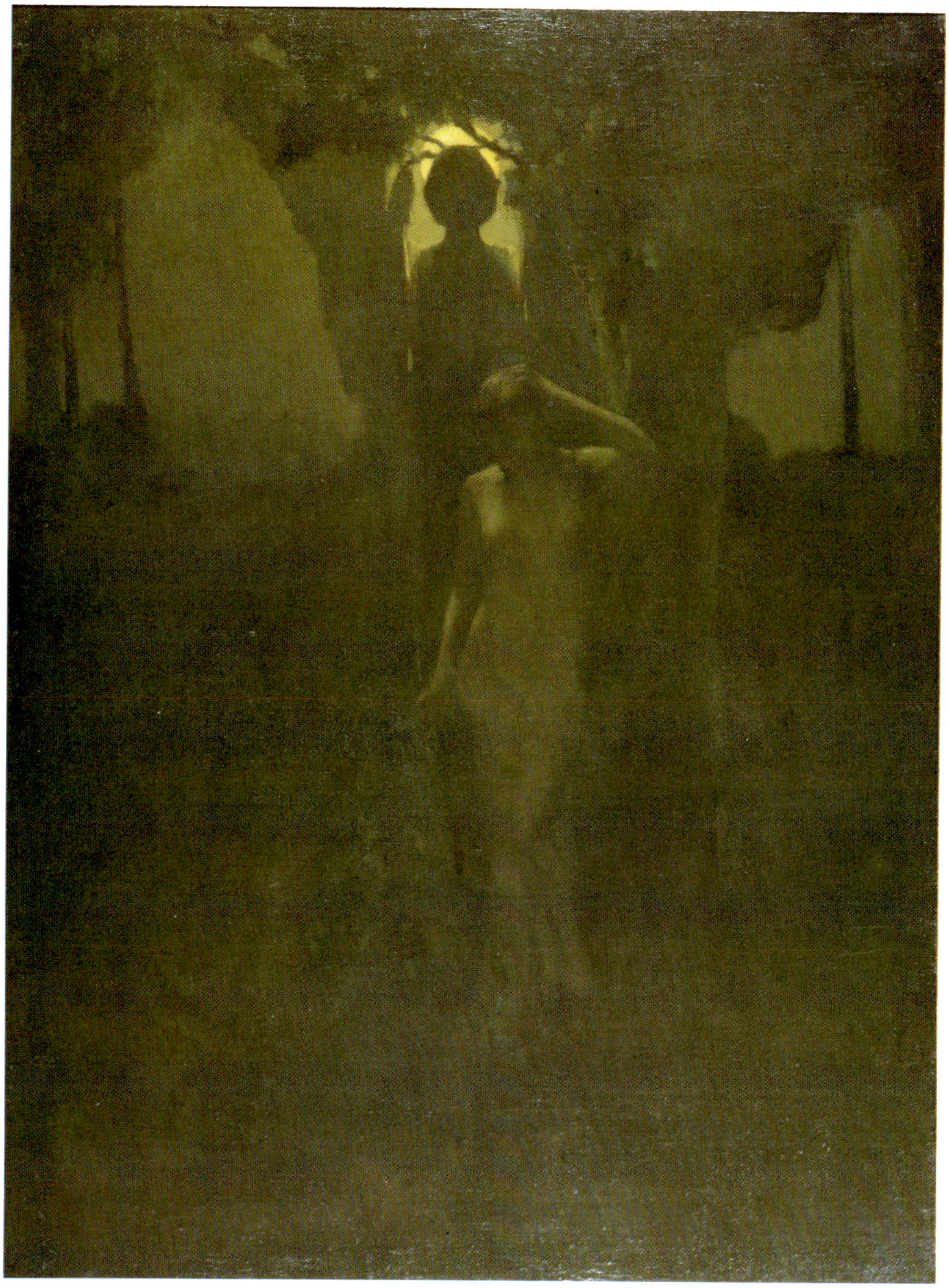

II. Arthur F. Mathews, *Eve,* cat. no. 41.

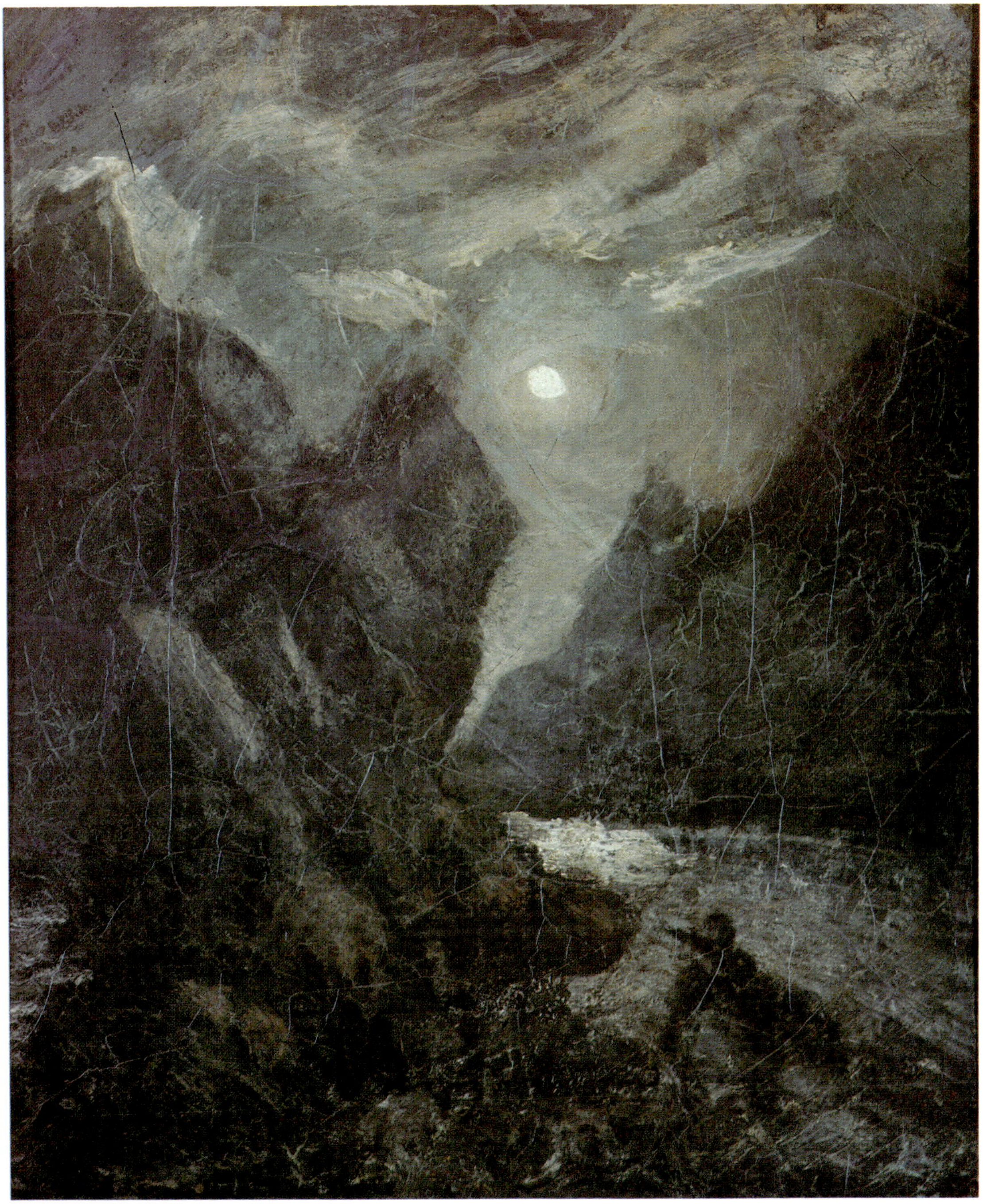

III. Albert P. Ryder, *The Lorelei,* cat. no. 52.

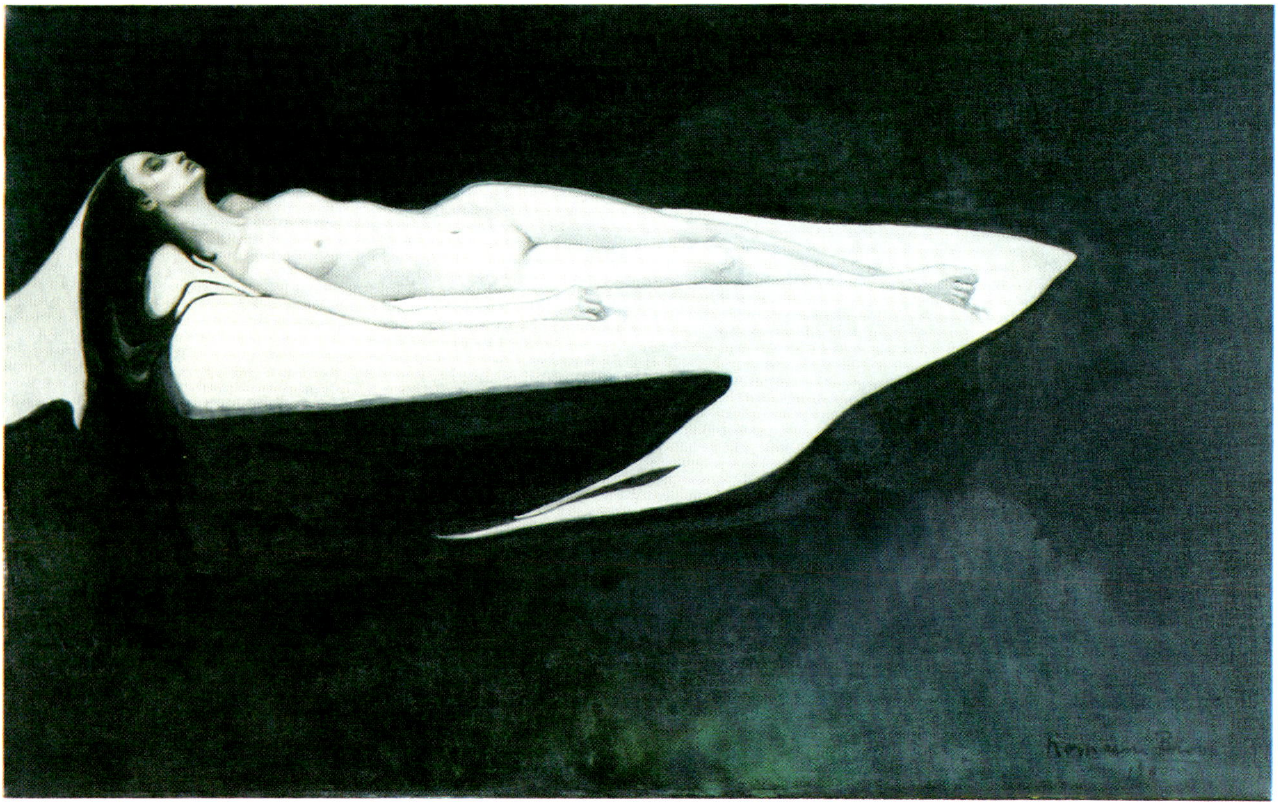

IV. Romaine Brooks, *Le Trajet,* 1911, cat. no. 5.

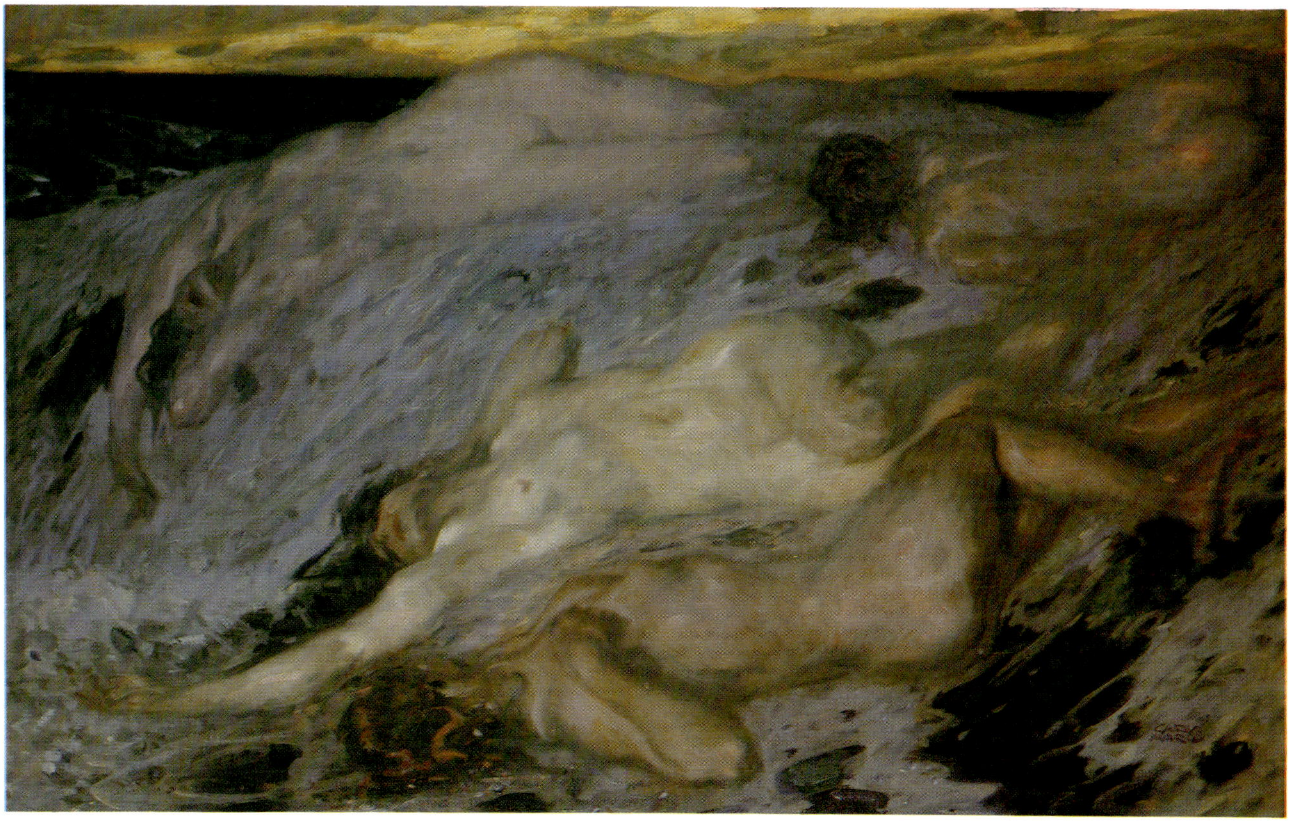

V. Carl Marr, *Mermaids,* cat. no. 39.

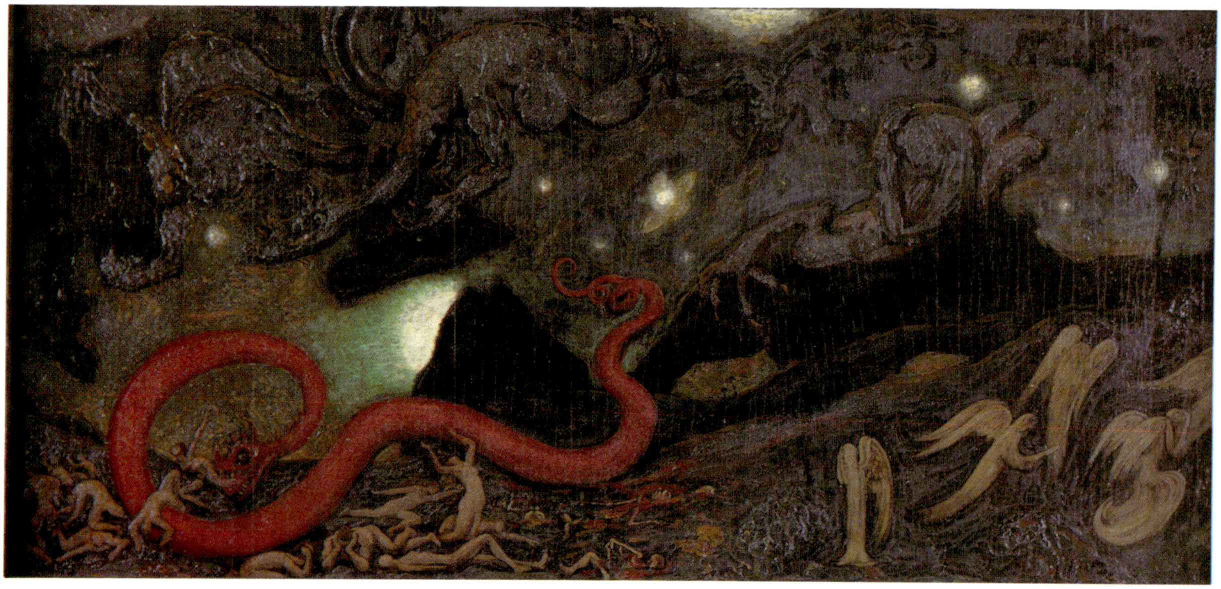

VI. Claude Buck, *The Conqueror Worm,* 1920, cat. no. 8.

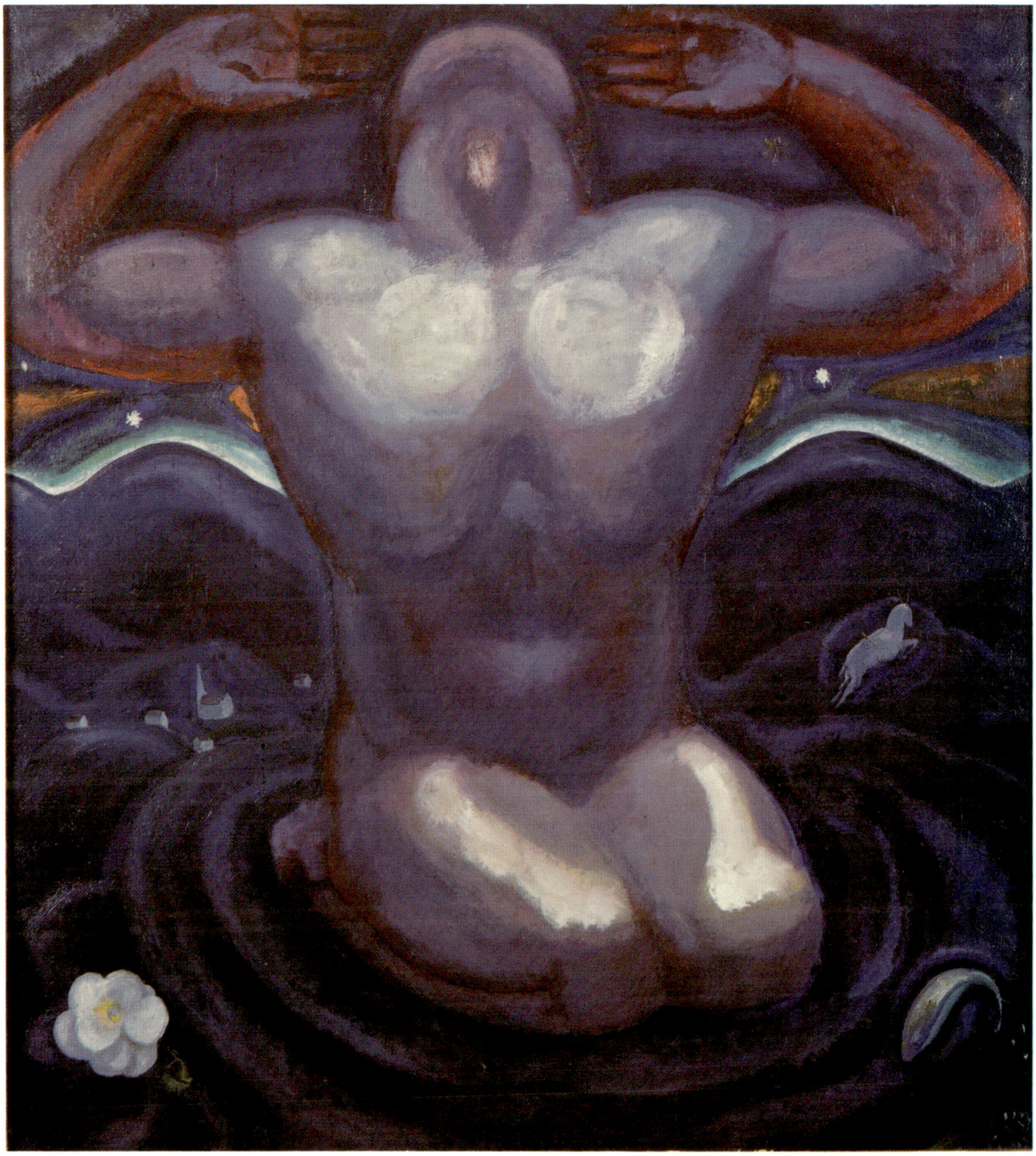

VII. Rockwell Kent, *Man Kneeling*, 1915, cat. no. 33.

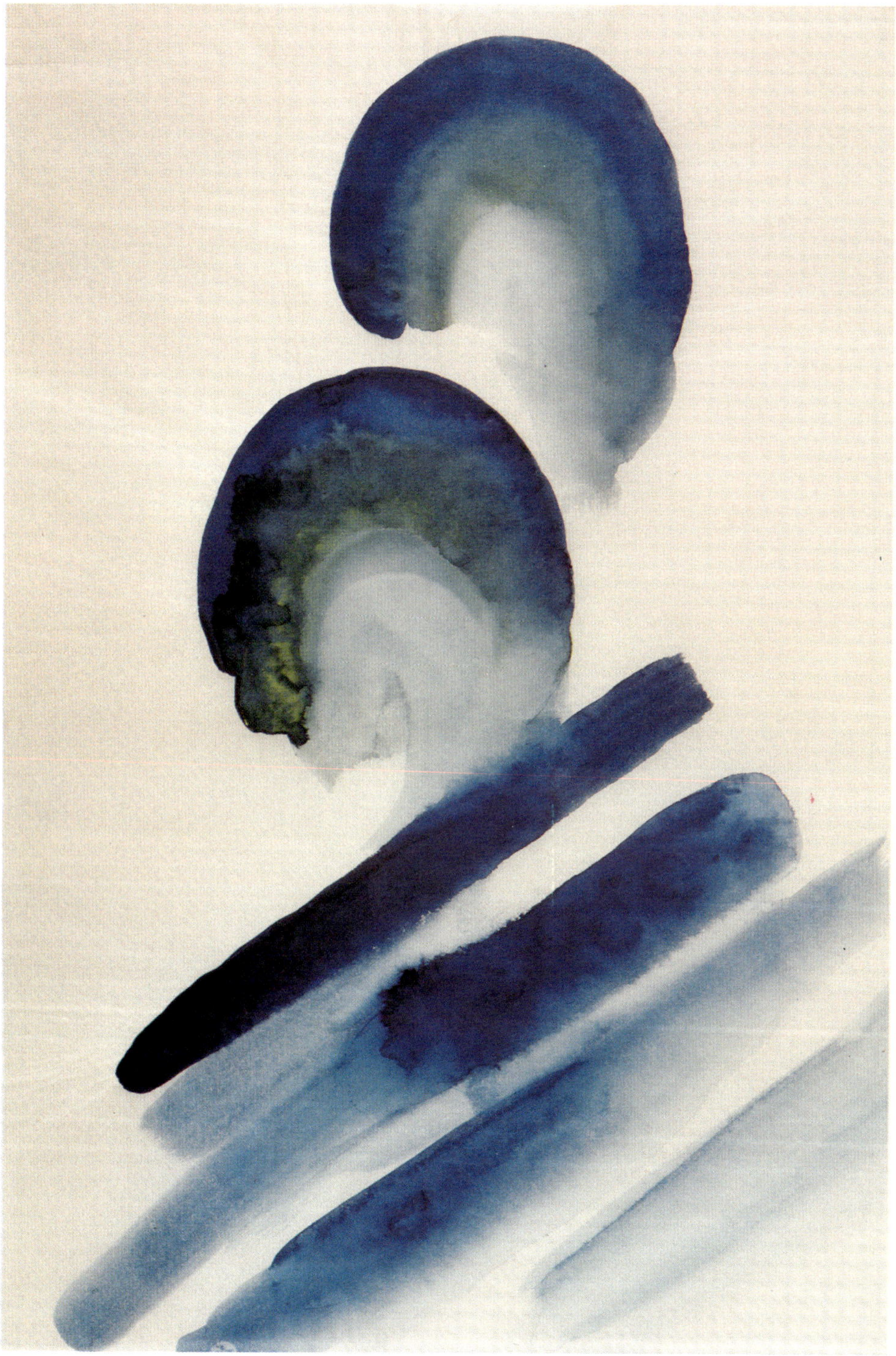

VIII. Georgia O'Keeffe, *Blue No. II,* 1916, cat. no. 46.

IV: Catalogue of the Exhibition

JOHN WHITE ALEXANDER
Allegheny, Pa., 1856-1915, New York City

Began career in New York as illustrator for *Harper's Weekly,* 1875. To Munich for study at Royal Academy in 1877, joining Duveneck and other Americans at Pölling, Bavaria, the next year. In 1879 to Venice with "Duveneck boys," where he was befriended by Whistler and Henry James. Returned to New York, 1881, and pursued portraiture for next decade. Settled in Paris, 1891, where Whistler introduced him to Mallarmé, Rodin, Mirbeau, Gide and others; marked change in his style in 1890s, due to association with Parisian Symbolists and aesthetes. Returned to New York, 1901. Elected to presidency of National Academy in 1909, a post he held until his death. Major mural commissions for Library of Congress (1895) and Carnegie Institute (1905).

1 **Memories,** 1903
Oil on canvas, 61¾ x 52″
Loaned by The Brooklyn Museum, Museum Collection Fund
(Shown in New York only)

Selected Bibliography:

Gabriel Mourey, "An American Painter in Paris: John W. Alexander," *International Studio,* 11 (August 1900), 71-77.

Charles H. Caffin, "John W. Alexander," *The World's Work,* IX:2 (December 1904), 5682-5698.

John W. Alexander, "The Art Outlook," *Art and Progress,* III:7 (May 1912), 573-580.

Address of Mr. John G. Agar . . . and Resolutions Adopted at the Testimonial to John W. Alexander (New York: Fine Arts Federation, 1916).

Cincinnati Museum, *Memorial Exhibition of Work by John White Alexander* (Cincinnati, 1917).

City Art Museum, *Memorial Exhibition of Paintings by John White Alexander* (St. Louis, 1917).

Mary Anne Goley, *John White Alexander (1856-1915)* (Washington: National Collection of Fine Arts, 1976).

ALICE PIKE BARNEY
Cincinnati, 1857(?)-1931, Los Angeles

Born to a wealthy and cultured family, Barney was raised in Ohio and New York City. First foreign travel to London, 1873-74, where she met and became engaged to explorer Henry Morton Stanley. Married railroad heir Albert Clifton Barney in 1876. Met Oscar Wilde in America in 1882; visited Wildes in London in 1885, where she socialized with Sargent, Zorn, Abbey and other artists. Resided primarily in Paris, 1886-89, and wintered there until 1902. Studied painting with Carolus-Duran at suggestion of Elizabeth Nourse, 1887-88; introduced to Whistler by John W. Alexander, and enrolled at Whistler's Academy Carmen, 1898. Befriended by Symbolist artists including Lévy-Dhurmer, who inspired her use of pastels, and Aman-Jean, and by Remy de Gourmont. Established American home in Washington, D.C. in 1890s, and moved there following husband's death in 1902. Built Studio House about 1902, to serve as culture center for capital, patterned after Whistler's White House. Leader in Washington art circles, as well as prominent in charitable and humanitarian projects. To Hollywood, California, 1925; built another studio, and organized the Theater Mart. Work includes portraiture (including G. B. Shaw, Whistler, Ruth St. Dennis, Alice Roosevelt Longworth, Wanda Landowska, and the Barney daughters, Natalie Barney and Laura Dreyfus-Barney) as well as figure studies, landscapes and imaginative themes.

2 **Woman and Peacock**
Oil on canvas, 28¾ x 46¼"
Loaned by the National Collection of Fine Arts, Smithsonian Institution, Gift of Laura Dreyfus Barney

Selected Bibliography:

Delight Hall, *Catalogue of the Alice Pike Barney Memorial Lending Collection* (Washington: National Collection of Fine Arts, 1963).

Donald R. McClelland, *Where Shadows Live: Alice Pike Barney and Her Friends* (Washington: National Collection of Fine Arts, 1978).

GEORGE RANDOLPH BARSE, JR.
Detroit, 1861-1938, Washington, D.C.

In Europe, 1879-1885, where he studied with Cabanel, Boulanger and Lefebvre at Ecole des Beaux-Arts and Academie Julian. Awarded Academy Prize in Paris, 1882. Worked in Rome, where he was befriended by Vedder. Elected to National Academyof Design, 1899; also a member of the Architectural League. Best known for portraits and figure paintings, and for murals (including Library of Congress commission). Committed suicide.

3 **Night and the Declining Day**, 1897
Oil on canvas, 80 x 40"
Loaned by Stuart Pivar

RALPH ALBERT BLAKELOCK

New York City, 1847-1919, near Elizabethtown, New York

Earliest surviving drawings, from circa 1865, show initial interest in landscape art, which persisted throughout career. Largely self-taught, possibly with the encouragement of James H. Johnson, a family friend and amateur painter. Enrolled in the Free Academy of the City of New York, 1864, where his physician father had urged him to study medicine; dropped out in 1866. Embarked on extensive trip through American West, 1869, which stimulated life-long interest in Indian motifs and landscape imagery; returned to New York, 1871. Married and moved to East Orange, N.J., 1877; employed briefly as painter of placques and decorative panels for Newark art factory. After late 1870s, paintings became less specific in locale; developed generalized moonlit landscape as central and definitive image. First breakdown in 1891 followed period of great poverty and little recognition; subsequent series of breakdowns culminated in severe one of 1899, after which he was committed to Middletown State Hospital for the Insane at Middletown, N.Y. Remained there almost continuously until his death. Reputation increased dramatically after he was institutionalized. Elected a full member of National Academy of Design in 1916; the same year he was given one-man show in New York, and Toledo Museum purchased painting for record price by living American artist.

4 **Vision of Life** (or **The Ghost Dance**), circa 1895
Oil on canvas, 21 1/8 x 39 3/8"
Loaned by The Art Institute of Chicago, Gift of Charles H. and Mary F. S. Worcester

Selected Bibliography:

Elliott Daingerfield, *Ralph Albert Blakelock* (New York: Frederick Fairchild Sherman, 1914).

J. W. Young, *Catalogue of the Works of R. A. Blakelock and Marian Blakelock* (Chicago: 1916).

Lloyd Goodrich, *Ralph Albert Blakelock Centenary Exhibition in Celebration of the Centennial of the City College of New York* (New York: Whitney Museum of American Art, 1947).

David Gebhard and Phyllis Sturman, *The Enigma of Ralph A. Blakelock 1847-1919* (Santa Barbara: University of California Art Galleries, 1969).

Sheldon Memorial Art Gallery, University of Nebraska, *Ralph Albert Blakelock 1847-1919* (Lincoln: 1975).

BEATRICE ROMAINE (GODDARD) BROOKS
Rome, 1874-1970, Nice, France

Born of American parents, and raised and educated mainly in Europe. To Paris, 1893; strained relationship with mother ended with break in 1895, father having previously abandoned family. To Rome to study art, 1896; enrolled at La Scuola Nazionale, which she left soon after, being uncomfortable as only woman in school. Summer in Capri, 1899; rented studio in abandoned chapel, and befriended by collector Charles Lang Freer, painter Charles C. Coleman, Somerset Maugham, poet John Brooks, and other members of Anglo-American community. At Freer's urging returned to Paris for study, 1899. Large inheritance after mother's death in 1902 insured financial security. Returned to Capri, 1903, and married Brooks, a celebrated homosexual; left him in 1904 and moved to London. Established friendship with Charles Conder; painted at St. Ives artists' colony, with palette newly restriced to Whistlerian grays. To Paris, 1905; befriended by Robert de Montesquieu, Paul Valery, Jean Cocteau, André Gide and other literary and artistic celebrities. One-woman exhibition at Durand-Ruel a critical success, 1910. Met Gabriel D'Annunzio in Paris, 1909; ensuing affair complicated by her relationship with Ballet Russe star, Ida Rubenstein, whom she met in 1910, and who served as model for a number of paintings. Met author Natalie Barney, circa 1915, and began enduring relationship which provided inspiration for both. Returned to Capri, 1918, and for several ensuing summers, where she was friendly with the Fitzgeralds, D. H. Lawrence, pianist Renata Borgatti, and other artists. Portraits of aristocrats and artists acclaimed during 1920s. Began distinctive drawings which rely on subconscious sources, mid-1920s; 50 drawings exhibited at Chicago Arts Club, 1935, occasioning extended and final visit to America. Essentially abandoned painting after 1930s.

5 **Le Trajet,** 1911
Oil on canvas, $45\frac{3}{8} \times 75\frac{3}{8}$"
Loaned by the National Collection of Fine Arts, Smithsonian Institution, Gift of the Artist

Selected Bibliography:

Paul Morand, Edouard MacAvoy and Michel Desbrueres, "Romaine Brooks," *Bizarre* (Paris), #46 (March 1968), entire issue.

Adelyn Breeskin, *Romaine Brooks, "Thief of Souls"* (Washington: National Collection of Fine Arts, 1971).

Meryle Secrest, *Between Me and Life: A Biography of Romaine Brooks* (Garden City, N.Y.: Doubleday, 1974).

ETHEL ISADORE BROWN
1871-?

Little is known about the artist. From 1897 to 1899, the Boston City Directory records her as living at 98 Chestnut Street in that city. Apparently travelled to Europe during that time: the painting in the exhibition is inscribed "Paris 1898," and in 1897 she exhibited "Luigi, Venice" at the National Academy of Design. From at least 1902-1906, taught painting, drawing and the history of art at St. Agnes School, Albany, N.Y. Her place of birth, and her place and date of death remain unknown.

6 **The Vision of St. John at Patmos,** 1898
Oil on canvas, 54¼ x 46"
Loaned by the National Collection of Fine Arts, Smithsonian Institution, Gift of Frances Smyth

---

CLAUDE BUCK
New York City, 1890-1974, Santa Barbara, California

Studied at National Academy of Design with Emil Carlsen, George DeForest Brush and Francis Jones, circa 1905-1912. Supported self as portraitist; painted imaginative compositions for own enjoyment, especially drawing upon Poe, circa 1907-1925. Organizer of The Introspectives inaugural exhibitions in New York in 1917 with Benjamin Kopman and Jennings Tofel. To Chicago in 1918, where he continued Introspectives exhibitions (1921) and taught at Chicago Art Institute and at Academy of Fine Arts (1920-1925). First trip to Europe in 1927. Urban genre scenes and portraiture of renewed importance from mid-1920s onward. Frequent exhibitor in Chicago area shows; awarded Shaffer Prize (1929) and Logan Medal (1932) by Art Institute of Chicago. To California in mid-1940s.

7 **Salome,** 1917
Oil on plywood, 8½ x 13½"
Loaned by Mrs. Claude Buck

8 **The Conqueror Worm,** 1920
Oil on plywood, 14 x 30"
Loaned by Mrs. Claude Buck

Selected Bibliography:

M. Knoedler & Co., *Imaginative Paintings by Thirty Young Artists of New York City* (New York, 1917).

Thurber Galleries, *Paintings by Claude Buck* (Chicago, 1920).

Claude Buck, "What is Art?" *Palos in Autumn,* no. 2 (1923), 3, 14.

Fred Koch-Wawra, *Who is Claude Buck?* (Chicago, n.d.).

FREDERICK STUART CHURCH
Grand Rapids, Michigan, 1842-1924, New York City

Directed by his parents toward a business career, Church worked from age thirteen to seventeen for the American Express Company in Chicago. Served in Union artillery during the Civil War, after which he settled in New York. Studied art with Walter Shirlaw and worked in commercial art and as illustrator for *Harper's Weekly*. Early illustrations often featured animals and were marked by humorous note. Active in foundation of Art Students League in 1875. First allegorical compositions produced in mid-1870s; feminine themes predominate from 1880s onward. Although a strong believer in academic training, Church did not visit Europe until late in life and felt that foreign art had little to teach Americans.

9 **Mermaids,** 1887
Oil on canvas, 13½ x 27″
Loaned by J. Harris Hudson

Selected Bibliography:

Walter Montgomery, editor, *American Art and American Art Collections*, II (Boston: Walker & Co., 1889), 529-540.

William St. John Harper, "F. S. Church: A Painter of the Ideal," *The Outlook* (November 25, 1905), 750-760.

WILLIAM BAXTER CLOSSON
Thetford, Vermont, 1848-1926, Hartford, Connecticut

About 1870, Closson was introduced to wood engraver's art, a medium in which he chose to instruct himself; subsequently apprenticed to wood engraver in Boston, and quickly developed expertise and reputation in medium. Studio in same Boston building as George Fuller, who became close friend and whose work he frequently engraved; also engraved works by G. F. Watts, C. W. Stetson, J. F. Millet, W. Rimmer, E. Burne-Jones and others, as well as his own compositions. Engraved independently for numerous publications in 1880s; Harper & Bros. sent him to Europe to engrave Old Masters, 1882. Engravings exhibited widely and often gained awards, including Paris Exposition, 1889, World's Columbian Exposition, Chicago, 1893, Graphic Arts Exposition, Vienna, 1901. Achieved acclaim for new engraving technique which he invented. With rise of photoreproductive techniques and demise of wood engraving, turned to painting in oil and pastel, 1894. Concentrated on landscapes and figure paintings; exhibited at Museum of Fine Arts, Boston, with Augustus Tack, 1910.

10 **The Angel,** 1912
Oil on canvas, 57⅛ x 37⅜″
Loaned by the National Collection of Fine Arts, Smithsonian Institution

Even an angel might find the coming into The Presence—
Into The Great White Light—too overpowering,
And clutch her wings to arrest her upward flight,
Turning away her face with closed eyes. W. B. C.

Selected Bibliography:

William B. Closson, "Fuller's Work Judged by an Engraver," in *George Fuller: His Life and Works* (Boston: Houghton, Mifflin, 1886), 80-85.

Vose Galleries, *The Closson Memorial Exhibition,* (Boston: 1927).

Earl Marlatt, "Multiple Personality in Art," *The Journal of Expression,* I:2 (September 1927), 93-97.

CHARLES COURTNEY CURRAN
Hartford, Kentucky, 1861-1942, New York City

Initial art training at Cincinnati School of Design. Studied in New York at the National Academy of Design and Art Students League, in 1880s, and in Paris at Académie Julian. Feminine subjects predominate in his painting, with images drawn both from contemporary life and from myth and imagination. A leader of the Cragsmoor, N.Y., artists' colony in early years of this century, specializing in rural genre scenes painted with lightened palette and loose stroke. Elected to membership in National Academy, 1904.

11 **Bacchanal,** 1890
Oil on canvas, 12½ x 15½"
Loaned by Kennedy Galleries

12 **Scent of the Rose,** 1890
Oil on panel, 4½ x 12"
Loaned by Beverly and Ray Sacks

ELLIOTT DAINGERFIELD
Harper's Ferry, Virginia, 1849-1932, New York City

Raised in Fayetteville, N.C., where father was Confederate army officer; apprenticed to local photographer. Ambition for further training took him to New York in 1880, where he studied with Walter Satterlee and attended Art Students League. Moved into Holbein Studios, New York, in 1884, where he befriended George Inness and Kenyon Cox. First trip to Blowing Rock, N.C., 1886, where he later built three studio homes. Early Inness influence on his landscape painting replaced after mid-1890s by religious and allegorical subjects. First trip to Grand Canyon, 1911, inspired series of visionary landscapes. Late in life returned to Blowing Rock studio and rustic, Barbizon-like imagery of his youth. In addition to easel paintings, worked as muralist, art teacher, poet and author.

13 **The Mystic Brim,** 1893
Oil on canvas, 30 x 36⅛″
Loaned by Robert P. Coggins, M.D.

14 **The Sleepers,** 1914
Oil on canvas, 36 x 48⅛″
Loaned by Robert P. Coggins, M.D.

Age on age the Sleepers rest,
To see in dreams the Canyon's splendor rise
Height on height, from river bed to golden crest.
Gods are they!—as you and I—
Who see in spirit what the eyes deny. E.D.

Selected Bibliography:

Elliott Daingerfield, *George Inness: The Man and His Art* (New York: Frederick Fairchild Sherman, 1911).

Elliott Daingerfield, "Nature Versus Art," *Scribner's Magazine,* XLIX (February 1911), 253-256.

Elliott Daingerfield, "Color and Form—Their Relationship." *The Art World,* III (December 1917), 179-180.

Grand Central Art Galleries, *Memorial Exhibition: Paintings, Water Colors, Drawings by Elliott Daingerfield* (New York: 1934).

Robert Hobbs, *Elliott Daingerfield Retrospective Exhibition* (Charlotte, N.C.: Mint Museum of Art, 1971).

ARTHUR BOWEN DAVIES

Utica, New York, 1862-1928, Florence

Began art studies with Dwight Williams in Utica, 1877; with family moved to Chicago following year, and continued studies at Chicago Art Academy and at Art Institute of Chicago. Worked as engineering draftsman in Mexico, 1880-1882. To New York to work as illustrator, 1886; studies continue at school of the Gotham Art Students and at Art Students League. First exhibition with American Art Galleries, New York, 1888; showed at National Academy, 1893, selling first painting. To Europe for first time, 1893, on trip sponsored by Benjamin Altman; European works included in Macbeth Gallery show on his return, beginning a long association with the dealer. First one-man show at Macbeth, 1896; persuaded Macbeth to exhibit "The Eight", 1908. California trip, 1905, where the landscape inspired many of his best-known works. President of the Association of American Painters and Sculptors and primary organizer of the Armory Show, 1913; modernist influences apparent in work from circa 1913-1920. Renewed interest in printmaking circa 1918. Late works included tapestry design for Gobelin Works in France, rediscovery of Greek theory of "inhalation" with Gustavus Eisen, and paintings of Italy in 1920s. Developed large personal art collection, reflecting eclectic tastes: Puvis de Chavannes, Blake, Redon, Maillol, Picasso.

15 **Chalice**, 1897
Oil on canvas, 31 x 22½″
Loaned by the Everson Museum of Art, Gift of the Children of Mrs. William S. Ladd

16 **Sleep**, circa 1905
Oil on canvas, 18⅛ x 40″
Loaned by the Worcester Art Museum

17 **Dream** (or **Measure of Dreams**), 1909
Oil on canvas, 18 x 30″
Loaned by The Metropolitan Museum of Art, Gift of George A. Hearn

Selected Bibliography:

Macbeth Gallery, *Loan Exhibition of Paintings, Watercolors, Drawings, Etchings and Sculpture by Arthur B. Davies* (New York: 1918).

Arthur B. Davies: Essays on the Man and his Art, Phillips Collection Publications #3 (Cambridge, Mass: Riverside Press, 1924). Reprinted with new illustrations as *Arthur B. Davies: Essays on His Art* (New York: Arco Publishing Co., 1974).

Munson-Williams-Proctor Institute, *Arthur B. Davies, 1862-1928* (Utica: 1962).

Brooks Wright, *The Artist and the Unicorn: The Lives of Arthur B. Davies (1862-1928)* (New City, N.Y.: Historical Society of Rockland County, 1978).

MANIERRE DAWSON

Chicago, 1887-1969, Sarasota, Florida

Born to a cultured Chicago family, Dawson was raised in an atmosphere where artistic pursuits were encouraged as an avocation but not as a profession. At parents' urging attended Armour Institute of Technology and joined design department at Holabird and Roche architectural firm, 1909. Self-taught in painting, which he began in 1903 and continued as his major interest until 1920. Early Whistlerian nature studies followed by "cartoon" or "play" paintings, 1906-1908, which emphasized simplified figurative compositions; aware of Davies' work, through mutual Chicago friend, and Davies' influence appears after about 1906. By 1909, aware of Cézanne, and in early 1910 produced a series of virtually non-objective paintings. First trip to Europe, 1910; introduced to Gertrude Stein in Paris, to whom he made first sale. Returned to New York, where he met Davies, who introduced him to Ryder. In Chicago, 1911, worked independently on futurist-like variation of cubism. Included in Chicago exhibit of Armory Show, 1913; encouraged by reception of work, left Holabird and Roche, to pursue painting career. Included in Davies' *Exhibition 14* and Milwaukee Art Society's *Art in the Modern Spirit* shows, 1914. Same year, moved to Ludington, Michigan, to manage his farm property in summer, paint in winter; farm and family responsibilities curtailed time for painting, which he abandoned after 1920.

18 **Figures on Pale Blue**, 1906
Oil on canvas, 26 x 16″
Loaned by Dr. and Mrs. Edwin J. De Costa

Selected Bibliography:

Museum of Contemporary Art, *Mannierre Dawson (1887-1969): A Retrospective Exhibition of Painting* (Chicago, 1976).

THOMAS WILMER DEWING
Boston, Massachusetts, 1851-1938, New York City

During Boston childhood received little formal education; worked briefly for a lithographer, and studied music to the point that he played violin in theater orchestra. Moved to Albany, where he established self as portraitist, working in chalks. With accumulated savings from portrait commissions travelled to Paris, 1876; studied with Boulanger and Lefebvre at Académie Julian, and at École des Beaux Arts. To New York City, 1880, where he taught at Art Students League, 1881-1888. Summers spent at art colony in Cornish, N.H., 1885-1902, with Saint-Gaudens, Brush, Cox, Metcalf, and others. Elected to Society of American Artists, 1880, and to full membership in National Academy of Design, 1888. Frequent exhibitor of decorative compositions based on women in interiors and landscapes, which were influenced by Whistler and Oriental art. With Weir and others founded Ten American Painters, 1898. Patronised particularly by Charles Lang Freer, founder of Freer Gallery of Art which includes many of his paintings.

19 **The Garden** (or **Spring Moonlight**), circa 1891
Oil on canvas, $20\frac{5}{8}$ x 35″
Loaned by the National Collection of Fine Arts, Smithsonian Institution, Gift of John Gellatly

Selected Bibliography:

Royal Cortissoz, "Some Imaginative Types in American Art," *Harper's New Monthly Magazine,* XCI (July 1895), 165-179.

Charles H. Caffin, "The Art of Thomas W. Dewing," *Harper's Magazine,* CXVI:695 (April 1903), 714-724.

Nelson C. White, "The Art of Thomas W. Dewing," *Art and Archaeology,* XXVII (June 1929), 253-261.

Durlacher Brothers, *A Loan Exhibition: Thomas W. Dewing, 1851-1938* (New York: 1963).

ARTHUR GARFIELD DOVE

Canandaigua, New York, 1880-1946, Huntington, New York

A precocious student, Dove began art lessons at age nine with Newton Weatherly in Geneva, N.Y., where he also attended school. Attended Hobart College and graduated from Cornell University, 1903. Worked as illustrator before going to Europe for further art study in 1908. Worked with Alfred Maurer in Paris; exhibited in Salons of 1908 and 1909. Returned to New York, 1909, and met Stieglitz, who included his paintings in 1910 group show. Created first abstractions, circa 1910. Worked on pastels of abstract symbols of natural forces, generically titled *The Ten Commandments,* 1910-1912. First one-man show at Stieglitz's gallery, 1912, was subsequently exhibited at Thurber Galleries, Chicago. Sponsored by Stieglitz and exhibited often with him thereafter. Included in Forum Exhibition of Modern American Paintings, 1916. Lived in Westport, Conn., 1910 to 1920, when he left his family; bought yawl about 1920, and lived on it in Huntington Harbor with second wife, the painter Helen Torr, 1920-1933. Began series of collages, mid-1920s. Duncan Phillips purchased two paintings from Stieglitz's 1925 Dove exhibition, beginning his lifelong interest in the artist. Growing critical acclaim in 1930s. Returned to family home in Geneva, N.Y., 1934; productive four-year period ensued, despite poor finances and health. Returned to Long Island, 1938, and lived in Centerport until death.

20 **Movement No. 1,** circa 1911 (from *The Ten Commandments*)
Pastel on canvas, 21⅜ x 18″
Loaned by the Columbus Museum of Art

Selected Bibliography:

Frederick S. Wight, *Arthur G. Dove* (Berkeley: University of California Press, 1958).

Barbara Haskell, *Arthur Dove* (San Francisco Museum of Art, 1974).

FRANK VINCENT DUMOND

Rochester, New York, 1865-1951, New York City

Enrolled at Art Students League in 1884; combined studies with illustration for *The Daily Graphic* and *Harper's Weekly.* Studied in Paris with Boulanger, Lefebvre and Benjamin-Constant, 1886. Began teaching at Art Students League, 1892, a post he held for 59 years; students included John Marin, Georgia O'Keeffe, Eugene Speicher and other prominent painters. Specialized in portraiture and landscape painting, which was often done near his studios in Pownal, Vt., and Old Lyme, Ct. Associated with the Old Lyme art colony from its early days until 1941, when he moved to New York City.

21 **Figures in Landscape,** 1902
Oil on canvas, 16 x 22″
Loaned by Lyme Historical Society, Inc., Gift of Mrs. Roger Griswold

---

LOUIS MICHAEL EILSHEMIUS
near Newark, New Jersey, 1864-1941, New York City

Born to a wealthy and socially prominent family, Eilshemius often travelled to Europe, where he received his early education. Art training at Art Students League and Académie Julian, after two years at Cornell University. Returned from Paris to New York in 1888; produced landscapes in Barbizon mode. Inheritance from father allowed for extensive travel to Europe, North Africa (1892), California and the Southwest, and Samoa (1901-1902). Established permanently in New York about 1911, with little travel thereafter; prolific period ensued, marked by New York City views and distinctive and comical nudes. Despite productivity, achieved little recognition until "discovered" by Marcel Duchamp at 1917 exhibition of Society of Independent Artists; acquired reputation among avant garde, and received first one-man show with Société Anonyme in 1920. Critical and public hostility to exhibition led to abandonment of painting, and began long period of mental and physical decline. Paralyzed by auto accident and confined to his room as his brother's dependent from 1932 to his death.

22 **Afternoon Wind,** 1899
Oil on canvas, 20 x 36″
Loaned by The Museum of Modern Art, New York, given anonymously

23 **The Demon on the Rocks,** 1901
Oil on cardboard, 20 x 15⅛″
Loaned by The Museum of Modern Art, New York,
Gift of Fania Marinoff Van Vechten in memory of Carl Van Vechten

Selected Bibliography:

Paul Karlstrom, *The Romanticism of Eilshemius* (New York: Bernard Danenberg Galleries, 1973).

Paul Karlstrom, *Louis Michael Eilshemius* (New York: Abrams, 1978).

KAHLIL GIBRAN
Besharri, Lebanon, 1883-1931, New York City

Emigrated to America and settled in Boston, 1895. Met F. Holland Day, photographer, publisher and aesthete, 1896, who introduced him to circle of Boston artists and writers. Influenced by Blake, Beardsley and Burne-Jones, as well as Maeterlinck and Richard Hovey. To Beirut to complete education, 1898. Returned to America via Paris, 1902. Exchanged Arabic and English poetry and drawings with poet Josephine Peabody, who helped arrange exhibition of his visionary drawings at Wellesley College, 1903. To

Paris for art study at Académie Julian, 1908; left Académie for art lessons with Pierre Marcel-Beronneau, a Gustave Moreau disciple, 1909. Impressed by work of Puvis de Chavannes and Eugene Carriére. To London, summer 1910, where he discovered Turner. Drew portraits of prominent artists for *Temple of Art* series, including Rodin, Paul Bartlett, Debussy. Returned to Boston, autumn 1910; moved to New York, 1911, where he continued interest in poetry and contact with Arabic literary and political events, as well as pursuing his art. Met Davies, who admired his work, 1913. One-man exhibition at Montross Gallery, 1914, drew praise of Ryder, who became a friend. Rodin influence apparent in wash drawings first exhibited in one-man show at Knoedler's, 1917. Growing emphasis on poetry, much of which he illustrated; published *The Prophet,* 1923.

24 **The Ages of Women,** 1910
Oil on canvas, 38 x 57"
Loaned by Jean and Kahlil Gibran

Selected Bibliography:

Jean Gibran and Kahlil Gibran, *Kahlil Gibran: His Life and World* (Boston: New York Graphic Society, 1974).

CARL GUTHERZ

Schoeftland, Switzerland, 1844-1907, Washington, D.C.

Brought to America in 1851, Gutherz was raised near Cincinnati and in Memphis. Father died at early age, leaving son to support self as mechanical draughtsman; with his savings, embarked for Paris in 1868 for art study at Académie des Beaux-Arts, and later with Pils, Lefebvre and Boulanger. During Franco-Prussian War worked in Brussels, Munich, and Rome; returned to Memphis, 1872, thence to St. Louis in 1874 to teach art at Washington University. Returned to Paris, 1884, for twelve year residence, the most productive phase of career, with concentration on large salon paintings and mural compositions; close friend of leading Parisian academicians, and of Puvis de Chavannes. Moved to Washington in 1896 to complete mural commission for Library of Congress, and lived there until his death. In addition to religious and allegorical compositions, worked as portraitist, painting such notables as Gen. Robert E. Lee, Jefferson Davis and Susan B. Anthony.

25 **Arcessita ab Angelus,** 1889
Oil on canvas, 60 x 78"
Loaned by the Brooks Memorial Art Gallery, Gift of Marshall F. Goodheart

Selected Bibliography:

Lilian Whiting, "The Art of Carl Gutherz," *The International Studio,* XXIV:96 (February 1905), 1xxxi-1xxxvii.

Joseph S. Czestochowski, Jr., *Carl Gutherz: Designs for Memphis Celebrations 1873-1881* (Memphis: Brooks Memorial Art Gallery, 1974).

PHILIP LESLIE HALE
Boston, 1865-1931, Boston

Part of a distinguished New England family, whose lineage traced back to the colonial period, Hale was born into the elegant, aristocratic world he often portrayed in his paintings. Studied art at Boston Museum School, at Art Students League and with Weir in New York, and in Paris at École des Beaux-Arts and Académie Julian. Exhibited with Durand-Ruel in Paris in 1891; first one-man show in New York at Durand-Ruel, 1899. Successful career as teacher at the school of the Museum of Fine Arts, Boston, for over thirty years; frequent exhibitor and award winner at major international expositions after 1900, contributing mainly figurative works. Married painter Lilian C. Westcott, 1902. Periodically acted as art critic for Boston press; published study of *Jan Vermeer of Delft*, 1913, an artist he especially admired.

26 **Moonlit Pool,** circa 1918
Oil on canvas, 47½ x 72″
Loaned by Franklin P. Folts

Selected Bibliography:

Vose Galleries, *Paintings & Drawings by Philip Leslie Hale, 1865-1931, from the Folts Collection* (Boston, 1966).

MARSDEN HARTLEY
Lewiston, Maine, 1877-1943, Ellsworth, Maine

Childhood in Maine; later moved to Cleveland where he began study at Cleveland School of Art. To New York, circa 1898; studied at Chase School and with Mora, DuMond. Enrolled in National School of Design, 1900. Summers in Maine and winters in New York, 1901-1909, painting small impressionist mountain scenes in Segantini manner, then "black landscapes" influenced by Ryder. First exhibition at Stieglitz's "291" Gallery, 1909. First European trip, made with help of Stieglitz and Davies, 1912-1913; experimented with cubism, and exhibited with Der Blaue Reiter in Munich. Exhibited in Armory Show, 1913. Returned to Europe, 1914; in Berlin, 1915-1916, continuing experiments with abstract paintings, which were exhibited in one-man show at house of Max Liebermann. Returned to America, 1916, and during next two years painted in Provincetown, Mass., Ogunquit, Me., and Bermuda as well as New York. First trip to New Mexico, 1919-1920. To Europe, 1922, where he lived in Berlin (1922-1923), Paris and Venice (1924-1926), Aix-en-Provence (1926-1928), Paris and London

(1929). Returned to New England, 1930, with renewed interest in native landscape. Travel to Mexico, 1932-1933, where he painted deeply colored landscapes which often included esoteric symbols; subsequently to Germany, where produced series of Bavarian mountain views. To New York and Maine, 1934, which thereafter formed the poles of his seasonal painting. Renewed importance of Maine landscape in late works. In addition to painting published poetry and criticism.

27 **Musical Theme (Oriental Symphony)**, 1912-1913
Oil on canvas, 39⅜ x 31¾″
Loaned by the Brandeis University Art Collection, Rose Art Museum,
Gift of Samuel Lustgarten

Selected Bibliography:

Gallery of the Photo-Secession, *An Exhibition of Paintings by Marsden Hartley* (New York: 1914).

Marsden Hartley, *Adventures in the Arts: Informal Chapters on Painters, Vaudeville and Poets* (New York: Boni & Liveright, 1921).

Museum of Modern Art, *Lionel Feininger/Marsden Hartley* (New York: 1944).

Elizabeth McCausland, *Marsden Hartley* (Minneapolis: University of Minnesota Press, 1952).

Stedelijk Museum, *Marsden Hartley* (Amsterdam: 1961).

C. BERTRAM HARTMAN
Junction City, Kansas, 1882-1960, New York City

Initial art studies at Art Institute of Chicago; early work depicted midwestern, especially native Kansas landscape. Subsequent residence and study in Paris and Munich, circa 1911-13; influenced by post-Impressionist innovations in development of fanciful European works. Returned to Chicago, 1913, thence to New York which was his home from 1915 onward. Designed batiks, circa 1915-1919; later turned to urban views, and New England landscapes, which were frequently exhibited in New York in 1920s and '30s. Participated in government art projects (WPA/FAP) for Oneonta Hospital and New York University, 1930s.

28 **Pearls,** 1911
Oil on canvas, 40⅜ x 40½″
Loaned by the Spencer Museum of Art, The University of Kansas
Gift of Mr. and Mrs. Ralph L. Weir

GEORGE HITCHCOCK
Providence, Rhode Island, 1850-1913, Insel Marken, Holland

Originally trained as lawyer. Abandoned that profession to study painting with Boulanger and Lefebvre at Académie Julian, Paris, and with Mesdag in Holland. Worked with Gari Melchers at Egmond-aan-Zee, Holland, on the North Sea, from circa 1885 until after 1900. First exhibited at Paris Salon, 1887; awarded gold medal at Paris Exposition, 1889, for Dutch subject of type which brought him popular acclaim at end of century. Also painted religious themes, often posed in Dutch guise.

29 **Blessed Mother,** 1892
Oil on canvas, 62¼ x 44″
Loaned by The Cleveland Museum of Art, Gift of Mr. and Mrs. J. H. Wade

30 **The Annunciation**
Oil on canvas, 65 x 39½″
Loaned by the Raydon Gallery

GEORGE INNESS
near Newburgh, New York, 1825-1894, Bridge-of-Allen, Scotland

Apprenticed as map engraver in New York City, 1841, but interest soon shifted to painting. Brief instruction from Regis Gignoux, circa 1843. Began regular participation in annual exhibitions of National Academy of Design, 1844; exhibited regularly with American Art Union, 1845-1851. Opened first studio in New York, 1846, where he worked until 1859; frequent trips to Italy and France, where he was influenced by Barbizon landscape painters. Moved to Medfield, a Boston suburb, 1859, thence to Eagleswood, N.J., circa 1864. In New Jersey, influenced by his neighbor, William Page, in use of layered transparent glazes, and introduced by him to Swedenborgianism. Resident in England, France and Italy, 1870-1875. Moved to Montclair, N.J., 1878, and began association with the prominent collector, Thomas B. Clarke. Achieved financial and popular success in 1880s, while living in Montclair; maintained New York studio and frequently traveled throughout the United States, and in Canada, Mexico and Cuba. Continued study of Swedenborg's doctrines, which came to have pronounced effect on late paintings. Worked in California, 1891, with William Keith, also a landscapist and Swedenborgian. Final trip to Europe, 1894, visiting Germany and France before unexpected death in Scotland.

31 **The Gleaners,** 1893
Oil on canvas, 26 x 36″
Loaned by the Spencer Museum of Art, The University of Kansas,
The William Bridges Thayer Memorial

Selected Bibliography:
Elliott Daingerfield, *George Inness: The Man and His Art* (New York: Frederick Fairchild Sherman, 1911).

George Inness, Jr., *Life, Art and Letters of George Inness* (New York: Century and Co., 1917).

Elizabeth McCausland, *George Inness, An American Landscape Painter, 1825-1894* (Springfield, Mass.: The George Walter Vincent Smith Art Museum, 1946).

LeRoy Ireland, *The Works of George Inness, An Illustrated Catalogue Raisonné* (Austin: University of Texas Press, 1965).

Nicolai Cikovsky, Jr., *George Inness* (New York: Praeger, 1971).

Marjorie Dakin Arkelian and George W. Neubert, *George Inness Landscapes: His Signature Years, 1884-1894* (Oakland, Cal.: Oakland Museum, 1978).

ROCKWELL KENT

Tarrytown Heights, New York, 1881-1971, Plattsburgh, New York

Best known as painter and illustrator, Kent began by studying architecture at Columbia University; painting instruction from William M. Chase, and later from Robert Henri. Summer, 1905, painted with Abbott Thayer in New Hampshire; two of the resulting canvases accepted into winter National Academy exhibition, and resulted in his first sales. To Monhegan Island, Maine, at Henri's suggestion in 1906, where he painted for several years; 1907 exhibition of Monhegan paintings in New York a critical success but financial failure. Alternated architectural drafting jobs with New England landscape painting. First trip to Newfoundland, 1910, followed by several year's residence in Brigus, 1915-1917. Arctic landscapes also painted in Alaska and Greenland. Published books on his travels and art, which also detail a philosophy drawn from William Blake and Nietzsche; designed his books as complete entities with concern for compatible typeface, illustrations and binding design. Prolific work in illustration and printmaking, especially during 1920s and '30s. Established studio at Ausable Forks, N.Y., 1920s, which was to remain his home until death. Political involvement with liberal causes in 1930s led eventually to attacks by Sen. McCarthy in 1953, resulting in Kent's ostracism. Received Lenin Peace Prize, 1967, and assigned monetary award to the people of North Vietnam.

32 **Nocturnal Dance,** circa 1905
Oil on canvas, 22 x 42¼″
Loaned by the Baker-Pisano Collection

33 **Man Kneeling,** 1915
Oil on canvas, 30 x 28″
Loaned by the Spencer Museum of Art, The University of Kansas

Selected Bibliography:
Rockwell Kent, *It's Me O Lord: The Autobiography of Rockwell Kent* (New York: Dodd, Mead & Co., 1955).

JOHN LA FARGE
New York City, 1835-1910, Providence, Rhode Island

Born to a cultured emigré family, La Farge's liberal education was encouraged by his father, who also supported his early artistic training. Travelled to Europe, 1856; modelled for Puvis de Chavannes and studied with Thomas Couture in Paris, 1857. Impressed by Velasquez and pre-Raphaelites during Continental travels prior to returning to America, late 1857. Continued his earlier legal training before opting for art. Studied with Couture's friend, William Morris Hunt, in Newport, R. I., 1859. Landscapes and still lifes as well as illustrations during 1860s show influence of pre-Raphaelites and Japanese art. European trip, 1873; visited with Burne-Jones, F. M. Brown and the Rossettis. Career as decorator began with commission to decorate Trinity Church, Boston, 1876. Began experiments with stained glass, 1877, a medium in which he pioneered in America. Maintained friendships with numerous leading painters in Europe and America, as well as with American literary and social leaders such as Henry and William James and Henry Adams. Accompanied Adams and Ernest Fenollosa to Japan, 1886; increased interest in Oriental religion and in Japanese art, which he avidly collected. Travelled with Adams to the South Seas, 1891. Lectured and published frequently on art history and aesthetic theory.

34 **The Strange Little Thing Kiosai Saw in the River,** 1897
(from *Fantasies on Oriental Themes*)
Watercolor on paper, 12¾ x 18″
Loaned by The Metropolitan Museum of Art, Purchase, Rogers Fund
(Shown in New York only)

Selected Bibliography:
John La Farge, *Considerations on Painting* (New York: Macmillan, 1895).

John La Farge, *An Artist's Letters from Japan* (New York: The Century Co., 1897).

John La Farge, *The Higher Life in Art* (New York: McClure, 1908).

Royal Cortissoz, *John La Farge: A Memoir and a Study* (Boston: Houghton Mifflin, 1911).

John La Farge, *Reminiscences of the South Seas* (New York: Doubleday, Page & Co., 1916).

MARY LIZZIE MACOMBER

Fall River, Massachusetts, 1861-1916, Boston

Born in a city noted for its still life painting, Macomber's early art lessons were from the fruit and flower painter, Robert Dunning; later studied figure painting at school of Museum of Fine Arts, Boston, with Otto Grundmann and Frank Crowninshield. Poor health interrupted studies for nearly three years, after which resumed instruction with Frank Duveneck. Opened sudio in Boston in late 1880s; first exhibited at National Academy of Design, 1889, after which 25 of her pictures were shown in a fourteen year period. Concentrated on allegorical compositions, circa 1889-1899, with strong pre-Raphaelite overtones; working technique altered about 1898, resulting in broader style in later pictures. Despite Quaker background, many paintings had religious, even Roman Catholic subjects; after 1898 pursued portraiture as well as allegorical themes. Made only one brief visit to Europe, circa 1899, where she particularly admired Rembrandt's lighting.

35 **Memory Comforting Sorrow,** 1905
Oil on canvas, 30 x 25″
Loaned by the Fall River Public Library

Selected Bibliography:

"Paintings of Mary L. Macomber," *New England Magazine,* 29: (November 1903).

Herbert C. Vose, "Macomber's Memory Comforting Sorrow," *Art and Progress,* 1910-1911, 204.

Charles A. Parker, "Mary L. Macomber," *International Studio,* 47:188 (October 1912), 1xi-1xiv.

EDWARD MIDDLETON MANIGAULT

Charleston, South Carolina, 1887-1922, San Francisco

New York exhibition debut, 1909; showed regularly thereafter at Daniel Gallery and Montross Gallery. Close friend and pupil of Kenneth Hayes Miller. Early fantasy themes abandoned for cubist style, about 1919; later abjured cubist work and destroyed about 200 of his pictures. Injuries from World War I service left him in poor health until his death. Moved to San Francisco, 1919; died of self-imposed starvation, to which he subjected himself in belief that it would enable him to see new colors previously invisible to him.

36 **Procession,** 1911
Oil on canvas, 20 x 24″
Loaned by the Columbus Museum of Art

Selected Bibliography:

Norton Gallery of Art, *Paintings by E. Middleton Manigault* (West Palm Beach, Fla., 1963).

PINCKNEY MARCIUS-SIMONS
(*né* Marius Antes Simons)
New York, 1865-1909, Bayreuth, Germany

Birthdate variously given as 1867 and circa 1863; correct date of 1865 provided by Mary Clare Altenhofen, on basis of death certificate and passport. Probably born in New York City; taken to Europe as infant, and only returned once to America in his first 25 years. Childhood in Spain and Italy, as well as France, where he was educated by Jesuits at Vaugirard College, Paris. While still a collegian, began to study painting with J. G. Vibert, as the youngest of his pupils. Produced sentimental genre scenes and historical paintings, with which he made Paris Salon debut in 1882. Early academic style changed in late 1880s and early '90s, due to influence of Turner, Wagner, French Symbolists, and Alma-Tadema and Moore (whom he encountered in London circa 1891). Exhibited four times in Salons de la Rose+Croix in 1890s, and had one man shows in New York, Boston and Chicago in mid-1890s. Showed *Parsifal Tone Pictures* at Knoedler Gallery, New York, 1904. Worked as set designer at Wagner Theater, Bayreuth. Enjoyed patronage of President and Mrs. Theodore Roosevelt.

37 **Cupid and the Flowers**, circa 1895
Oil on panel, 8 x 5½″
Loaned by Victor Spark

38 **Porcelain Towers**
Oil on canvas, 35 x 44½″
Loaned by the National Park Service

Selected Bibliography:

George William Sheldon, *Recent Ideals of American Art* (New York: D. Appleton and Company, 1888), 27-30.

Avery Galleries, *Symbolistic Paintings by P. Marcius-Simons* (New York: Republic Press, 1896).

Frances Keyzer, "Some American Artists in Paris," *International Studio*, 4:16 (June 1898), 246-252.

M. Knoedler and Company, *The Parsifal Tone Pictures by P. Marcius-Simons* (New York: 1904).

CARL MARR

Milwaukee, Wisconsin, 1858-1936, Munich

From an artistic German immigrant family, Marr's talent was encouraged by his father, who was a fine art engraver; youthful art training with Henry Vianden in Milwaukee, circa 1867. John Marr desired to send son for study with his friend, George Inness, with whom he had worked in Hartford; Carl too young for lengthy trip, and worked instead in father's engraving business. At sixteen, hired by Northwestern Railroad Co. to sketch Wisconsin scenery for travel publications. Vianden submitted Marr's sketches to Royal Academy of Fine Arts, Weimar, to which he was admitted; subsequently studied in Berlin and at Royal Academy, Munich, under G. Max and Piloty. Awarded silver medal in annual Christmas prize competitions for figure work open to students of all royal academies in Europe, 1879. Returned to Milwaukee, 1880, but found reception discouraging; moved to Boston and worked as illustrator for *Harper's Magazine.* Returned to Munich, 1882, and lived in Europe rest of life; returned to America biennially to visit family and retain American citizenship. Professor of art in Munich, and subsequently director of Royal Academy of Fine Arts. Frequent exhibitor and award winner in international expositions, 1889-1917. Knighted by King Ludwig III of Bavaria, Kaiser Wilhelm and King Victor Emmanual of Italy; in 1909, was privileged by Kaiser to use title "von."

39 **Mermaids**
Oil on canvas, 19 x 33″
Loaned by Elvehjem Museum of Art, University of Wisconsin-Madison, Gift of Mrs. Albert G. Bardes, Lenore T. Zinn, Robert J. Zinn and Walter G. Zinn

Selected Bibliography:

Fame Without Claim: Carl Marr (n.p., n.d.) (copy of publication in files of FA/PG Library, Smithsonian Institution, Washington, D.C.)

ARTHUR FRANK MATHEWS

Markesan, Wisconsin, 1860-1945, San Francisco

Grew up in Oakland, Cal., where family settled in 1867, and worked initially in Bay area as architectural draughtsman, designer and illustrator. Studied painting in Paris at Académie Julian with Boulanger and Lefebvre in late 1880s. Specialized in subjects from mythology which combined interests in art and nature; paintings exhibited in Paris Salons of 1887-1889. Influenced by figurative murals of Puvis de Chavannes, Whistler's color tonalities, and Japanese woodblock prints. Returned to San Francisco, 1889; director of California School of Design, 1890-1906. Married his student Lucia Kleinhans, 1894, and with her developed "California Decorative Style" in creations ranging from paintings to furniture to book design;

together they exercised major influence on California art and design from late 1890s to early 1920s. Operated The Furniture Shop, a design collaborative, 1906-1920, which flourished with demand for quality custom-designed interiors following San Francisco earthquake and fire. Helped establish *Philopolis,* 1906, a monthly magazine designed to consider the artistic and ethical aspects of San Francisco's rebuilding; frequent contributor to magazine. Achieved distinction as muralist; won gold medal from American Institute of Architects for murals in California State Capitol, Sacramento.

40 **The Wave**
Oil on canvas, 38¾ x 35¾″
Loaned by The Oakland Museum, Gift of the Art Guild, The Oakland Museum Association

41 **Eve**
Oil on canvas, 66 x 53½″
Loaned by The Oakland Museum, Gift of the Art Guild, The Oakland Museum Association

Selected Bibliography:

Harvey Jones, *Mathews: Masterpieces of the California Decorative Style* (Oakland, Cal.: Oakland Museum, 1972).

California Design 1910 (Pasadena: California Design Publications, 1974).

FRANK BLACKWELL MAYER
Baltimore, 1827-1899, Annapolis, Maryland

Studied art with Alfred Miller in hometown, and subsequently with Gleyre and Brion in Paris, where he resided 1864-1870. Worked as portraitist and history and genre painter. In his own day best known for colonial subjects; his pictures of the Plains Indians are best remembered today. Visited Minnesota in 1851; sketched Indians, and ultimately completed murals for State Capitol in St. Paul. Most of career based in Baltimore-Annapolis area.

42 **Vigilance, The Gryphon,** 1896
Oil on canvas, 22½ x 16¼″
Anonymous loan

EDITH KROGLER NAGLER
New York City, 1895 (or 1890?)-1978, Dallas

Little is known about the artist. Studied at National Academy of Design, and at Art Students League with Frank DuMond, and with Robert Henri and Douglas Volk. Exhibited at National Academy, 1925. Lived in Spuyten Duyvil, N.Y., in 1920s and '30s.

43 **Vivitur Ingenio Caetera Mortis Erunt,** 1914
Oil on canvas, 54 ½ x 77″
Loaned by Rozelle Cooper

ROBERT LOFTIN NEWMAN
Richmond, Virginia, 1827-1912, New York City

Began painting by copying prints in mid-1840s; first work sold through American Art Union, 1849; with proceeds traveled to Europe for first time, 1850, intending to study in Düsseldorf. Met William M. Hunt in Paris, who convinced him to enroll in Couture's classes; also spent much time visiting Louvre collections. Returned to Clarksville, Tn., home after five months. Second trip to Paris, 1854; with Hunt met Millet at Barbizon. Maintained studio in Clarksville, offering art instruction and painting portraits, late 1850s. Conscripted into Confederate army, 1864; moved to New York following Civil War, where he made his home for most of the rest of his life. Third European trip, 1882. In New York, 1882-1892, part of time living with Wyatt Eaton at the modern Benedict Chambers which also housed Ryder, Weir and other younger artists. Work was admired by prominent collectors and younger painters, who helped support him. Only exhibition of his paintings during his lifetime presented by Knoedler's, New York, 1894; 87 of the 109 works subsequently displayed at Museum of Fine Arts, Boston. Exhibition warmly received by critics and public.

44 **Sappho**
Oil on canvas, 12⅝ x 18⅝″
Loaned by Victor D. Spark

Selected Bibliography:

Marchal E. Landgen, *Robert Loftin Newman* (Washington: National Collection of Fine Arts, 1974).

GEORGIA O'KEEFFE
Born, Sun Prairie, Wisconsin, 1887

Early schooling in Wisconsin and Virginia, followed by instruction at Art Institute of Chicago with John Vanderpoel, 1905. Attended Art Students League, 1907-1908, studying with Chase, More and Cox. Summer classes with Alan Bemont, a disciple of A. W. Dow, University of Virginia, 1912. Classes with Dow and Bement at Columbia University, 1914-1916. Intermittently employed as commercial artist, Chicago, 1909-1910; as supervisor of art in public schools, Amarillo, 1912-1914; head of art department, West Texas State Normal College in Canyon, 1916-1918. First exhibition with Alfred Stieglitz, 1916; first one-woman show at his "291" Gallery, 1917, the last exhibition for the gallery. Abandoned teaching for Stieglitz's sponsorship, 1918, with whom she continued to exhibit regularly until his death in 1946. Married Stieglitz, 1924. Early abstractions of 1910s, followed by floral themes beginning circa 1923. Summer in Taos, N.M., 1929; she returned to New Mexico seasonally most years thereafter until 1946. First paintings of bleached desert bones, 1931. Purchased house in Abiquiu, N.M., 1945, and moved there permanently following settling of Stieglitz estate, 1949. First trip to Europe, 1953, followed by frequent travels there and in Orient, Latin America and Near East. Presently works in New Mexico, continuing Southwestern landscapes and abstractions which have preoccupied her since 1930s.

45 **Blue No. I,** 1916
Watercolor on paper, 15⅞ x 11″

46 **Blue No. II,** 1916
Watercolor on paper, 15⅞ x 10$^{15}/_{16}$″
(Nos. I and II shown in New York only)

47 **Blue No. III,** 1916
Watercolor on paper, 15⅞ x 10$^{15}/_{16}$″

48 **Blue No. IV,** 1916
Watercolor on paper, 16 x 10$^{15}/_{16}$″
(Nos. III and IV shown in Lawrence only)

Loaned by The Brooklyn Museum, Bequest of Miss Mary T. Cockroft.

Selected Bibliography:

Ralph Flint, "The Georgia O'Keeffe Drawings and Paintings at '291'," *Camera Work,* No. 49-50 (June 1917), 5.

Daniel Catton Rich, *Georgia O'Keeffe* (The Art Institute of Chicago, 1943).

Anita Pollitzer, "That's Georgia," *The Saturday Review of Literature,* XXXIII (November 4, 1950), 41-43.

Worcester Art Museum, *Georgia O'Keeffe* (Worcester, Mass.: 1960).

Mitchell Wilder, ed., *Georgia O'Keeffe: An Exhibition of the Work of the Artist from 1915 to 1966* (Fort Worth, Tex.: Amon Carter Museum of Western Art, 1966).

Lloyd Goodrich and Doris Bry, *Georgia O'Keeffe* (New York: Whitney Museum of American Art, 1970).

Georgia O'Keeffe, *Georgia O'Keeffe* (New York: Viking, 1977).

CHARLES ROLLO PETERS
San Francisco, 1862-1928, San Francisco

Early training with Jules Tavernier and at San Francisco School of Design, followed by six years in Paris. Enrolled at Ecole des Beaux Arts, with Gérôme and Cormon, and at Académie Julian, with Boulanger and Lefebvre. Exhibited at Paris Salon, 1889, and received encouragement from Whistler and Alexander Harrison. Returned to San Francisco by 1890. Successful one-man show in New York, 1891, advanced painting career and led to return to France in same year. Resided in Brittany, 1891-1895; executed series of paintings of Napoleon, his favorite theme of that period. Returned to successful career in California, 1895; studio and home at his Monterey estate became focal point for area artists. In England, 1909-1911, where he painted and exhibited views of peasant cottages executed in same Whistlerian manner as his familiar pictures of California adobes. To San Francisco, 1911, but returned frequently to Europe during last decade of life.

49 **Visitation (Angels Appearing to the Shepherds)**
Oil on canvas, $24\frac{7}{8} \times 35\frac{1}{2}$"
Loaned by The Oakland Museum, Gift of The Kahn Fund

Selected Bibliography:

Betty Lochrie Hoag, *The Gifted Peters Family* (Carmel, Cal: Carmel Museum of Art, 1968).

GOTTARDO PIAZZONI

Intragna, Switzerland, 1872-1945, Carmel Valley, California

Came to California at fifteen, to join father who had preceded him to Carmel Valley. Attended California School of Design, San Francisco, 1891-circa 1893, studying under Arthur Mathews. Further training in Paris at Académie Julian and Ecole des Beaux Arts, 1895-1898. Returned to California, 1898. Opened Piazzoni Atelier d'Art, San Francisco, 1901. Active in formation of First Secessional Art Exhibition, 1902, and of California Society of Etchers. Taught at California School of Fine Arts, 1919-1935. Frequent travels to Europe. Worked primarily as landscapist and muralist.

50 **Lux Eterna,** 1914
Oil on canvas, $42\frac{1}{2} \times 60\frac{1}{2}$"
Loaned by The Fine Arts Museums of San Francisco, Gift of Mrs. Philip Wood, in Memory of Ethel A. Voorsanger, to The Patrons of Art and Music

---

HENRY PRELLWITZ

New York City, 1865-1940, East Greenwich, Rhode Island

Pupil of Dewing and at Art Students League before Parisian study at Académie Julian. Awarded Third Hallgarten Prize at National Academy of Design, 1893; exhibited Shakespearean subject at N.A.D., 1897. Lived and worked in New York City and Peconic, Long Island. Painted summers in Cornish, N.H. Member and treasurer of National Academy.

51 **Ariel Sings** (from *The Tempest*), 1906
Oil on panel, 16½ x 33½″
Loaned by the Raydon Gallery

ALBERT PINKHAM RYDER
New Bedford, Massachusetts, 1847-1917, New York City

Initially self-taught, Ryder began formal study of art under William Marshall in New York City, where his family had moved about 1868. Entered classes of National Academy of Design, 1871; exhibited first work at N.A.D., 1873, and often showed in their annual exhibitions thereafter. Invited to exhibit with four other young artists at Cottier and Company in New York, circa 1875, which was first step toward founding of Society of American Artists, of which he was a charter member in 1877; exhibited with S.A.A. throughout 1880s. Early landscape motifs increasingly supplanted by marine views and by imaginative motifs from mid-1880s onward; themes drawn from Bible, classical legend, Wagner, Poe, Shakespeare, Coleridge, Chaucer, often with emphasis upon visionary imagery. First European trip, 1877, lasted only one month, in London; second trip of several months' duration, 1882, touring Mediterranean countries and Paris with Daniel Cottier and Olin Warner. Three later brief trips more important for experience of sea voyage than Continental travel. After circa 1898 attempted few new compositions; instead retouched earlier paintings, often with bitumen, which led to rapid deterioration of works. Befriended by younger Americans, including Warner, Weir, K. H. Miller, Hartley and others, who cared for the aging and eccentric recluse.

52 **The Lorelei**
Oil on panel, 22½ x 19¼″
Loaned by the Guennol Collection

53 **Stag in the Forest of Arden,** (or **Landscape with Centaur**), circa 1897
Oil on canvas, 12¹⁄₁₆ x 12¹⁄₁₆″
Loaned by the Hyde Collection

Selected Bibliography:
Lloyd Goodrich, *Albert P. Ryder* (New York: George Braziller, 1959).

REX SLINKARD
Bicknell, Indiana, 1887-1918, New York City

Initial study at Los Angeles Art Students League; awarded scholarship for further training in New York, 1908. Studied with Henri, 1908-1910, and shared studio with George Bellows. Returned to Los Angeles and was elected director of L.A. Art Students League, 1910, in which post he served until 1913. Economic circumstances forced return to family ranch, Saugus, Cal., where his father discouraged artistic activity. Working independently developed innovative modern style, influenced by Chinese art, Renaissance masters, European modernists, and California landscape. Drafted into army, 1917, and died in influenza epidemic while stationed in New York. Posthumously acclaimed by Marsden Hartley and William Carlos Williams; letters to Carl Sprinchorn and others published by Williams in 1920-1921.

54 **My Song,** 1915-1916
Oil on canvas, $37\frac{1}{2} \times 51\frac{1}{2}$"
Loaned by the Stanford University Museum of Art, Estate of Florence Williams

Selected Bibliography:

M. Knoedler and Co., *Rex Slinkard, 1887-1918: Memorial Exhibition* (New York: 1920).

"Rex Slinkard's Letters," *Contact,* No. 1 (December 1920), 2-4; No. 2 (January 1921), n.p.; No. 3 (Spring 1921), 1-8.

John Alan Walker, "Rex Slinkard," *The Los Angeles Institute of Contemporary Art Journal,* No. 3 (December 1974), 20-23.

PAMELA COLMAN SMITH
1877 or '78-circa 1950, England

Accounts of Smith's early years differ; most sources agree, however, that she was born in America, possibly in Massachusetts, and that she spent her childhood in Jamaica and England. Lived in New York City from 1893-1899; enrolled at Pratt Institute, 1893-1897, where she studied with Arthur Wesley Dow. Early work in theater design, illustration, miniature stage design, and as author; artworks sold through Macbeth Gallery, New York. Returned to England in 1899, where she resided thereafter. Associated with literary circle including John Masefield, AE and the Yeats family, sharing their interest in mysticism and the Celtic Revival. W. B. Yeats sponsored her membership in Irish Literary Society and the Hermetic Order of the Golden Dawn, about 1901-1905. Introduction to Rosicrucianism led to use of synaesthetic principles in her art, beginning in 1900. Her "music pictures" exhibited at Little Galleries of the Photo-Secession in 1907, in Alfred Stieglitz's first show of non-photographic work; additional shows with

Stieglitz in 1908 and 1909. Designed new tarot card deck for occult scholar Edward Waite in 1909; continued her book illustration and theatrical interests in London and, after World War I, in seaside artists' colony called the Lizard, to which she retired.

55 **The Wave,** 1903
Watercolor on paper, 10¼ x 17-¾"
Loaned by the Whitney Museum of American Art, Gift of Mrs. Sidney N. Heller

56 **Beethoven Sonata No. II,** 1907
Watercolor on paper, 13½ x 9"
Loaned by Alfred Stieglitz Archive, Collection of American Literature, Beinecke Rare Book and Manuscript Library, Yale University

57 **The Blue Cat,** 1907
Watercolor on paper, 11 x 14"
Loaned by Alfred Stieglitz Archive, Collection of American Literature, Beinecke Rare Book and Manuscript Library, Yale University

Selected Bibliography:

Alfred Stieglitz, "The Editor's Page," *Camera Work* (January 1907), 37-38, 49.

"Pictures in Music," *The Strand Magazine,* 35:210 (June 1908), 534-638.

"Pictured Music," *Current Literature,* XLV:2 (August 1908), 174-177.

M. Irwin Macdonald, "The Fairy Faith and Pictured Music of Pamela Colman Smith," *The Craftsman,* XXIII:1 (October 1912), 20-34.

Pamela Colman Smith and Hon. Mrs. Forbes-Sempill, "Music Made Visible," *The Illustrated London News,* 170 (February 12, 1927), 258-260.

Melinda Boyd Parsons, *To All Believers—The Art of Pamela Colman Smith* (Wilmington: Delaware Art Museum, 1975).

EDWARD J. STEICHEN

Luxembourg, 1879-1973, New Redding, Connecticut

Emigrated to America at age two; settled in Milwaukee, 1889. Apprenticed as commercial designer for four years, mid-1890s. Finding inadequate art instruction organized with friends the Milwaukee Art Students' League to give members opportunities for life drawing and criticisms. Purchased first camera, 1895, and explored photography simultaneously with painting study. Influences of Mallarmé and Stieglitz's *Camera Notes* led to experiments with pictorial photography and comparably moody effects in painting. Three photographs exhibited in Second Philadelphia Salon, 1899, drawing praise of Clarence White; included in first Chicago Photographic Salon, 1900. Quit commercial art to travel to Paris for study, 1900; visited Stieglitz en route in New York, who bought three of his photographs. Resided in Paris, 1900-1902, an eclectic period in both his painting and photography. Introduced to Rodin by Fritz Thaulow, 1901. Shared studio with F. Holland Day, whose portrait he painted and exhibited in Salon of 1901. Returned to America, 1902, and established portrait photography studio in New York at 291 Fifth Avenue, in space which later housed Stieglitz's Photo-Secession Gallery. Achieved acclaim for photographic portraits and landscapes in Whistlerian manner. Paintings continue similar vein, generally in landscape motifs. Returned to Paris, 1906. Championed Matisse's Fauvism, 1908, and recruited his work and that of other American and European moderns for exhibition in Stieglitz's "291" Gallery. First one-man show of paintings and photographs at Worcester Art Museum, 1910. Forced to return to America by outbreak of war, 1914. Served with American forces in France, 1917-1919, then returned to French country home at Voulangis to resume painting and photography. Shortly thereafter abandoned painting and destroyed many canvases, dedicating himself to photography for which he is best remembered today.

58 **Shrouded Figure in Moonlight,** 1907
Oil on canvas, 24 x 25⅛"
Loaned by the Sheldon Memorial Art Gallery, University of Nebraska, F.M. Hall Collection

Selected Bibliography:

A. E. Gallatin, "The Paintings of Edward J. Steichen," *International Studio* (April 1910), x1-x1ii.

Museum of Modern Art, *Steichen the Photographer* (New York: 1961).

Edward Steichen, *A Life in Photography* (London: W. H. Allen, 1963).

William Innes Homer, "Edward Steichen As Painter and Photographer, 1897-1908," *The American Art Journal,* VI:2 (November 1974), 45-55.

CHARLES WALTER STETSON

Tiverton Four Corners, Rhode Island, 1858-1911, Rome

As child moved frequently in Massachusetts and Rhode Island as preacher-father served different Baptist congregations; family settled in Providence in 1869. Self-taught as artist; early Ruskinian landscapes followed by broader, coloristic technique in 1878, when he opened first studio in Providence. Paintings accepted into exhibitions at Pennsylvania Academy, Boston Art Club and elsewhere, attracting praise of J. J. Jarves, Charles DeKay, and Champney. Taught self etching, circa 1882. Married Charlotte Perkins, author and feminist, 1882, the same year as first one-man exhibition at Providence Art Club. With Sydney Burleigh built Fleur de Lys studio building and established artists' guild, 1885. Attracted to Venetian old masters and to G. F. Watts, which he encountered in New York in early 1880s. First trip to sourthern California, 1888. Divorced Perkins and married Grace Ellery Channing, poet, 1894; moved to Pasadena and resided there, 1894-1901. First visit to Europe, 1897, where he was enchanted by Italy. In Boston, 1901-1902, before moving to Rome. Befriended by Vedder in Italy, and painted his portrait. Most frequently worked as landscapist and figure painter, particularly concentrating on imaginative themes.

59 **A Pagan Procession,** 1892
Oil on canvas, 12 x 20″
Loaned by the Rhode Island School of Design Museum of Art, Bequest of Isaac C. Bates

Selected Bibliography:

Providence Art Club, *A Catalogue of the Pictures and Sketches Exhibited by Charles Walter Stetson* (Providence: 1884).

Corcoran Gallery of Art, *Catalogue of the Memorial Exhibition of Works by the Late Charles Walter Stetson* (Washington, D.C.: 1913).

AUGUSTUS VINCENT TACK

Pittsburgh, Pennsylvania, 1870-1949, Deerfield, Massachusetts

Initial art training at Yale School of Fine Arts, and in New York with H. Siddons Mowbray and John La Farge; subsequent studies in Paris with Luc Olivier Merson. Academic influences strong on his early work, as well as eclectic borrowings from contemporary Europeans, *e.g.* Segantini, Le Sidaner, Martin. Career divided between society portraiture and innovative color inventions. Met Duncan Phillips in 1913; enjoyed his patronage for the balance of his life. His work outside of portraiture marked by strong colorism, emphatic mood and increasingly abstract forms.

60 **Madonna of the Everlasting Hills,** circa 1914
Oil on canvas, 56 x 46″
Loaned by The Phillips Collection, Washington, D.C.

61 **Mystical Crucifixion,** before 1924
Oil on canvas, mounted on plywood, 21 x 49″
Loaned by The Phillips Collection, Washington, D.C.

Selected Bibliography:

Jessie Lemont, "Old Subjects in New Vestments," *The International Studio,* LIV:213 (November 1914), iii-x.

Duncan Phillips, "The Romance of a Painter's Mind," *The International Studio,* (March 1916), xix-xxiv.

Deerfield Academy, *Augustus Vincent Tack, 1870-1949,* special supplement to the Deerfield Journal, 24:3 (Deerfield, Mass., 1968).

Eleanor Green, *Augustus Vincent Tack, 1870-1949: Twenty-six Paintings from The Phillips Collection* (College Park: University of Maryland Art Gallery, 1972).

HENRY OSSAWA TANNER
Pittsburgh, Pennsylvania, 1859-1937, Paris

Son of a respected minister and later bishop in the African Methodist Episcopal Church, Tanner's early artistic aspirations were supported by parents. Entered Pennsylvania Academy of the Fine Arts in Philadelphia, 1880, studying under Thomas Eakins until 1882. Worked with modest success in Philadelphia as portraitist and illustrator, 1882-1888. To Atlanta, 1888, to establish photography studio and teach drawing for two years. To Europe, 1891, where he enrolled at Académie Julian in Paris; studied under Benjamin-Constant and J. P. Laurens. First painting accepted into Paris Salon, 1895; received honorable mention in Salon, 1896, for a religious picture, which inspired further essays on Biblical themes. Travels to Egypt and Holy Land sponsored by Philadelphia patron, 1897, the first of several journeys to the Levant. Awarded third class medal in 1897 Salon for *Resurrection of Lazarus,* which French government purchased for the Luxembourg Museum. Thereafter continued the religious themes which brought him acclaim as America's first important black artist. First summered at Trepied, a French artists' colony, 1904, and later built studio there. Lived in France with only occasional brief trips to America.

62 **Salome with the Head of John the Baptist**
Oil on canvas, 46 x 35⅛"
Loaned by the Museum of African Art, Gift of Jesse Tanner

Selected Bibliography:

Helen Cole, "Henry O. Tanner, Painter," *Brush and Pencil,* VI:3 (June 1900), 97-107.

Henry O. Tanner, "The Story of an Artist's Life," *World's Work,* XVIII:2 (June 1909), 11661-11666, and XVIII:3 (July 1909), 11769-11775.

Marcia M. Mathews, *Henry Ossawa Tanner, American Artist* (Chicago: University of Chicago Press, 1969).

ELIHU VEDDER
New York City, 1836-1923, Rome

Childhood spent in New York with frequent stays in Cuba; early art instruction with Tompkins Matteson in Sherbourne, N.Y. First European trip, 1856; after winter in Paris settled in Florence, 1857-1860. Friendly with young Italian artists who frequented Caffè Michelangiolo. In New York, 1861-1865; associated with literary and artistic bohemians at Pfaff's cafe. Exhibited at National Academy of Design, especially enigmatic paintings marked by a concern for mystery and the illogical. Returned to France, 1865, thence to Italy, 1866; produced small genre scenes and landscapes on Breton and Italian themes, as well as continuing fanciful, evocative themes. Lived in Italy for rest of life, with periodic visits to America. Introduced by his friend Edwin Ellis, a student of the occult, to FitzGerald's translation of the *Rubaiyat of Omar Kháyyám*, 1871. Worked on illustrations to accompany FitzGerald translation, 1883-1884, which was published by Houghton Mifflin, 1884; *Rubaiyat* drawings drew popular and critical acclaim and provided imagery for subsequent paintings. Persian and Indian legends, Old Testament and classical mythology provided inspiration for paintings of 1880s and 1890s, many of which dealt with themes of death or states of mind. Growing interest in decorative arts—stained glass, metalwork, mosaics, mural and illustration—1880s; mosaic and mural commissions for Library of Congress, 1896. Published and illustrated autobiography (1910) as well as two volumes of verse.

63 **The Cup of Death,** 1885
Oil on canvas, 44⅜ x 20¾″
Loaned by The Virginia Museum of Fine Arts

64 **Underwater Fantasy,** circa 1885
Oil on board, 15½ x 10″
Loaned by Graham Gallery

65 **Morning Glory,** 1899
Oil on paper, 20⅛ x 19⅞″
Loaned by the Museum of Fine Arts, Boston

Selected Bibliography:

Elihu Vedder, *The Digressions of V.* (Boston: Houghton Mifflin Co., 1910).

American Academy of Arts and Letters, *Exhibition of the Works of Elihu Vedder* (New York: 1937).

Regina Soria, *Elihu Vedder: American Visionary Artist in Rome (1836-1923)* (Cranbury, N.J.: Fairliegh Dickinson University Press, 1970).

National Collection of Fine Arts, *Perceptions and Evocations: The Art of Elihu Vedder* (Washington: Smithsonian Institution Press, 1979).

JULIAN ALDEN WEIR
West Point, New York, 1852-1919, New York City

Received early art lessons from father, Robert W. Weir, professor of drawing at U. S. Military Academy. At eighteen entered classes at National Academy of Design; admitted to J. L. Gérôme's atelier in Paris, 1873; befriended by Bastien-Lepage who worked and travelled with him and introduced Weir to Parisian art life. To New York, 1877, with frequent summer trips to Europe. After marriage in 1883 established summer studio at Branchville, Ct., near his friend John Twachtman. Although active in formation of Society of American Artists, 1877, was elected to membership in more conservative National Academy of Design, 1886; served as president of N.A.D., 1915-1916. First one-man show at Blakeslee Galleries, New York, 1891. Frequent exhibitor and award winner in annual exhibitions in New York, Philadelphia and elsewhere. Showed with Twachtman, Monet and Besnard at American Art Galleries in New York, 1893; founding member of Ten American Painters, 1898.

66 **The Open Book,** 1891
Oil on canvas, 31¾ x 29⅛″
Loaned by the National Collection of Fine Arts, Smithsonian Institution, Gift of John Gellatly

Selected Bibliography:

Phillips Collection, *Julian Alden Weir, An Appreciation of His Life and Works,* Phillips Publications #1 (New York: E. P. Dutton, 1922).

Dorothy Weir Young, *The Life and Letters of J. Alden Weir* (New Haven: Yale University Press, 1960).

GEORGE ALFRED WILLIAMS

Newark, New Jersey, 1875-1932, Biddeford, Maine

After apprenticeship in business, pursued art career, beginning at age 20 as illustrator for *St. Nicholas Magazine.* Subsequently studied painting at Art Students League with Douglas Volk and Kenyon Cox, and in W. M. Chase's classes. Continued career as illustrator, including work on English classics and on Richard Le Gallienne's translation of Wagner's *Tristan and Isolde* (1909). After 1909, concentrated exclusively on painting career. Early paintings were small in scale, mainly of landscape and figure compositions. First larger compositions with *Drama of Life* series, 1913-1914. One man show at Montross Gallery, New York, 1910. Exhibited ten works in Panama-Pacific Exposition, 1915, where he was awarded silver medal for watercolor. Painted at Maine summer art colonies, first Ogunquit, later Kennebunkport, 1910s onward.

67 **The Drama of Life—The Marginal Way,** 1913
Oil on canvas, 22 x 30″
Loaned by The Art Institute of Chicago, Friends of American Art Collection

Selected Bibliography:

George Alfred Williams, "Principles," *American Magazine of Art,* 8:5 (March 1917), 197-199.

Cincinnati Museum, *Special Exhibition of Paintings by George Alfred Williams* (Cincinnati: 1920).

CHARLES ALLEN WINTER

Cincinnati, 1869-1942, Gloucester, Massachusetts

Entered Cincinnati Art Academy at fifteen, where he studied painting for nine years; won Academy's Foreign Scholarship Competition, 1894, and embarked for three years' study in Paris. Taught by Bouguereau and William Ferrier at Académie Julian; also attended Colorossi night school. Study in Paris and later in Rome followed by travel in Italy and Germany, 1897-1898. Exhibited in Paris Salon, 1896 and 1898. Returned to America, 1898, to teach portraiture at St. Louis School of Fine Arts. To New York, 1901, where he worked as painter and illustrator for 30 years. Summers spent in Gloucester, Mass., 1914-1931; year-round resident of Gloucester thereafter. Circa 1915, began study of color theory, working with Henri, Sloan, Bellows, Hardesty Maratta and others, which continued to interest him for more than 20 years; lectured on simplified methods of color study at Art Students League. Worked as muralist for Public Works of Art Project in Gloucester, 1930s.

68 **Fantasie Egyptienne,** 1898
Oil on canvas, 93½ x 32½"
Loaned by Barry Friedman

Selected Bibliography:

"Charles Allen Winter: Biographical Sketch," 1936, typescript in C. A. Winter Papers, Archives of American Art, Smithsonian Institution, Washington, D.C., 5 pp.

List of Illustrations

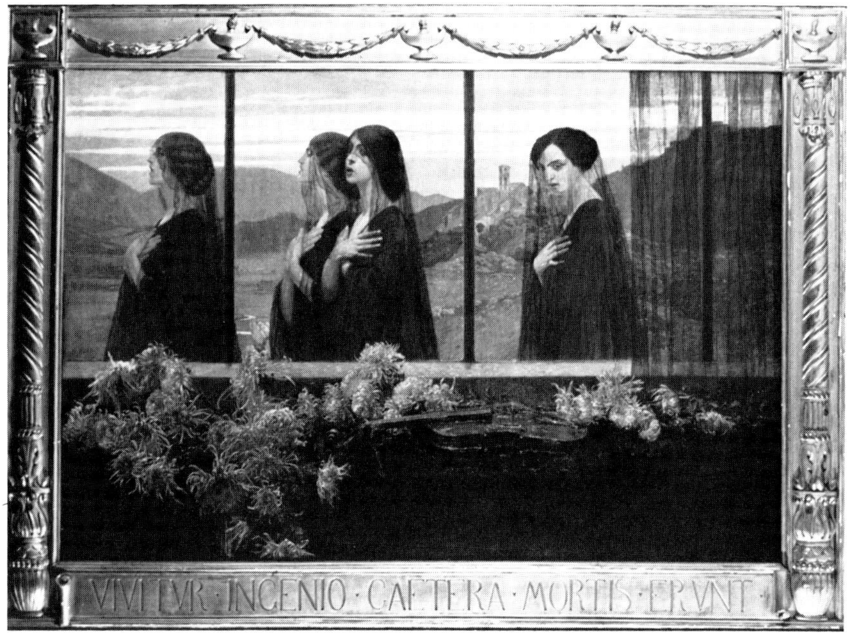

84. Edith K. Nagler, *Vivitur Ingenio Caetera Mortis Erunt,* 1914, cat. no. 43.

Works in the exhibition are indicated in italics and include parenthetical reference to the painting's numbering in the Catalogue of the Exhibition *in* Part III. *Collateral illustrations of works not included in the exhibition are used marginally throughout the text.*

Exhibition Staff
Grey Art Gallery and Study Center

Robert R. Littman
Director

Gary A. Reynolds
Assistant Director for Curatorial Affairs

Michael Boodro
Assistant Director for Public Affairs

James Clearwater
Gallery Manager

Rina Paz
Administrative Assistant

Gladys Collins
Senior Citizen Liaison

Exhibition Staff
Spencer Museum of Art

Charles C. Eldredge
Director and Curator of Exhibition

Dolo Brooking
Director of Museum Education

Janet Dreiling
Registrar

Ruth Lawner
Publications Editor/Designer

Carolyn Chinn Lewis
Clerk-Typist

Mark Roeyer
Exhibition Designer/Preparator

Douglas Tilghman
Assistant Director/Administration

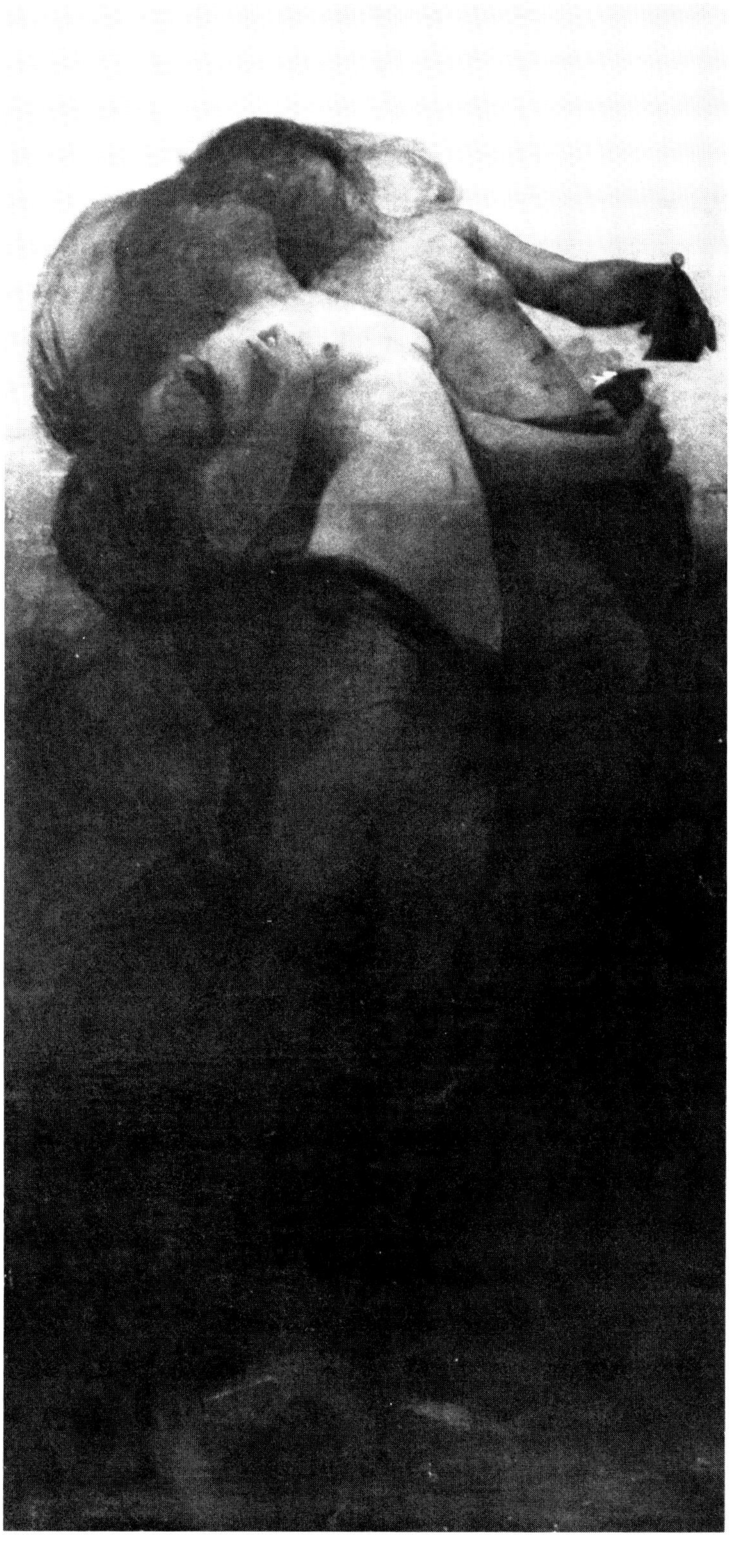

85. George R. Barse, *Night and the Declining Day,* 1897, cat. no. 3.